# A HISTORY OF REDFERN LEGAL CENTRE

FRANCES GIBSON

*'There's glory for you!'*

*'I don't know what you mean by "glory",' Alice said.*

*Humpty Dumpty smiled contemptuously.*

*'Of course you don't — till I tell you.'*

For all my Redfern Legal Centre colleagues who made working there a joy and Stephen O'Neil with love and admiration.

There's Glory for You: A History of Redfern Legal Centre
ISBN (paperback): 978-0-6456392-6-1
ISBN (hardback): 978-0-6456392-7-8

©2023 Frances Gibson

All rights reserved. No part of this book may be reproduced in any form or by any electronic or mechanical means, including information storage and retrieval systems, without written permission from the authors, except for the use of brief quotations in book reviews and promotional material.

July 2023. Published by Frances Gibson.

Lamingtone Publications
www.lamingtone.com
Email: francesgibson@me.com

Production: ARMEDIA

Published and produced on the land of the Wangal people.

A catalogue record for this work is available from the National Library of Australia

# CONTENTS

ABOUT THE AUTHOR ................................................................................................... 7
GLOSSARY ................................................................................................................... 9
PREFACE .................................................................................................................... 10
A HISTORY OF REDFERN LEGAL CENTRE .................................................................. 12
    The suburb of Redfern ........................................................................ 14
    Historical context: The 1960s and 1970s ........................................... 17
    The legal profession in Australia ........................................................ 22
A BEGINNING ............................................................................................................. 30
    The role of the Faculty of Law: the University of New South Wales ........ 30
    Redfern Town Hall ............................................................................... 40
    1977–1979 ........................................................................................... 42
    Early cases: the environment, Mardi Gras, crime ............................. 55
    Relationships with the Law Society and judges ................................ 68
    Redfern Court ...................................................................................... 73
    Magistrates .......................................................................................... 74
    Management and Community Control ............................................... 76
    Consolidation: 1980s and 1990s ........................................................ 83
    HIV/AIDS ............................................................................................. 90
    Clients .................................................................................................. 96
    Working with non-lawyers .................................................................. 98
    Volunteers .......................................................................................... 100
    Temporary relocation and abolishing of the management committee ..... 108

# THE WORK OF THE CENTRE ... 110
## Pro bono alliances ... 110
## Specialist areas of work at RLC ... 112

# A NEW CENTURY 2000-2022 ... 140
## Funding ... 150

# 2020: A PANDEMIC ... 156

# SOCIAL INNOVATION AT REDFERN LEGAL CENTRE ... 170
## Methods of identifying legal need ... 172

# 'THE BABIES': SPECIALIST SERVICES DEVELOPED AT RLC ... 184
## The Prisoners Legal Service ... 184
## Intellectual Disability Rights Service ... 195
## Redfern Legal Centre Publishing ... 205
## Women's Domestic Violence Court Assistance Scheme (WDVCAS) ... 223
## Welfare Rights Centre ... 234
## The Accommodation Rights Service (Seniors Rights) ... 238

# CONFERENCES AND SOCIAL LIFE ... 242

# INDEX OF PEOPLE ... 251

# ENDNOTES ... 262

## ABOUT THE AUTHOR

 **FRANCES GIBSON** has worked in and with community legal centres since 1988. She was solicitor and joint principal solicitor at Redfern Legal Centre from 1988–1995. From 1996, she was Director of Kingsford Legal Centre, University of New South Wales, and was invited to be the first Visiting Clinical Scholar at New York University in 1999.

She was appointed as Coordinator of the new School of Law Program at La Trobe's Bendigo campus in 2004. During her time in Victoria, she worked one day a week as a solicitor at the Loddon Campaspe Community Legal Centre on community legal education and direct legal service provision to people in remote areas affected by drought.

She then returned to Sydney to take up a position as Director of Experiential Learning at UNSW and completed a PhD, which formed the basis for this history. She is also a member of longstanding independent pop band, the Cannanes which have toured in Australia and the world for decades.

This history begins with an overview of the way the Centre was established and the work of the Centre up to 2022. It covers specialist areas of the Centre's work and then details, in a separate section, a selection of the services that started at RLC and then became separate organisations—the RLC "babies" as they are known.

> particular view.
>
> AH  Ideological assessment(?) is essential for all. Difficult to define RLC ideology except negatively or blandly, dont think we should do so. Dont think we should recognise vastly different ideologies. Whilst we can have a political position on a particular issue we cannot line up politically in a party political way, it would leave us open to attack. Some of the best/most client-sensitive volunteers have been politically Liberals.
>
> JA  Agree difficult to have centre ideology - only very general statement(s) - eg only employ people who think anti-discrimination is a good thing, not employ express racists.
>
> **HM  If people are saying politics is unimportant to the way a person does their job here I disagree. There have been problems as to how we select volunteers in this area. Previous decisions seem to be that a volunteer is OK so long as they are not stark raving mad. This is an inadequate criterion.**
>
> JT  It's important to define ideology and if we try hard enough we can do it. A person who is employed needs to know. Nothing to stop us putting it in the job description. There are different versions of left ideology - how far left? We should do one of the two things Carol has suggested in the recommendation. Service ideology should be consistent with staff ideology.
>
> JA  Round the table again, focussing on whether we should spell out an RLC ideology.
>
> R  We should not do so. We should spell out policies on different issues, eg anti-discrimination, law reform/social change as a goal, etc. People come from

# GLOSSARY

| | |
|---|---|
| ALS | Aboriginal Legal Service |
| AMS | Aboriginal Medical Service |
| ANU | Australian National University |
| AVO | Apprehended Violence Order |
| CLC'S | Community legal centres |
| CLE | Community legal education |
| DDLC | Disability Discrimination Legal Centre |
| DV | Domestic violence |
| ICLC | Inner City Legal Centre |
| ISLS | International Student Legal Service |
| IDRS | Intellectual Disability Rights Service |
| ISTAAS | Inner Sydney Tenants' Advice and Advocacy Service |
| PIAC | Public Interest Advocacy Centre |
| PLS | Prisoners Legal Service |
| RLC | Redfern Legal Centre |
| TARS | The Accommodation Rights Service |
| UNSW | University of New South Wales |
| WDVCAS | Womens Domestic Violence Court Advocacy Scheme |
| WRC | Welfare Rights Centre |

# PREFACE

> One of the deep secrets of life is that all that is really worth the doing is what we do for others.
>
> *Lewis Carroll*

The business of the historian, it has been said, 'is to remember what others forget.'[1] The history of the early community legal centres is not yet forgotten but it soon may be. Legal centres are not good at recording their past. Centres are understaffed, resources are stretched, the demands of the work seem urgent and unrelenting. There's no time for looking back, reflecting on experiences, honouring past workers, no space for archiving or even storing old records. At the time the early centres were established, their mode of operation was slightly anarchic. As Gerard Craddock comments, 'We weren't recording history, we were making it.'[2] But their work leaves significant traces and there have been many varied sources for this history.

My first encounter with community legal centres was in 1984. I was studying law at ANU and one evening someone suggested a trip to the outskirts of Canberra where members of a conference of community legal centres were having a party. I don't remember much of the scene—just a large round room full of hippyish type people dancing enthusiastically to some rather bad music. At the time as a fervent afficionado of punk and new wave, I looked at them with some curiosity but felt little affinity.

I did note two things from that night however. One, community legal centre people liked parties and two, they were strangely fond of bad music. Both of these observations turned out in later years to have substance. It took more than this night to convince me that community legal centres were to be a major part of my future but it was a start.

The opportunity I had to work in the community legal centre movement for many years commencing in 1988 was a privilege. My colleagues in the centres were intelligent, funny, empathetic and committed. I note my admiration for them—in particular those with whom I worked closely while at Redfern Legal Centre, including Jane Goddard, Mick Hillman, Ben Slade, Cathy Kerr, Danae Harvey, Pam Anderson, Janet Loughman, Andy Haesler, Harriet Grahame, Beth Jewell, Pat McDonough, Louise Blazejowska and Mary Perkins, as well as many others.

This work arose from a PhD thesis and my supervisors for that work—Francine Rochford, David Nichols and Mary Anne Noone, contributed so much to my work and have always been knowledgeable, helpful, encouraging and provided clarity where needed—I am in their debt. Thanks to Robin Gibson for editing support and encouragement. UNSW law students Yasmin Alali, Bronwyn Dyer and Cherilyn Herbert provided fabulous assistance.

Thanks to all the interviewees particularly Robyn Lansdowne who has been a valuable archivist. This is a biased collective memoir and any faults in the telling of this tale are probably mine.

*Frances Gibson*

# CHAPTER 1
# A HISTORY OF REDFERN LEGAL CENTRE

'The story of the Redfern Legal Centre is of course a distinctly Sydney history. This is, however, important: the micro-histories of people and political organisations, and the philosophies that drive them, in each state are too often glossed over in an attempt to reflect what is perceived to be a national or transnational experience. Often the specificities of time and place contribute greatly to the social contests that influence conceptual developments within discourses such as law; and paradoxically, looking closely at such contests can only help reveal the interplay of ideas and political currents that emerges from international intellectual exchange, and that assists in creating a uniquely national political experience.'[3]

*Ann Genovese*

Hearty congratulations to Mary Anne and Joe on the occasion of their engagement. Mary Anne a barrister and Joe (in the final year of his LLB) first met while interviewing a client who was charged with rape. Due to the couple's valiant efforts—the client (who will act as best man at the wedding) was held to be innocent.

*RLC News Vol 1 No 1*

Memory is life. It is always carried by groups of living people, and therefore it is in permanent evolution.[4]

*Eric J. Hobsbawm*

## THE SUBURB OF REDFERN

By the late 1960s, Redfern was described as 'an economically and socially depressed area. Sydneysiders, on the whole, regarded it as a slum, an attitude shared by many of its residents.'[5] This however had not always been the case.

The traditional owners of the land are the Cadigal and Wangal bands of the Eora but in 1817 Dr William Redfern received a grant of 100 acres of land from Governor Macquarie. The land was described as a rich alluvial flat, surrounded by and partly encroached upon by sand hills. In 1842, after the area was subdivided, Pitt Street was one of the finest streets in the area with grand Victorian terraces and the courthouse, police station, post office and fire brigade station all built on the land between Pitt and George Streets.

In the twentieth century, Redfern had become a centre for a diverse set of populations. Early that century, many Lebanese people (known as Syrians) had settled in Redfern, establishing retail, warehousing businesses and factories. These businesses often supplied suitcases of drapery and manchester to Lebanese hawkers. These hawkers, unable to gain employment in other industries, would travel with these goods, often aiming to raise capital to set up their own businesses in the area.[6]

Other residents worked in the Eveleigh train workshops and the manufacturing businesses in the area.[7] Max Neutze describes Redfern before World War II as a 'stable working class inner suburb.' After the war, however, with the availability of better working class housing in outer suburbs, it became common for families to live in Redfern in rented premises while waiting to save the deposit on a new cottage or move into public housing. During this period, the suburb became a gateway for Greek, Italian and Maltese migrants arriving in the country.[8] From the 1950s onwards, the area experienced significant change. There were two major sources of this change—the displacement of old housing by the Housing Commission towers, and large-scale movement of migrants into the area. In the mid-1950s[9] there was an exodus of manufacturing from the central city. Slum clearances and the many Lebanese people settling further away from the CBD in the western suburbs destroyed the heart of the old Lebanese quarter.[10] Many people, however, stayed in the area due to rent control provisions introduced after the war and there were also large numbers of single people living in boarding houses.[11]

Since white settlement, no large Aboriginal population had settled in Redfern until the 1920s, when Indigenous people from rural areas moved in looking for work. Aboriginal people moved to the inner city in the 1960s after closure of rural reserves[12] and estimated numbers for Aboriginal people living in the Redfern area by 1971 ranged between 4,000 (by a government commissioned survey) to 9,000 by Aboriginal estimates.[13] In 1973, houses occupied by Aboriginal people on the Block[14] near Redfern station were bought by the Commonwealth Government and given to the Aboriginal Housing Company. There had long been ongoing conflicts between the police and Aboriginal people of Redfern.[15] In the 1960s, discriminatory policing practices had even led to the establishment of a curfew for Aboriginal people. Reflecting on the period Justice Wootten noted:

> I found, as most people do, it [the curfew] a little hard to believe when I first heard it, but when I observed it operating with my own eyes, I was left with little doubt. The simple position was that any Aboriginal who was on the streets of Redfern at a quarter past ten was simply put into the paddy wagon and taken to the station and charged with drunkenness, and that was something that was just literally applied to every Aboriginal walking along the street, irrespective of any sign of drunkenness

> in his behaviour. This and the associated problems gave rise to very strong feelings amongst Aborigines here.'[16]

In 1970, as a response to the ongoing conflict between Aboriginal people and the police, Aboriginal activists and lawyers set up the Aboriginal Legal Service in Redfern. The service was staffed by volunteers, including law students, to provide advice to Indigenous people in the area.[17] A number of these students and lawyers were associated with the University of New South Wales. Clare Petre has argued that Redfern Legal Centre was set up later than Fitzroy Legal Service in Victoria because activist lawyers were first involved in setting up the Aboriginal Legal Service and the chamber magistrates in NSW[18] and the Public Solicitor did already provide some legal advice to the public.[19] At this same time, South Sydney Community Aid was also running tenants' rights projects in the area which led to the establishment of the Tenants Union in 1976.[20]

The NSW Law Society Young Lawyers committee was dedicated primarily to sporting competitions and cocktail parties. In 1971, however, Terry Purcell, a young lawyer interested in services to disadvantaged clients and inspired by stories of young lawyers in the US providing legal aid in poor neighbourhoods, put a proposal to the Law Society to set up a legal service one night a week with volunteer lawyers in Redfern. This first legal volunteer advice service in NSW—possibly in Australia—started at Redfern Town Hall in February 1971. 'We used the Alderman's room (the room on the right as you enter the Town Hall). We had a constant stream of people with stories about bad landlords and police. We didn't have a lot of capacity, but we gave advice and referred them to lawyers.'[21]

## HISTORICAL CONTEXT: THE 1960S AND 1970S

'Law and legal services are usually stereotyped as bringing stability rather than innovation to institutional structures. However, the development of legal services since the 1960s demonstrates that this stereotype is not true.'[22]

*Erhard Blankenberg*

Redfern Legal Centre was established in 1977. Community legal centres (CLC's) developed in Australia in the 1970s as an inheritance from the international waves of change in the 1960s and 1970s. Lawyers were 'the vehicle of social change' in this time.[23] In western democracies, community protests and activism, the rise of feminism, politicisation of the youth, the lowering of the voting age, gay rights, the generation gap, rock music and abolition of university fees created and reflected movements for change which all had an influence on the development of centres.[24]

It has been noted in relation to the 1960s that

> as difficult as it is to assess the eventual structural and cultural impacts of a particular movement on a single society at a specific later date, it is even more challenging to determine the lasting effects of an entire decade of collective action spanning several movements—student, anti-war, nuclear disarmament, anti-imperialism, communist, revolutionary, liberation, anti-apartheid, environmental, women's, and civil rights movements—located in several countries including Canada, France, Germany, Pakistan, South Africa, the United Kingdom, and the United States[25]

Australia could, of course, be included in this list. From the 1960s, in Australia, post-war prosperity created the conditions for the rise of a new, more educated middle class, which articulated new liberal perspectives in public debate—questioning the cultural cringe, calling for reform to censorship and the White Australia Policy, campaigning for the abolition of the death penalty, the improvement of Aboriginal rights, and changes to abortion law.[26] Challenging and contesting the boundary between public and private life was central to the liberation movements of the 1970s.[27] One effect of these forces was a heightened consciousness in the community and universities, and by lawyers and law students, of the failings of our legal system and the possibilities law held for change.

The direct genesis of CLCs in Australia is tied to the actions of many who had been students in the 1960s and 1970s. Demand for university education increased in Australia during this period when the first wave of "baby boomers" started to complete secondary education.[28] After World War II, means-tested Commonwealth Scholarships in Australia upheld a meritocratic ideal, assisting the poor but intrinsically talented student to get into university.[29] In 1972, Australia's first Labor Federal government in 23 years came to power. It abolished university fees and introduced a means-tested assistance scheme for all full-time students. The total number of students enrolling at university increased dramatically.[30]

Student radicalism in Australia emerged in demonstrations against the apartheid system.[31] The coincidence of the civil rights and antiwar movements in the United States in the 1960s helped create a generation of students dedicated to social activism[32] and this was also the case in Australia. Sit-ins were held at Australian universities in 1968 at the same time as student uprisings across the western democratic world.[33]

The Australian Government's decisions in 1964 and 1965 to introduce a conscription system and send troops to Vietnam led to a widely based mass movement against both the war itself and conscription.[34] In Australia in the early 1970s, there were mass demonstrations against the war and also against apartheid in South Africa. The introduction of free tertiary education in 1974[35] had an effect on student radicalism by allowing students from different social backgrounds to study at university and therefore to engage in university activism.[36] Although studies indicate that there was relatively little change in the socioeconomic background composition of students following the abolition of fees, the participation of women and mature age students did increase markedly during this period.[37]

Civil liberties organisations were revitalised and many of those involved would become active in the community legal centre movement. Crowley describes the 1970s in Australia as 'a time of street protest that would have been unthinkable 20 years before except protests by waterside workers.'[38] Arrow describes the decade as 'an extraordinary era of social reform.' Migration had changed many communities, in the inner cities but also in some suburban areas.[39] Ethnic organisations were advocating for change along with Indigenous people and gay rights activists. These 'special interest groups' also, of course, included advocates of feminism (the term Women's Liberation[40] was abandoned approximately 1973–74).[41]

Of this period in Australia it appears however that 'what was most distinctive and original about sixties radicalism was its attempt to create a "lived radicalism", with consistency between its ends and means, within the womb of civil society rather than through violent revolution or conventional party politics.'[42] This is certainly the approach taken by the early CLC movement. The birth and significance of CLCs cannot be understood unless they are seen 'as part of the outburst of social activism in the late 1960s and early 1970s, which arose outside the framework of political parties and the established welfare system, although always associated with the left.'[43] There were signs of protest in many sectors across the nation. There were prison riots at Bathurst Gaol in the 1970s and uprisings in other gaols.[44] Grass roots activists and unions joined forces in protest in the anti-nuclear movement.[45] The precursor to the Greens party, the United Tasmania Group was formed in 1972 to oppose proposed environmental destruction at Lake Pedder. This group was the world's first political party based on environmental concerns to contest elections.[46] It has been noted in the context of women's health centres established in this same period that

> some political contexts facilitate change while others retard it. The environment in which the Australian women's health movement emerged presented perhaps a 'once in a lifetime' policy opportunity. Internationally, change was in the air as radical challenges to the status quo were mounted in all Organisation for Economic Cooperation and Development (OECD) countries. Equality-seeking social movements—interested in such issues as civil rights, peace, sexuality, the environment, self-help, and consumer, student, worker and women's issues—were generating proposals for root-and-branch reform of existing power relations.[47]

The new Whitlam government elected in December 1972, focused activities on 'the progressive elements of Australia and New Zealand and prioritised human rights, international organisations, racial equality, decolonisation and *détente* ... heavily influenced by the new left social movements.'[48] Chesterman's history of Fitzroy Legal Service argues that the objectives of that centre were a product of volunteers attempting to marry the politics of the New Left to the workings of the law, though the author admits that supporting this argument is problematic.[49] One problem is, as Cahill noted in 1969, that no one can agree what the term New Left means in the Australian context. Barcan used the term in 1960 to refer to the socialist left that appeared around 1956 which was not connected to the Communist or Labor parties. Cahill points out that by 1969 this movement was seen as the old establishment left and a 'new' New Left was established.[50] Guidance can perhaps be obtained from Oz magazine offering readers a guide to the Left including a 'new new left, old left etc, the old new left.[51]

Barcan describes the New Left in Australia as being made up of two streams in that the first, post 1956, New Left, many of them ex-communists, sought a democratic, self-managing socialism. 'The bulk of the second New Left lacked any strong commitment to socialism. They were clearer about what they opposed than what they wanted; they were inclined to settle for an expansion of the welfare state.'[52] It is this approach that in retrospect seems the more influential on the CLC movement.

Felicity Faris, reflecting on the establishment of Fitzroy Legal Service says:

> Fitzroy was part of a social movement. It combined revolutionary and radical politics and infused these into the legal service.'[53]

The notion of alignment with what was known as a New Left movement is possibly more apposite when considering the establishment of Fitzroy Legal Service in 1972 than five years later when RLC was being established in a different political and social environment in Sydney. No matter what labels may have been used to describe the early CLC workers, it is certainly the case, as Chesterman contends, that the methods and approaches of the people involved with CLCs were in line with what were seen as New Left approaches of participatory democracy, activism and protest.[54]

## THE LEGAL PROFESSION IN AUSTRALIA

Activism and protest were not the norm in Australia's legal profession in the 1970s. The practice of law in Australia has always been associated with the upper middle class[55] and until the early 1970s, the Australian legal profession was almost exclusively the domain of white men from privileged backgrounds.[56] Encel, writing in 1970, pointed out middle class, Protestant males were responsible for the establishment of the Bar[57] and the superior courts in general.[58] A survey of lawyers in New South Wales and Victoria in 1976 revealed that over a third had private school backgrounds and that the profession was politically conservative in its voting preference and identification.[59]

Comments in 1978 by Sir John Young, Chief Justice of Victoria, that 'the better the lawyer the less likely he is to propose extensive or substantial reforms'[60] probably reflected the view of many in the profession. Sexton and Maher comment that the legal profession was not representative of the Australian community, non-Anglo Australian ethnic groups were underrepresented, and lawyers had a strong tendency to be from families where other members were lawyers. Even in 1989, Weisbrot's survey of Australian lawyers notes that lawyers were disproportionately drawn from high status backgrounds and he draws attention to the strong dynastic/family connections for lawyers entering the profession.[61]

The profession had been very successful in resisting external (including state) interventions in attempts to change its restrictive practices. Weisbrot claims this was due to the influence of lawyers in parliament and senior bureaucracy, a virtual monopoly on judicial appointments, and the persuasiveness of the rule of law ideology which demands the independence of the profession from the state. Christine Parker's survey of regulation of the legal profession in New South Wales includes the observation:

> The first (and perhaps most compelling) challenge to the self-regulatory bargain came in the early 1970s with the widespread recognition that lawyers' justice was not available, affordable or accessible to the poor and the disadvantaged. The private profession was criticised from without by the reformist Whitlam government and by the Commission of Inquiry into Poverty as it expanded to examine the legal system. It was challenged from within by a rapidly growing movement of activist lawyers influenced by the welfarist new left politics of the day.[62]

The New South Wales Inquiry into the Legal Profession commenced in 1976 on a reference from Attorney–General Frank Walker and was initially aimed at a restructure of the profession but final recommendations did not go that far.[63] The Inquiry, however, did criticise restrictive practices[64] such as requirements that clients could only hire a barrister by hiring a solicitor first; and that if Queens Counsel (QC) was hired, a client must add a junior barrister at two thirds the QC's fee. The divided nature of the profession requiring both solicitors and barristers produced duplication of effort and increased legal costs.[65] The Commission further found that that lawyers were prohibited from using advertising to inform clients of their fees or the services they offered; that qualified conveyancers could not compete with lawyers and that solicitors' costs were governed by a scale of fees, and it was prohibited to charge less than the scale fee. They found that "individual lawyers were often uninformative and unhelpful to clients, particularly in explaining their billing practices, and showed insensitivity to client needs."[66] It could be strongly argued, on these findings that the way the profession regulated itself and disciplined its members failed to address the issues that most frequently concerned clients. Proposals to regulate barristers and solicitors through a single body with representation from the public as well as the profession were bitterly opposed in NSW. The President of the NSW Bar Association described these suggestions as a "threat to traditional legal values and … a great step towards the attainment of anarchy."[67] In contrast to the profession's approach, legal centres ignored or attacked traditional models of legal practice such as bans on advertising and more extensive use of paralegals, they blurred the distinction between barristers and solicitors and were initially viewed with trepidation and hostility by professional bodies in Australia.[68]

The election of a Federal Labor government in 1972 with its detailed law reform program 'jolted the legal profession as a whole.'[69] Law reform initiatives changed the legal landscape including the establishment of the Law Reform Commission, introduction of the *Family Law Act 1975* (introducing, amongst other measures, no fault divorce), Indigenous land rights and the *Trade Practices Act 1974*.[70] Administrative law was revolutionised with two pieces of legislation: the *Administrative Appeals Tribunal Act 1975* and the *Ombudsman Act 1975*.[71] The advent of the Whitlam government was a mixed blessing for activists for while the new Commonwealth government 'adopted some of the rhetoric of the left and implemented radical policies such as the abolition of university fees, abolition of conscription, and the recognition of China, it may have dissipated support for more radical change … The New Left survived the fall of the Whitlam government in November 1975. Indeed, Whitlam's dismissal might even have given it a renewed lease of life. But by the late 1970s right-wing or moderate students were gaining strength. But the New Left did not experience a dramatic collapse. It dispersed gradually, leaving its influence in a wide area of social activities.'[72]

Although legal aid was not at the forefront of issues debated at the time, it is clear there was 'increasing public awareness that a significant proportion of the population lived in poverty, especially single mothers, unskilled recently arrived migrants, the permanently unemployed, the aged and the Aborigines.'[73] This poverty, then as now, led to social problems such as evictions, violence, unscrupulous finance deals, discrimination, family breakdown, imprisonment—all matters in which the law played a major role.[74] The legal centre lawyers were part of moves directed at achieving change in many spheres across the country.

It was not only in the legal world that the effect of these forces was being felt. Parallel developments in health and welfare organisations, for instance, reflected the same recognition that the time was ripe for change to create a more equal society. Activists in these fields were forging innovative organisations and practices that are surprisingly similar to developments in community legal centres. The first Indigenous community-controlled health and legal services were set up in Redfern in 1971 by Indigenous activists and others.[75] Fitzroy Legal Service was established in Melbourne in 1972. These developments all laid a groundwork for a series of events which were to eventuate in the establishment of Redfern Legal Centre.

# THE LAW by Malcolm Turnbull

## Oasis in the legal wilderness

CLARE PETRE is an unlikely part of a law office, but the Redfern Legal Centre is an unlikely institution. The centre, which opened its doors in March, 1977, was founded by staff and students of the University of NSW Law School. It provides free legal aid to any citizens who can't afford a private solicitor and the South Sydney Council provides it with accommodation in the old Redfern Town Hall as well as a number of full-time officers.

One of these officers is Clare Petre, a social worker. Her appointment to the centre is unique in legal aid services. John Basten, a lecturer at the University of NSW and a founder of the centre, said: "As a lawyer you have to deal with many sorts of problems, like minor criminal matters, domestic assaults, consumer rip-offs, in which the law is only a peripheral part of the problem. My experience as a lawyer was completely inadequate when dealing with non-legal problems like these. A social worker can provide the expertise that lawyers simply do not have."

Clare Petre has a distinguished background in social work. She graduated from the University of Sydney in 1969 with a Bachelor of Social Studies, took a Diploma in Criminology in 1971 and in 1975 took a Master of Science, in social work administration, from the London School of Economics.

She has worked as a social worker in

*Clare Petre: many legal anomalies facing the poor*

less true here than in most places, is that they don't know what community

Family Law Act a couple can live in the same house and share some chores but so long as they live essentially separate lives they are legally living separately. But if this couple were each collecting separate pensions, the Social Security Department would probably withdraw one on the grounds that they were living together.

"The Australian Council of Social Services has a committee examining these problems and we have some representatives on that. In another area, that of tenancy law, we have also done some work and Sid Einfeld, the Minister for Consumer Affairs in NSW, has promised to set up a committee to look at proposals for a new Landlord and Tenant Act. We hope to have some representation on that committee too."

One of the centre's three full-time solicitors, Garth Symonds, is preparing a community legal education program. It will take small groups of citizens, migrants, workers, women and aged people and discuss legal problems with them.

One of the major requests the centre

```
                                    170 Phillip Street,
                                    SYDNEY.  2000.

                                    18th February, 1971.

T. Duggan, Esq.,
c/- South Sydney Municipal Council,
73 Garden Street,
ALEXANDRIA.  2015.

Dear Tom,
            I am enclosing a draft News Release which
either you or the Mayor might like to place with the local
newspapers, any foreign language newspapers circulating in
the area and perhaps the News Letter of the South Sydney
Junior Rugby Leage Club or like organisations.  Also I am
enclosing six circulars which I would like you to give to
Ron Williams to hand around the Welfare Centres.

            Further, would it be possible for a small
sign to be placed underneath the sign about the local members
saying that the Legal Assistance Service operates each
Wednesday evening from 6.30 p.m. to 9.30 p.m.

                Kind regards,

                                    Yours sincerely,


                                    John H. Mant.
```

1. Frank Walker, NSW Attorney–General, launching the *Legal Resources Book* at Redfern Town Hall in 1979.
2. Heather McGilvray, Andy Haesler, Jane Goddard.
3. Clare Petre, Willa McDonald, John Kirkwood.
4. John Terry, Clare Petre.
5. One of the several 'back yard' gatherings of RLC staff and volunteers to discuss the Centre's operation, future, and issues.
6. Andy Haesler, Debbie Whitmont, Roger West, Michael O'Donnell, 1980/81.
7. Annual Report cover: Gough Whitlam, Clare Petre and Mr Santalab.
8. Redfern Local Court.

1. Jane Goddard, Clare Farnan, Heather McGilvray, Mick Hillman, Gordon Renouf, Simon Rice, Jill Anderson, Penny Harrington, Ben Slade, Andy Haesler.
2. Penny Harringon and Andy Haesler.
3. Mick Hillman, Gordon Renouf, Ben Slade.
4. Redfern Town Hall repairs, 1980s.
5. Andy Haesler.
6. Redfern Legal Centre recreation.
7. Meetings... meetings... and more meetings, 1990s.
8. Roger West.

Mr Andrew Haesler, principal solicitor with the Redfern Legal Service and a South Coast resident, said he had undertaken initial work for the town and was preparing a submission on residents' behalf to the Premier and the Legal Aid Commission.

CHAPTER 2
# A BEGINNING

## THE ROLE OF THE FACULTY OF LAW: THE UNIVERSITY OF NEW SOUTH WALES

> The concept that law could be an instrument for social justice not social control was a defining thematic link between people in the Faculty.
>
> *Terry Buddin*

In 1971 UNSW established a new Law School in Sydney. The first UNSW Vice-chancellor, Sir Phillip Baxter, believed that 'the University ... must endeavour to meet the needs of a changing society, not be afraid of innovation, and be radical rather than conservative in its attitude to its responsibilities.'[76] This approach was reflected in his choice for appointment of the first Dean of the Law School. Hal Wootten was committed to social justice and determined to create a Law School with a difference.[77] Harry Whitmore was the next Dean 'responsible for creating from the fledgling institution established by Hal Wootten a full scale and dynamic Australian Law School.'[78] Wootten and Whitmore, made the decision to hire academics with a social justice outlook and made personal approaches to law graduates who were doing a postgraduate degree or working in the UK, USA and Canada.

Photograph courtesy UNSW Archives.

When the UNSW Law School was formed it was given leeway to forge a critical legal education. A number of legal academics disenchanted with positivism and a trade school approach to law became founding staff members at UNSW.[79]

Academic literature and activist programs relating to 'poverty law' and law reform, originating in the United States and the United Kingdom, were influential on legal academics at UNSW.[80] Two Faculty members (John Basten and Julian Disney) were NSW editors of the *Legal Services Bulletin*[81] and were in contact with the new Fitzroy Legal Service established in 1972 in Melbourne.

The UNSW Law School wanted to be 'different and innovative and not based so much on the big end of town.'[82] Kelsey describes the approach:

> The impetus of the Law School, when it opened in 1971, was towards liberation. Liberation from lectures, textbooks, examinations with a commitment to small-group teaching, varied assessment, wide-ranging inquiry into the law as a social and political process, all within an easy framework encouraging free communication between teacher, student and administrator.[83]

Andrew Haesler, a student at the time, comments: 'barriers between some of the lecturers and students were low in terms of age and experience of the law ... People were pushing the boundaries about what was taught, what was learnt and what classes were ... Students were taking an active role. Academics were encouraging research that had a practical outcome.'[84] Academics and students mixed socially. Disney remembers 'We used to go to the pub every Friday afternoon with the students.'[85]

Influences on the UNSW law course had many sources. A "Law and Social Justice' subject run by Upendra Baxi at Sydney University had influenced UNSW academics who were students at the Law School at that time including Terry Buddin, Eddie

Neumann, and John Kirkwood.[86] The assessment for this course was in a form at that time unheard of—a long essay. These three did a project including fieldwork on the law on demonstrations in Australia including anti-apartheid demonstrations—looking at whether there had been selective law enforcement.

In 1965, Sargent Shriver, director of the Office of Economic Opportunity and architect of President Johnson's War on Poverty, had picked Bamberger as the first director of legal services at the federal Office of Economic Opportunity USA. The position empowered Bamberger to devise the first national program to help the poor with civil legal problems. It was the predecessor agency for what in 1974 was established by Congress as the Legal Services Corporation, a non-profit that today provides funding to 134 legal aid organisations across the USA.[87] Later, he travelled the world, spreading the gospel of legal services and clinical legal education, from Europe to Nepal to Australia to apartheid South Africa.[88]

Clinton Bamberger came as a visiting professor to UNSW Law School around 1978.[89] There were contacts in the Law School with US academics Marc Galanter and Rick Abel. John Basten had studied at Oxford and taught law at the University of Chicago for a year and had a year in practice as a solicitor in Sydney. He joined the UNSW Faculty of Law in 1974. Basten had met a London activist named Tom Fawthrop so was aware of the developing situation in law centres in the UK.[90]

'There were different groups at the Law School—the Law Revue, the Law Journal and the practical do things in the community group who were thinking about alternative ways of practice. There was of course some merging of those groups.'[91] Robyn Lansdowne remembers: 'I didn't feel I had much in common with most law students. I hadn't been to a private school and I was not interested in balls or skiing parties…but there was a cohort of mature age students… Bob Bellear, Helen Golding.'[92]

On campus, legal academics, John Basten, Dave Brown and George Zdenkowski were involved with the Prisoners Action Group and were very politically engaged.[93] They were assisting people in gaols including those involved in the Bathurst riots cases.[94] Simon Rice observes:

> Many of the same people who started the [legal] centres were at the time or later members of organisations such as the Australian Legal Workers Group, the Feminist Legal Action Group, the Prisoners Action Group, and Women behind Bars. They defended the Gay Mardi Gras campaigners and established a prisoners' legal service, they campaigned for drug reform and against police verbals. And they were there, on duty day and night, for local people in trouble or need.[95]

Legal academics at the Faculty worked with prisoners and students on practical legal problems such as assisting at the Children's Court.[96]

It was not long before discussions were held between academics and a group of interested students about the possibilities of setting up either a legal clinic for students as part of the UNSW curriculum or a stand-alone legal service—a community legal centre. In 1975, a meeting was held in Redfern at St Luke's Community Centre in Regent Street to discuss ideas about community controlled legal services. Not everyone was enthusiastic. In the morning session one local resident stood up repeatedly and complained about lawyers and how dreadful they were.[97] By 1976, the idea of setting up a legal advice centre became a focus of the group at UNSW partly stemming, it seems, from debates about assessment at the Law School. UNSW lecturer Dave Brown's recollections as to this are as follows:

## A BEGINNING

In 1976 Richard Chisholm, Brian Kelsey and I in particular were campaigning against exams and in favour of what we then saw as much more student centred and anti-authoritarian forms of assessment, such as Pass/Fail (non-grading); self-assessment by students; and group assessment. This should be seen in the light of the then UNSW Law School opposition to honours, which was militant and strongly supported by a majority of the school and was a bit of a marker of the new UNSW approach to teaching. As well as arguing for these sorts of policies within the Teaching Committee and School, in one particular session, either session one or two in 1976, Brian, Richard and I were all proposing to our classes some of these then subversive forms of assessment.

The school requirement was that the proposed assessment program for individual courses had to be discussed with students in the first class. Mostly this was treated as a formality, but we three, and perhaps others, took it more seriously. In my Criminal Process class I was proposing to the students elements of self or group assessment and had issued a short discussion sheet to this effect.

As a new young lecturer, I was somewhat surprised to be summonsed out of the middle of a class by one of the secretaries, who said I had to report to the Dean immediately. I attended the Dean, Prof Harry Whitmore's office, to be confronted by a red faced Dean waving my assessment discussion sheet about and shouting that if this ever got out to the profession, it would be the end of the UNSW law degree. After some time, Brian Kelsey and Richard Chisholm turned up having also been summonsed and a general discussion/argument took place. Brian Kelsey took the running on this as he was a very cool and calm character and much less over-awed than I was.

The upshot of this was a public debate on whether UNSW should liberalise assessment policy. It took place in one of the large lecture halls in Clancy and was packed out with virtually the whole law faculty including students. Brian and Richard spoke in favour, running all the then anti-institutional lines common to the 1960s and 1970s counter culture and anti-institutional movements and speaking against were Professors Whitmore and Sackville who argued basically that the legal profession (admittedly at that time very conservative) would withdraw accreditation from the UNSW degree if such policies were adopted. There was a vote of all attending and my recollection was we got around 40 per cent of the vote and they got 60 per cent. My take at the time was that their argument was supported by a majority of students worried about the status of their degree, rather than on the merits of the educational arguments being put.

After this vote a rumbling dissatisfaction among the more radical staff and students continued, given expression by a piece Brian Kelsey wrote in Tharunka, 'What's Wrong with the Law School',[98] in which he argued that the school was departing from its original critical mission. This article was the trigger for a mass meeting of law students and staff, on the then 9th floor common room in the old library tower block building. The room was packed and debate free ranging about what was or should be the ethos or mission of the UNSW Law School. I have a strong recollection of a wonderful exchange between Prof Julius Stone arguing that people needed to move up the ladder of experience and knowledge rung by rung and not rush too fast, and Peter Livesey who was one of the most radical and outspoken law students, arguing in opposition to this 'take it easy', work your way up the hierarchy approach.

At some point, I don't recall who it was, but someone threw in the suggestion that the students and staff should concretise this debate by establishing a community legal centre and there was some discussion of this, with subsequent spin off meetings taking the argument further. I didn't take part in these.[99]

The meeting 'What's wrong with the Law School?' was held on 26 October 1976. The thrust of the meeting was 'that the law course was not sufficiently in touch and not focused on practice and particularly poverty law practice.'[100] At this meeting a 'straw vote confirmed overwhelming acceptance of the idea of establishing a Law School clinic to provide legal advice and assistance to the community'[101] and a solicitor from Fitzroy Legal Service was sponsored to attend the second meeting.[102]

George Zdenkowski went to Sydney Law School and graduated in 1971. He did articles at a large city firm (now called Ashursts) and became involved in the Council of Civil Liberties and the Aboriginal Legal Service (ALS) which at the time was a voluntary service in Redfern. The partners allowed him to assist people who had been arrested in anti-apartheid protests. Hal Wootten and Richard Chisholm were involved in the ALS also and were organising the roster of volunteers from the large firms. After going overseas, he was offered a lectureship by Hal Wootten and started at UNSW in February 1974 at the same time as John Basten and Julian Disney. Zdenkowski says:

> There was a small group of us who became involved in the formation of RLC. There was a cross fertilisation in what was happening in practice and the universities. The lecturers at UNSW would encourage the students to get involved. There was a proliferation of elective courses which didn't really exist at traditional law courses such as Sydney. At UNSW there was a whole range of optional courses—I taught a trial process option which had simulated trials based on actual trials. Some students became very engaged and it led some students to get involved at RLC. The Council for Civil Liberties involved a lot of lawyers from Sydney and there were links between them and RLC and there were links between UNSW and Redfern. It wasn't an exclusive club.[103]

At the meeting of the Law School on the 26 October 1976, it was resolved that approval in principle be given for the setting up of a legal aid clinic as soon as practicable and that a committee be set up to consider the models for such a clinic. The membership of the committee was John Basten, Phil Burgess, Terry Buddin, Julian Disney, Kim Swan, Robyn Lansdowne and Susan Churchman.[104] A further general meeting to discuss the legal centre was held on 19 November 1976 at the Law School in the Library Tower. Phil Molan from Fitzroy Legal Service came and described how that Centre operated. Richard Chisholm contributed a farsighted discussion paper that included ideas about community legal education and test cases. There was discussion about whether to provide clinical legal education for students of UNSW or a service for 'needy members of the community.'[105] The service approach was selected. It was decided that a community legal centre was the priority and a clinic would be further down the track. Terry Buddin believes that reasons for this included concerns that the Faculty did not have the financial resources or necessary skill set to run a clinic at that stage, and that there were other people interested in setting up a legal centre who were outside the Law Faculty.[106] As Jeff Giddings points out though, 'Although Redfern did not become the site for the UNSW clinic, a clear culture of voluntary involvement among students had been established.'[107]

In 1977, George Zdenkowski and Brian Kelsey set up a clinical program at UNSW which took the form of a placement program. This was taken over by Terry Buddin. It was understood that this was a holding operation until a clinic got off the ground. It was not to be until 1981 that Kingsford Legal Centre was established in the Faculty of Law at UNSW.[108]

Roger West comments; RLC 'was very similar to Fitzroy. It had more law students due to the connection with UNSW. A year or so after I arrived there was talk about starting a formal clinical program at RLC. This was rejected and Kingsford was started instead… We didn't want the students to be going there with the motive of getting credit for their law degree. We wanted people who were going because they were passionate about it with no other motive. We thought it could undermine the independence of the Centre.'[109]

There was discussion about where the service would operate and potential areas were narrowed down to Waterloo, Maroubra and Kingsford with the final decision to be dependent on the availability of accommodation. People were selected to investigate those areas and were to report back on 30 November 1976. Julian Disney recalls 'There were about five or six staff who agreed to take action. I remember that Sue Armstrong said, "Why don't we go and look today."' Disney had a car and they set off. First, they looked at Botany. 'We drove around looking at public transport routes and how practitioners and students could get there. The transport was very limited and we thought it might be necessary to go nearer to a train station and the CBD where volunteer lawyers would be coming from after work.'[110] Disney adds:

> After I went to the Law Reform Commission on 1 December 1976, most of the others were away for a month or so over Christmas but I kept looking at the places South Sydney Council told us might be available. I went to some bizarre places including one in Darlinghurst which had been a boarding house for girls from the bush but was in a very primitive condition. There was a building on the corner of Crown and Foveaux Streets which would have been perfect but we missed out on it. We looked at Alexandria Town Hall as well and some space linked with Rachel Forster Hospital in Redfern that might become available.[111]

Redfern was seen as an epicentre of disadvantage, and finally the UNSW group decided that Redfern Town Hall was a good spot for a centre.[112] Discussions were held with the Aboriginal Legal Service and the Aboriginal Medical Service. Bob Bellear who was a Director of the AMS and Paul Coe and Chris Kirkbright from ALS were students at UNSW.[113] In early 1977, Purcell was contacted by Frank O'Grady from South Sydney Council in relation to the legal advice service run at the Town Hall saying 'there's a bunch of people from the University of New South Wales who want to use the town hall. The town hall wasn't being used then due to the changes in the councils. I said, 'This is going to be much better than anything we are doing" and he said "great.""[114]

Terry Buddin describes the experience of dealing with the council as being somewhat cloak and dagger. 'For reasons that were never explained meetings had to be conducted away from the public gaze usually in some obscure back room.'[115] Negotiations were conducted with one of the councillors, Terry Murphy, in early 1977. The council had a number of under-utilised halls after the 1968 amalgamations of local suburban councils into the City of South Sydney, so Redfern Town Hall was available. It was suitable because it was close to the city for volunteer lawyers, was close to a court and the railway station. Probably the deciding factor, however, was that the council offered free rent. Council was interested in a deal—the RLC group was offering to provide free legal advice to people the council felt a responsibility for.

## REDFERN TOWN HALL

Redfern Town Hall, at 73 Pitt Street Redfern, is an imposing building designed in 1870 by George Allen Mansfield.[116] The suburb of Redfern, one of the most famous in Australia, is now closely associated with the Aboriginal community of Sydney but the hall has another history, separate yet connected. It has long been the site of significant community, political and protest events. Labor party luminaries have chosen the hall for campaign launches and speeches.[117] The rugby league team South Sydney Rabbitohs was officially formed on the premises in 1908[118] and the Redfern All Blacks rugby team held large dances there in the mid-twentieth century.[119]

In 1943, Bill Ferguson hired the hall for a public meeting, where he launched his nomination for a place as the first Aboriginal person on the Aborigines Welfare Board. Anti-conscription meetings were held there in the 1960s. Anzac Day gatherings were held at the hall and it was often the site for polling booths in elections. Notable rugby union player Nicholas Shehadie remembers the time in 1947:

> When I was first selected to go to England with the football and the people of Redfern gave me a farewell at the Redfern Town Hall and Johnnie Wade[120] was the compere ... And they had this big function at Redfern Town Hall and I remember Johnnie Wade saying "This is a fun night. Everyone leave the hardware outside"—the guns and the knives were left outside. [121]

UK Legal Aid expert, Roger Smith visited Redfern Legal Centre in 1991 and noted of the Town Hall that 'The state of decoration gives an air of temporary occupation that has lasted longer than anticipated. The building is also redolent of an organisation saying that its priorities are people rather than paint.'[122] Large political meetings still go on in the upstairs hall, along with ballroom dancing sessions, cinema screenings, public talks, fashion shows etc. It is still a hub for the local community. But in addition to all of the above, in 1977, it opened its doors as Redfern Legal Centre and the Centre still operates from these premises today.

## 1977–1979

> The secret to getting ahead is getting started.
>
> *Mark Twain*

Once premises were found, work started on establishing the Centre. Andy Haesler remembers that there was a student committee that took over a room in the Library building (at UNSW) which eventually became the RLC room.[123] Room 1309 at the Law School was to be the contact point for the Centre.[124]

> We used to walk past it going to class. The RLC office was like a storeroom—a corner with no windows... When Terry Buddin had organised the premises, a roster of students was formed and the UNSW academics called on their mates to organise a roster of lawyers—this must have been done over the summer 1976–77.[125]

Dominic Gibson was a student at UNSW Law School in 1977.

> I started to see signs going up around the Law School about Redfern Legal Centre ... looking for volunteers.'[126] Another student—Peter Livesey, put posters up. 'I put posters up and I think they were done by Chips Mackinolty at the Fine Arts studio. The posters said Redfern Legal Centre—free legal centre. When I was putting them up people were asking me "Hey where's the band on?" They looked like band posters.[127]

The RLC group was highly organised and had a practical focus. Issues such as recruiting volunteer lawyers, liaison with local lawyers, and insurance were discussed prior to opening. A detailed paper prepared by Phil Burgess on 10 December 1976 raised the issue of whether the Centre should be established as an unincorporated association, a co-operative society or a company limited by guarantee[128] (the latter was selected). The working party to set up the Centre consisted of the original committee

## A BEGINNING

(listed above) with the addition of John Kirkwood, Russell Hogg, Steven Catt and Rick Raftos, with a number of other academics named to assist.[129] Another discussion paper canvassed issues such as the aims of the service, services to be provided/excluded, opening hours, rosters, role of non-practitioners, ideas about management, ('we feel there should not be any head as such'[130]) and a detailed description of the procedure to be followed when a client walked into the Centre.

The Centre opened on 14 March 1977. On 31 March 1977, the organisation was set up as an unlisted non-profit company limited by guarantee.[131]

Initially, RLC operated legal advice and assistance sessions[132] five weeknights and two afternoons a week on Tuesdays and Thursdays. Academic lawyers were often around during the day.[133] Andy Haesler was rostered on as a law student on the second day the Centre was open. At this stage, there were no paid staff.

> There were folders and a big table, and we must have had some training—probably out at uni the week before. Because it was alien but not totally alien. We had a phone and we had a number ... The phone rang and we answered it ... People were wandering in ... we took details and got information and clients could come back to get advice in the evenings. ... I can't remember sending anyone away. The advice was always free. There was never a means test ... Referrals were made to the ALAO and the Public Solicitor so we had information about them.[134]

The Centre's free legal assistance was provided to anyone who walked in and it was open out of normal office hours, usually in the evenings. A Greek interpreting service had started on Thursday afternoons in November 1977.[135] 'The Council paid for cleaning, maybe a few bits of furniture. Everything was donated. The first photocopier held together with a paperclip literally—to do a copy you had to move a paperclip. We got some old furniture from law firms who would give furniture as they were upgrading.'[136]

Michael Mobbs recalls:

> The dress was casual—there were barristers in jeans etc—there was a quasi-hippiness to it but a sense of pride. There was sense of the humanness of lawyers that was apparent not just to colleagues but for all the clients, and there was a sense of courtesy and respect for all clients. There was a sense that we have to do as good a job as any other lawyer.[137]

At first the Centre had little funding or assets but there was no shortage of clients. A letter from the Centre seeking funding noted: 'Our first four weeks of operations suggests that there is a strong demand for the type of service we are providing, as illustrated by the fact that with a minimum of publicity we have already assisted approximately 100 clients.'[138] The Centre was not run like any other lawyers' practice. A suggestion in September 1977 that there be a uniform manner of answering the phone for lawyers and legal assistants and that they give their names was rejected. "It was pointed out that this could become very artificial. It was resolved that things should stay as they are.'[139]

South Sydney Council had generously agreed it would pay for a social worker to staff the Centre[140] and Clare Petre, the first employee, started work on 1 August 1977. Petre had been working as Deputy Senior Social Worker at Royal Prince Alfred Hospital in Camperdown and had in addition to her social worker credentials, a Masters Degree in Social Administration and a Diploma of Criminology. Lansdowne recalls: 'I remember working on a refugee case with Clare and going to visit these people and being very impressed. She had a typewriter with her and was typing up the interview. She was very well organised, she was very charismatic, gorgeous and a dynamo.'[141] In 1977, Petre and John Basten visited Bob Ellicott, Commonwealth Attorney–General in Canberra. He had been to the USA, knew Clinton Bamberger and was receptive to their arguments for funding.[142] Advertisements for a lawyer and legal secretary were in the *Sydney Morning Herald* from 16 July 1977 after a $20,000 grant from the Federal government was secured.

John Terry was employed as RLC's principal solicitor and Susan Davitt as secretary.[143] A short description of Terry in the first ever RLC news in October 1977, describes him as 25 years, unmarried (and likely to remain so) but involved in a traumatic affair with a cat called Vera. Terry had allegedly become a lawyer 'for all the wrong reasons having drawn his inspiration from preposterous television programmes of dubious entertainment value. He feels that this is indicative of the general ignorance of law widespread in the community and sees the task of RLC as being broader than merely providing advice and representation to persons who are already in trouble.'[144] Terry is described as 'very inspiring and a great advocate.'[145] He was the Centre's first solicitor and worked at the Centre for about a year. David Buchanan, a barrister who knew Terry from ANU remembers that after Legal Workshop, Terry went to work for the Aboriginal Legal Service:

> He turned up with his brand new yellow car – a Ford Falcon with a black hood ...the car in which he was going to drive out west. He was very chuffed at getting the job...But he always had an interest in progressive causes...He was a very good advocate. He had a well-ordered mind, high intelligence, great curiosity about the world and was able to order his thinking so when he produced an argument or was cross examining, he was persuasive. He really enjoyed being an advocate.[146]

He had also been at the ALAO before taking the job at Redfern Legal Centre.

> John Terry, RLC's first solicitor, left RLC to work for many Indigenous clients and became a barrister in NSW. He was deeply impressed by Nora McManus, an American Catholic nun who settled in Wilcannia and who worked with Aboriginal people. He died at an early age in 1994. At his funeral it was said 'Many in the legal profession were encouraged by Terry and not a few saw him as a mentor and pioneer. As Terry's career in the law proceeded from the days at Wilcannia to Redfern and then to the private bar his intellect and style became finely tuned. He agonised over his cases because he so fervently believed in the dignity of the human person and a desire for due process and a just and fair outcome.'[147] When he died his will stated 'he wished to be buried 'at the feet of Nora McManus' in the Aboriginal section of the Wilcannia cemetery. Today you can see the solid granite grave of Terry lying at right-angles at the feet of Nora McManus in the Wilcannia cemetery.'[148]

That a social worker was the Centre's first employee was probably partially a result of the Council's offer to fund a position, but it was also in keeping with the Centre's ethos of offering a holistic service to clients. Academics at UNSW involved with the Centre had already demonstrated interest in the use of non-lawyers in the provision of legal services.[149] With the arrival of paid staff, the Centre changed slightly. 'When the paid staff came, they became the core and they were there every day ... the volunteers were not so crucial.'[150]

In 1977, Debbie Whitmont was a law student at Sydney university. She was not particularly enjoying it, then someone

## A BEGINNING

came to university and said RLC was opening up and looking for students to volunteer. She signed up for an afternoon shift. There were only two students from Sydney University—Penny Quarry and herself. Everyone else was from UNSW.

> For the first time I saw a way that the law I was studying could be useful or relevant... The course at Sydney University was very old fashioned... there were no electives...There were no tutorials... just big lectures to a huge lecture room... You would do exams and they would publish the list of results in descending order of success including those who failed... There was activism on campus about feminism, arts and theatre, political economy etc—but not so much about justice...I had a bad experience applying for a summer clerk position... They said to me at that interview "what sort of law are you interested in?" I said "I work at Redfern Legal Centre." The partner said "Well, we do some work for the Little Sisters of the Poor but charity work is not the bulk of our work"... I remember being on the 25th floor and going downstairs and crying my eyes out and thinking why am I doing law—what a dreadful thing to have done. He had also said "ah... Whitmont—we do have some Jews in the firm but not many"... I realised the big firms were not for me.'[151] Whitmont became more interested in the Centre. 'At some point I went on evening shifts and then became more and more involved... I loved it... I finished law... and I did work with a law firm in the city for a while in a small firm in general practice.'[152]

Penny Quarry worked as a volunteer at the Centre starting in 1977.[153]

> It was so great—Clare [Petre] was so open and charming and the place seemed full of light and really exciting. I remember everyone was very excited to get Clare and John Terry. There were a lot of rumours about people sleeping with each other but I didn't care about that. Rumours about solicitors bonking each other on the desk tops upstairs. I can remember one name but I won't tell you that.[154]

The lawyers at the Centre had a radical approach to legal practice, as Petre[155] recalls:

> They felt that a lot of people who came face to face with the legal system had a whole range of problems and a lawyer might represent them, get a plea in mitigation or get a reduced sentence but they still had all these other problems, domestic violence, income problems etc. We wanted to focus on helping clients with a range of other services and if you are a low-income disadvantaged person in poverty, almost by definition, they needed other services. We also wanted to help people not getting legal services, for example prisoners and tenants, gay people and other minority groups were identified as groups who were missing out ... We wanted to be proactive and reach out ... We wanted to set up a model that would be different, that would be holistic and wouldn't just look at the black letter law part of a person's problem because they wanted to focus on poverty law. The lawyers felt that there were people who fell through the gaps in traditional law and that's where they wanted to focus.

John Basten recalls: 'Everybody on the management committee played a role in file checking. We were paranoid about making mistakes ...Every file was checked on a regular basis...We were establishing a legal practice without a Principal Solicitor... John Kirkwood took out a full practising certificate. He was theoretically responsible for the work of all the volunteers which included students, as well as practitioners from town, as well as us'.[156] Quality control was managed by UNSW staff — The Gang of Six—Julian Disney, John Kirkwood, Terry Buddin, John Basten, Denis Harley and another were responsible for reviewing files allocated on an alphabetical basis. Comments by lawyers working at the centre at this time describe the nature of the work:

## A BEGINNING

> The roster at RLC at the beginning was unpredictable. Problems were related to homelessness, domestic violence, consumer issues, family and criminal law. A lot of judgements had to be made about advice on the spot or referrals. People had literacy issues, there were a lot of migrants, tenancy problems, contracts that people couldn't understand.[157]
>
> It was an eclectic mix—a lot of the work was dealing with bureaucracies.[158]
>
> It was hectic—people would come in drunk—a whole range of different people ... there was a sense of being on the edge as we were taking on cops, and practices which had never been systemically challenged. We were challenging the current way of doing things.[159]

Peter Cashman who had worked in private firms as well as Fitzroy Legal Service noted that RLC:

> wasn't as well organised as I would have expected. It is just endemic in the way legal centres operate ... there was no adequate typing or secretarial support ... there were endless debates about self-sourcing—doing your own typing etc. I was in a conventional legal practice where you had a dictaphone and secretaries ... There was a big move about people getting paid the same amount and having no demarcation between professionals and support staff ... the Centre was always under-resourced ... It was a pretty harmonious place ... people worked together well.[160]

In some of the Centre's criminal work, John Terry was briefing young barristers, Peter Livesey and Helen Golding. These two lawyers were acting for RLC clients many in the prisons of NSW, usually for free.

Peter Livesey describes himself as 'very naïve and idealistic,' attributing this to his religious Catholic family. Like many young people at the time, he was politically active from an early age. He had a number of early brushes with the law—including being arrested for offensive language and possession of a smoke flare at an anti-apartheid demonstration in Orange in 1971 where the Springboks were playing a country match. (He was found not guilty of the charges). After a year at Sydney Law School where he did not do well, he decided to apply to UNSW Law School. Due to his poor results, he was required to attend an interview at which he confessed his arrest at the demonstration, (a confession he feels may have helped his application), and was accepted and enrolled in an Arts Law degree.[161]

Livesey had been one of the group arguing for the establishment of RLC at UNSW and helped promote the Centre by putting up posters but was not involved in the day to day establishment of the Centre. He graduated in 1976 and went straight to the Bar in 1977, an unusual move. Garth Symonds describes him as 'a pretty radical kind of guy… a charming person.'[162]

Helen Golding had also been a student at UNSW Law School. She had more experience than many associated with RLC—had travelled overseas and had taught English as a second language to migrants. After travelling to central Australia in 1974, she was struck by the plight of Aboriginal peoples and decided to get legal qualifications. She enrolled at UNSW. Once admitted, she went straight into appearing in the courts particularly for prisoners. David Buchanan, barrister who knew her remembers her as a 'wonderful, exciting woman … I remember visiting her place round behind Taylor Square in Darlinghurst where she played host to many of us in her kitchen, many a time.'[163]

Briefed by Terry and others at RLC, the two barristers threw themselves into some of the momentous issues of the day. As Livesey remembers, 'It was a very political time.' Bodies such as the NSW Law Reform Commission were advocating significant change in the legal profession including doing away with distinctions between solicitors and barristers, advocating the abolition of restrictive practices such as barristers acting without instructing solicitors, abolition of wigs etc. Mr Justice Wootten saw dissatisfaction with the legal profession in Australia as part of a 'ferment around the world.'[164]

Neither Golding nor Livesey had barristers' chambers which was, of course, not usual practice. Livesey started doing cases on drugs and demonstrations and Golding focused on prisons and Indigenous cases. A client noted, 'I had some reservations about a woman barrister defending me. Those reservations vanished after I saw her legal expertise inside Central Court of Petty Sessions where my case was scheduled. Her instructing solicitor, John Terry, was another gem who helped prepare the case with the tenacity of a bulldog. Helen and John were a combination as tough as teak.'[165]

Both Golding and later Livesey, had a number of clients in Katingal, a notorious gaol. It opened in 1975, billed proudly by the NSW government as 'the country's first modern, purpose-built extreme maximum-security prison.'[166] But by 1978, the Nagle Royal Commission into NSW Prisons said that the State's newest prison should be shut down. The Report stated that 'It is clear that the cost of Katingal is too high in human terms. It was ill conceived in the first place, was surrounded by secrecy and defensiveness at a time when public discussion should have been encouraged. Its inmates are now suffering the consequences.'[167] The recommendation that Katingal be closed was only accepted after a hard fought campaign over a period of months. Golding was very involved with the campaign (which included burning a model of Katingal outside the District Court, traffic halted for demo on Sydney Harbour Bridge, a tent vigil set up outside Long Bay where Katingal was etc).

Prison activist, Bernie Matthews describes Golding:

> Helen was one of a new breed of feminist lawyers who had taken an active role in ventilating prison issues ...Helen had a buoyant personality. She could not be kept down. If she got a hard knock then she would just bounce straight back up again. Her energy and vitality was infectious. One minute she would be fronting Central Court over prison related issues. Then she would be at the Family Law Courts trying to salvage something out of the remnants of a marriage break up. Then out to a suburban court to stop an eviction order which would tip an impoverished family onto the street, or down to Darlinghurst cells to arrange bail for some hooker who had just been arrested and had no money to pay her own bail...Helen never seemed to be in the same place twice. Her principles, energy and vitality carried her through the hardships and disillusionments of life.

A notorious escape by a prisoner, Russell Cox, in November 1977, led to prisoners in Katingal suffering repercussions. One included prison officers photocopying all prisoners' mail including photos and Christmas cards so that prisoners received only photocopies. Golding, upset with this measure, did a media conference on the steps of Central Court regarding the photocopying of the cards. According to Bernie Matthews, a prisoner at the time, this incident had more impact in the Sydney media than all the disturbances, riots etc that had taken place.[168] The prison officials at Katingal issued an edict that legal visits were to be conducted in presence of two officers or with recording devices. Helen protested about infringement of lawyer/client confidentiality. She then took the 'unprecedented step' of allowing media interviews regarding legal visits inside Katingal. These televised interviews upset Corrective Services and the legal fraternity. Helen was hauled up before NSW Law Society where she was reprimanded and told to refrain from making public statements and to confine comments about

Katingal to the courtroom. She was called up by the Law Society more than once to justify outspoken comments.[169]

Garth Symonds adds: 'The first impression of Helen Golding I had was how altruistic she was. It was truly remarkable. I had never met someone like that before. She was a barrister and she found it hard to charge people. I don't know how she managed.'[170]

In about September 1977, Helen Golding took her friend Virginia Bell to enquire about volunteering at RLC.[171] Golding lived close by in William Street Redfern and Virginia had met her through people such as Hal Ginges, Janet Wahlquist and Daniel Brezniak, lawyers who were interested in setting up a poverty law practice—a private practice which would subsidise free work.[172] Bell studied law at the University of Sydney. While she was at university, she worked at the Settlement in Chippendale which was operating partly as a drop in for young kids in the area and spent time with people concerned about squats in Victoria Street and green bans. She had taken a job in a law firm which did nothing but second mortgage work for finance companies and files were parcelled out according to the initial of the client's name. Bell became a full-time volunteer and later staff member at the Centre. And as Symonds comments she 'stood out for her humour and dedication.'[173] Anne Healey commented: 'Virginia is very thoughtful, and has a huge amount of knowledge and compassion and understanding for people. When you asked for her opinion and she gave it, you always thought you could trust it... Virginia and Nanette [Rogers] and the other women at RLC were such wonderful role models.'[174]

Livesey and Golding were very proactive in their work but not in a way which accorded with traditional legal practice. Golding would say; 'Unless the Bar Association is complaining about us we are not really doing our jobs.'[175] Magistrates would complain about both of them for making speeches in court. Even supportive members of the legal profession were concerned. David Buchanan remembers:

> I had issues about Peter Livesey's approach to practice as a barrister. He was opposed to the concept of chambers. We were all opposed to wigs etc but he took that opposition to another level. He was opposed to the concept of being part of a Bar. I thought this was a mistake because I thought that you are a better barrister if you are able to work alongside and be with peers with whom you can consult and absorb law and practice skills.[176]

Livesey recollects: 'Judges hated me. I threatened the system. The head of the Bar Association told me 'if you don't get your hair cut they will disbar you…' Golding and Livesey were acting for some of the State's most notorious criminals—Edward 'Jockey' Smith, Steven Sellars, the Tidmarsh murder case (the robbery of Sydney bookmaker Lloyd Tidmarsh with two others which resulted in the death of Tidmarsh. The conviction for the murder of Tidmarsh was later rejected on appeal and Smith accused the police of verballing him). When questioned on why RLC would take on these cases for people who seemed like hardened criminals, Livesey reflects:

> I don't know exactly why we did those cases—at the time it seemed like the right thing to do…These cases were causes. Katingal was a cause as the Nagle Royal Commission had ordered Katingal gaol to be shut and they hadn't done that. Tidmarsh was a cause because it was clearly a frame up and we eventually charged police with conspiracy…A lot of this work was done on blind emotion. I knew the cops were bad. They had framed me. They framed these people. I had grown up with a belief in the law…and the whole process was just a perversion of that as far as I could see.[177]

Golding was indomitable, indefatigable and feisty but in a terrible twist of fate, in March 1978 while driving north at Easter time she had a head on collision and was killed.

The next issue of the *Alternative Criminology Journal* was dedicated to her. Dave Brown, legal academic at UNSW wrote:

> Women prisoners in particular not only benefited from her legal support, but from the deeply personal concern and friendship that went with it. Male prisoners and especially the former inmates of Katingal, will remember the courageous woman who championed their cause, smuggled out documents and complaints, and refused to be silenced in the face of intense personal, intimidation and poverty ...A moving non-religious ceremony, attended by many hundreds of people was held at Redfern Town Hall. The inside of the hall was decorated with red and black flags, and placards bearing slogans such as 'To Helen who not only appeared in courts but wrote on their walls.

Helen Golding's early death was a tragedy and a sad loss for the Centre and her clients. *RLC News* April 1978 notes: 'It must be said that there are many whose liberty was secured by her efforts. She was frustrated by the rigidity of the courtroom and the frostiness of the legal profession. She was a fine barrister and above all she was absolutely fearless in the interests of her clients.'

In the 1980s, a house on Liverpool Road, Burwood for women released from prison was named Golding House after Helen. Her daughter Joanne attended the opening.

## EARLY CASES: THE ENVIRONMENT, MARDI GRAS, CRIME

In 1977, in what was to prove a rare foray into environmental issues, the Centre decided to assist the Friends of the Earth and the Movement Against Uranium Mining in proposed actions under the *Atomic Energy Act* and another for misleading advertising under the *Trade Practices Act*.[178] Michael Mobbs instigated this uranium action which was later run under John Kirkwood's name with no professional connection with the Centre.[179] In

June 1977, demonstrators were trying to prevent the ship ACT6 taking 200 tonnes of yellowcake from Lucas Heights.[180] John Terry and David Buchanan assisted demonstrators arrested at Glebe Island container terminal in these actions.

## MARDI GRAS

The Centre was able to offer its services where access to private lawyers may have been difficult for clients to obtain. An early challenge for Redfern Legal Centre were the events of the first Mardi Gras march on Saturday 24th June 1978. The evening celebration was a planned street 'festival' calling for an end to discrimination against homosexuals in employment and housing, an end to police harassment and the repeal of all anti-homosexual laws. The event was met with unexpected police violence. The Mardi Gras' organisational history records:

> Several hundred gays, lesbians and straight supporters—some in fancy dress and some simply rugged up against the cold—gathered at Taylor Square and followed a truck with a small music and sound system down Oxford Street to Hyde Park. As revellers joined in along Oxford Street, the police harassed the lead float along the route and when the march stopped in Hyde Park, where telegrams of support were to be read, police confiscated the lead float truck and arrested the driver … Angered by this, 1500 revellers diverted up William Street to Darlinghurst Road, where the police had closed the road. At this point the police swooped and violently arrested 53 men and women, many of whom were beaten in cells.[181]

Virginia Bell remembers:

> I was with some friends and we joined it. I remember it turned ugly in Darlinghurst Road. The police were rounding people up and putting them in paddy wagons and taking them to Darlinghurst Police Station. I think it was using unlawful

assembly. I went to the police station and was there with David Buchanan and John Terry would have been there.[182]

Terry and Golding received calls about the arrests and Terry went straight down to Darlinghurst police station. In the morning he rang Livesey who appeared at Liverpool Street court. Garth Symonds and David Buchanan were also amongst those representing the accused.[183] Livesey says: 'I stood up and said: "these arrests are a disgrace to the administration of justice in NSW." There was a big cheer from the back of the court. … The magistrate threatened to throw me out.'[184]

Chris Ronalds:

> Everyone was taken to different police stations. We had no money to bail anyone out. In those days the legal left used to drink at the Criterion. John Terry and I went down and borrowed money from the publican at the pub. He lent us $1000. That was a huge sum of money in those days and we marched up the street with the cash terrified that something would happen to it. So when everyone went to court they had to give me their bail money and then I had to take it down to the pub and pay it back.[185]

Terry appeared on television speaking out against the arrests and made submissions to the Attorney-General. RLC acted for 19 of the people arrested and referred others to sympathetic solicitors and the Public Solicitor. Charges were laid under s45 of the then *Summary Offences Act* for taking part in an unlawful procession.

The second Mardi Gras event went on in 1979. Chris Ronalds remembers:

> This year John Terry organised to get money out of the bank and gave it to two gay boys to keep the money at home but they neglected to tell us they were going to the opera. The money was in their freezer and we had to wait for them to come home before bailing anyone out.[186]

It was not until 29 November 1979 that the police officially dropped charges against all RLC clients with assistance from many lawyers, including barrister Carolyn Simpson, after magistrate Mr Henderson SM found no prima facie case.[187]

The Centre was involved in acting in high profile criminal matters. In late 1978 Livesey was working on the Tidmarsh murder case. He describes the scenario; 'I had never done a murder trial and never done a committal. I am acting as the client had run out of money. Because I had started the Australia Marijuana Party in 1977, (a minor Australian political party that operated in the late 1970s and early 1980s campaigning for the legalization of marijuana), Lenny Nash, the magistrate hated me. I go down to the Coroners Court in Glebe. There are sharpshooters on the roof. My client had been brought down in a paddywagon, handcuffs and in a straitjacket. There were two police motorcycles in front and two behind. The court was full of police. We had to argue just to get one handcuff off so he could make notes. This case ended up going for 14 weeks.'[188] Livesey was told that a photo of him was used as a dartboard at Maroubra police station.

In January 1980, RLC joined a 'Campaign Against Police Verbals Group' which led active meetings including a meeting that year attended by 300 people at Redfern Town Hall organised by the Australian Legal Workers Group.

Bill Dickens notes:

> The police did not have much time for anyone from RLC. Back at that time there were issues about police verballing and Nanette [Rogers] was taking some litigation to do with verballing. There was a time when they fabricated records of interview and the armed hold up squad had people like Rogerson and Bourke and so that was a campaign that RLC was high profile in... 'I've got some vague memory of being out at Mullawa being in a

demo with Virginia Bell. I can't even remember what we were demonstrating about. We had placards etc.[189]

One landmark criminal case run by Nan Rogers in 1981 was reported in Redfone under the heading ' Nan Clean Sweeps the High Court.'[190] The case of *R v Donald Geoffrey McPherson* in the High Court found that High Court Judges are under an obligation to inform unrepresented accused persons of their rights. The judge presiding at a criminal trial is under an obligation to ensure that the trial is conducted fairly and in accordance with law. He must accordingly exclude evidence tendered against the accused which is not shown to be admissible. Particularly if the accused is unrepresented, once it appears that there is a real question as to the voluntariness of a confession tendered by the Crown, the judge must satisfy himself that the confession was voluntary, and if, as will usually be the case, this can only be done by holding a voir dire, he must proceed to hold a voir dire even if none is asked for.'[191]

In 1978, John Kirkwood approached lawyer Peter Stapleton to come onto the Centre's volunteer roster. Stapleton had been involved with the establishment of the ALS and had been on their management committee and assisted in drafting their Constitution.[192] He started on the roster in February 1978 from Sly and Russell,[193] later went onto the management committee and is still on the Board today. Craddock comments that: 'The person whom I think has contributed the most to the Centre over time is Peter Stapleton.'[194] Stapleton went onto the Thursday night solicitors' roster. 'It was great, it was demanding… a lot of the essence was how the people on the night bonded together.' The firm that he was working in at the time was conservative, (Peter was the first Catholic and the first Labor party voter to become a partner in the firm) but did not oppose his volunteer work at the Centre.[195]

> I was working in corporate law and takeovers and [at RLC] you are dealing with railway fines, tenancy problems etc…at Redfern you didn't have the support systems there at all compared to a law firm. At law firms you had a secretary, human resources…at Redfern you were everything… we established an audit system—there was an endeavour to establish quality systems whereby files were checked on a regular basis… The relationship between the Centre and UNSW was bonded…John Basten was a manager telling us all the things we were doing wrong… He had a great intellect and was very disciplined…John would pull us up on proper approaches to cases and the law…He was a leader in the legal practice… We would go for weekends planning meetings—the big discussion was focus on grassroots assistance or putting energy into reforming the system…this was always a huge topic at all those meetings.[196]

Paul Farrugia also started in early 1978. He started on a Wednesday night with Debbie Whitmont on duty.[197] 'There was a great buzz about the place… We were all young idealistic crusading lawyers—filling a gap in rudimentary legal aid program.'[198] Farrugia gave advice on evenings and later took time off his private practice to do advice on afternoons for an extraordinary 20-25 years.

> I was self employed so it was easier for me. It was dynamic—a lot of people were interested and keen and working with the students was a great innovation…We all formed friendships very quickly. I remember loving that we didn't have to think about costs. That I didn't have to think about money… The Centre was really well organised. In fact I think I adopted a few ways of doing things in my own practice from Redfern.[199]

Farrugia was aware of the value of RLC to the clients.

> I doubt there were any other late night advice services. Occasionally I would do home services—Getting wills signed for people who were not mobile….Redfern wasn't gentrified. I wasn't

ever actually scared but there were concerns about young students wandering streets late at night. Not a major factor. Redfern was a little bit wilder in those days. Some clients had mental health issues and there were a few who became well known.... We had a connection to the interpreter service. We could get them to come along or sometimes we would use the telephone interpreter service. Redfern was a practical working legal office and maybe adapted to changing technology faster than other legal firms as there were so many young people there. No one ever got dressed up. We were all very casual. It made the clients feel more comfortable. I adopted the same approach in my private practice and stopped wearing ties a long time ago. If lawyers talk down to people that doesn't encourage confidence. It is an important part of being a lawyer to make people feel at ease.[200]

## Roger West comments:

The Centre was run in a way that we didn't have to toe anyone's line or seek permissions from anyone. You could make the decisions you wanted to make. Owen Jessup and Michael Chesterman were very supportive in the Law School and guided us. We were very concerned to ensure that the quality of legal advice was as good as it could be. The Law Society was trying to come to terms with this strange beast. They were a bit hostile and were looking at the quality of the service. And the issue of who was going to control that quality. Every file had to be managed in a way that was consistent with having volunteers. Owen Jessup or Michael Chesterman had a roster whom we nicknamed the Gang of 6—to go through every file and check them systematically and attaching suggestions etc. It was a great quality control system. This was a way of ensuring the volunteer's advice was sound... We had no means test—just anyone who couldn't afford a private lawyer.[201]

## Simon Rice recalls:

Roger was working there. And Virginia. I was terrified of Virginia.

She was so tough, no nonsense and straightforward. Roger was so gentle and accommodating...There was a big book and you'd turn up and you'd open up the book and the book had instructions in it for students to work on. Rosters were for half a day but you were welcome. You could hang around longer. It was not overly regimented. Files were manila folders and you would put action on the files and put it down in the book for yourself or someone else to work on...I used to get in early as I lived in Redfern. You would catch Owen Jessup like an elf in the night going through the files. He was a volunteer lawyer there. He would go in early and check the files and make sure they had forward dates.[202]

Another full-time volunteer at this time was Garth Symonds.[203] Symonds was admitted in 1973 as a solicitor and went to Oxford. He then went to work at North Kensington Law Centre for a year or two in the mid-1970s—as a volunteer. 'Terry Buddin came over to the UK and told me RLC was starting up and I went back to Australia and became a full-time volunteer at RLC in 1978. At North Kensington Legal Centre people were not only interested in individual casework but interested in making a more profound difference—They were interested in social change, group work.'[204] When he arrived at RLC, 'The Centre was still trying to figure how to operate.'[205]

'The fundamental difference from North Kensington LC was that ...the dominant focus for the Centre as far as I was concerned was doing individual casework. This is where I differed from the others. There was a management committee and retreats and we would discuss our policy. I was hot off the boat from North Kensington and would say we should also be focused on social change—by test cases or by lobbying or by writing policy papers – No one was terribly interested in that. Nobody objected to my doing that type of work. I wrote a submission about Children's Legal Aid. People were fine if I did it but they weren't terribly interested in joining in.'²⁰⁶ Symond's outlook on RLC's work was articulated at many meetings. In meetings as Stapleton recalls 'Garth Symonds was very focused on reform—he could create a lot of heated discussion on his own.'²⁰⁷ Symonds adds: 'Virginia and I were responsible for supervising students and follow up work from clients attending. John Terry might ask us for help but then there were particular files which we had which we worked on ... I shared a house with John Terry, a stone's throw away from RLC and Helen Golding lived there for a while too. People would come over—the house was a bit of a lively social scene with some pretty interesting personalities...John [Terry] was gregarious, an extrovert, loved life. He took his legal work seriously.'²⁰⁸

In 1978, Debbie Whitmont had been offered two jobs as a lawyer and was conflicted about which one to choose.

> Many people told me not to go to Redfern Legal Centre. RLC was having a lot of trouble with the Law Society – accepting that working at Redfern could make you eligible for a practising certificate was difficult... The feeling was that private practitioners didn't like the Centre... I was told clearly I could kiss goodbye to my career if I decided my first job would be at Redfern Legal Centre. But I took the RLC job. John Basten referred to it as the "Earth Mother" position... it involved seeing people turned up for their shifts and checking people completed files properly... organising when we went on conferences... deal with clients etc...We went to Falls Creek with the Victorian CLCs around 1981. That was exciting 'cause we met all the Victorian CLC people. There was a lot of discussion... There were definitely disagreements... I always felt like I didn't have a social and political structure to fit the Centre in—not like someone like Robyn Lansdowne who seemed fearfully smart and to understand everything and have a lot to say—I always felt like a bit of a novice...There was a wonderful sense of equality

there... It was my whole life when I worked there...we would go to the pub...out to dinner after shifts.²⁰⁹

John Kirkwood was an activist who had studied at Sydney Law School. He was recruited by Tony Blackshield to do tutoring at UNSW before he had even finished his law degree.²¹⁰ He spoke German and French and was given a Swiss government scholarship to study international law in Geneva. He translated some radical texts into English and travelled in Africa as he had become friends with Sekai Holland (the former Zimbabwean Co-Minister of State for National Healing). He volunteered at the Aboriginal Legal Service and did some practical training with Bruce Miles and worked at the DPP.²¹¹ He and Buddin were long term housemates and had many late night discussions about the idea of a Law School clinic. John Kirkwood had boundless energy and was someone who drove ideas and action.²¹² He had a profound social conscience and was teaching social security law. One lawyer at the time noted: 'John Kirkwood was a remarkable guy. He was extraordinary. John was the great mediator, the great man trying to bring harmony. He had such a gentle and intelligent way about him. He was excellent in that way.'

'The Centre was really close to John's heart. It was the thing he wanted most to happen.'²¹³ John was involved with the Centre as a volunteer lawyer, a member of the management committee and one of the Directors of RLC Ltd and actively involved in the production of the Legal Resources Book. He was a very healthy man but was diagnosed with a brain tumour in 1979 at the age of 30. He was given a year to live but lived for seven years working all of the time at the Law School, the Centre and on the Social Security Tribunal. For him the work was the important thing and to keep contributing.²¹⁴ He set up the first course in social security law in Australia and wrote a book called

*Social Security Law and Policy*[215] which was not published until after his death on 4 January 1986.

> In RLC's Tenth Year Report it states 'When he died as a result of the tumour at the age of 37 Redfern Legal Centre lost part of itself.'[216] The John W. Kirkwood Memorial Scholarship was established to assist students who may be experiencing financial difficulty to undertake study in the Faculty of Law and Justice at UNSW.

The work of the Centre was not limited to case work. West comments:

> We wanted to push boundaries in a smart way. We could do legal education, we could do test cases in the High Court, we could do law reform—I am incredibly privileged to say we could do all of that. We were doing legal education and legal advice sessions in the Eveleigh train workshops at three in the morning as that was people's lunch times. Hardly anyone could speak English. They were mainly women were cleaning trains and scrubbing down the outside and inside of trains with buckets. And then at lunchtime they were coming out to go to legal education on family law, domestic violence, de facto rights etc. It was a really exciting thing to be doing. We had government interpreters lined up to do it.[217]

Work at the Centre for staff and volunteers was full on. In 1978 when a letter arrived from the Health Department offering places in a relaxation course. It was jokingly agreed that 'the Centre's full-time staff should undertake an intensive two-year course.'[218]

The Sydney CLC group though was known for having fun. Despite close links with colleagues at Fitzroy Legal Service in Victoria, the two centres took different approaches. One saying at the time was 'If you have an idea in Victoria you call a meeting, if you have an idea in Sydney you have a party.'[219] Despite this comment, evidence shows there were plenty of meetings at the Sydney centre and no end of discussion. 'There was a lot of discussion… There were definitely disagreements…'[220] Bell remembers:

> I enjoyed the work. We used to have regular staff meetings but I was a bit intolerant, I think, of some of the discussions. I remember when the union of social workers came to see us. They had all these ideas that we should only work 35 hours a week. Not that I am anti-union, but I didn't think solicitors who were endeavouring to help people needed that kind of help. My focus was always on the casework. There was the Public Solicitor and the ALAO—but there was a limited amount of legal assistance.[221]

> Redfone (RLC internal magazine) recorded that on the night of the Royal Wedding July 29 1981, there were less clients than any other evening at the Centre.

Simon Rice was a student volunteering at the Centre in the early 1980s. He remembers that in about 1980 between the traffic lights on Pitt Street and the Town Hall there were six or seven triple story terraces. In each of those terraces there would have been 50 or 60 single men living… the police station on Turner Street was an old yellow smelly police station with aggro coppers who were not always happy that lawyers were there…. The pub—the Cricketers Arms [now Tudor Hotel] was really run down. There were no cafes.'[222]

Gerard (Crash) Craddock started volunteering at the Centre around 1980 and was also on the management committee.

> The students were engaged in most Centre activities… I remember the first client I ever saw… I worked with Julian Millar. The client needed a will. Julian told me to take the client in and

get some instructions and draft a will. So I did. Had I ever drafted a will? No. I had done legal systems and criminal law. Had I ever seen a will? No. Anyway I drafted a will and gave it to Julian and he laughed and laughed and that was my introduction to legal practice... The general run of volunteer lawyers were those practitioners who were just a bit more socially aware.... there was never any thought on the part of anyone that it was worth doing as a career move... Eddie Neumann was involved in the early stages ...Eddie liked private practice and had helped set up the ALS and the South Coast ALS.' Though averse to private practice at the beginning, Craddock later ended up working with Eddie Neumann and Greg Murray—both volunteer solicitors at Redfern.[223] Craddock and Murray noted a growing conservatism over time in the student body at UNSW. 'We did a little survey in about 1985 and there was a movement towards people in the universities figuring it [volunteering at RLC] was a career enhancement and we got a different kind of student...and the students were a bit more interested in having a beneficial experience at the Centre for themselves as they wanted to put on their CV that they had had this practical experience.[224]

Debbie Whitmont was the administrator of the Centre for a couple of years before a position of community lawyer was created—the first such position created in Australia. The idea was to look beyond particular cases and identify issues and then to try and achieve change in that area of law or policy. Whitmont was successful in being employed in that role. 'One issue of concern that was identified early on was the elderly. We organised a phone in with complaints about nursing homes... The Centre started thinking about specialisations—disability, womens' issues, social security etc. Whitmont also worked with others in establishing Marrickville Legal Centre.

> What distinguished it was it was geographically elsewhere but also culturally elsewhere. I remember one of the first things we did...we were SO enthusiastic! We organised Turkish lessons

> for all the volunteers...I remember one of the things we taught people to say was "I'm sorry there are no lawyers here at the moment"... [Redfern Legal Centre] 'was a huge education for me. Wonderful people in charge, trying to fight for things to be better. Working with people who were incredibly committed ... and had fun and drank a lot. It changed everything for me....
>
> Redfern had a very important role in building a bridge between the legal system and people who didn't have the power to use it—real people—that was the huge strength of it. Lawyers who worked in big city firms would come out once a fortnight after working hard all day and see people who would walk in off the street—some of whom had very difficult problems ... Redfern Legal Centre was THE legal centre. The only legal centre we had to compete with was Fitzroy. The relationship was incredibly competitive as to who was the best provider of services.[225]

The centre was well accepted in the Redfern area. Petre points out that 'when people understood what we were doing there was huge acceptance of the centre ... Locals got used to everyone. We ended up very good mates with the publican. We developed good relationships with local doctors and local traders like Roger the Shoeman.'[226] The centre worked in collaboration with many local organisations such as the Newtown Neighbourhood Centre which had opened on December 3rd 1977 and the Kings Cross tenancy service which started in September 1977.

## RELATIONSHIPS WITH THE LAW SOCIETY AND JUDGES

Before RLC opened, Garth Nettheim, a legal academic from UNSW, had discussions with the NSW Law Society Council about the proposed operations of RLC but the lecturers at the Law School, aware of the obstructive attitude to community-based law centres taken by professional associations in England and Victoria,[227] decided not to seek Law Society approval before starting the Centre. On 22 February 1977, Don Harley from the Law Society contacted the Centre and spoke to Robyn Lansdowne. He said he would come and visit the Centre in its first week of operation. Her note of the conversation states that he seemed 'if not enthusiastic, quite interested and non-critical', but she recalls feeling 'indignation that the Law Society were poking their nose in.'[228] He wanted to know the names of lawyers who were rostered on for the first week. He raised some potential issues about supervision and wanted to participate on the management committee organising the Centre. This was going a step too far for the Centre workers and by April 1977 this offer had been politely refused [229] though he did attend the second meeting of the Management Committee as an observer.

In a letter dated 25 March 1977, the secretary of the Law Society advised that the Executive Committee was concerned that aspects of the proposed operation of the Centre might give rise to breaches of the *Legal Practitioners Act*. The Society made recommendations to RLC that notices be displayed prominently to those seeking advice noting that between 9am and 5pm the Centre is 'manned by students not qualified to give legal advice and that referral out from the Centre be directed to a qualified practitioner on a panel as had been the case with existing referral Centres.' RLC's files do not include the response if any to these requirements but neither requirement was acted upon. In March 1977, the Society also raised concerns with the Commissioner of Corporate Affairs about the use of the name Redfern Legal Centre on the letterhead but no evidence appeared that any action was taken by the Commissioner.'[230]

> **The Judiciary**
>
> The general attitude of some of the legal profession especially those in positions of authority is illustrated by the 'Dialectical Diatribe' in RLC News December 1977. This short piece also illustrates the ongoing confusion of the Centre with the Aboriginal Legal Service that still persists today.
>
> 'Scene: Any suburban Court of Petty Sessions
>
> Players: Magistrate, his attendants, a lone solicitor and client
>
> ACTION
>
> Solicitor: If Your Worship please I appear for the Defendant in this matter
>
> Magistrate: Your Name is M....?
>
> Solicitor: Terry, Your Worship from the Redfern Legal Centre
>
> Magistrate: From the what?
>
> Solicitor: Redfern Legal Centre, Your Worship
>
> Magistrate: What is that Mr Terry? Do you mean the Aboriginal Legal Service?
>
> Solicitor: No Your Worship its...
>
> Magistrate: Redfern Legal Centre?! It's extraordinary
>
> Solicitor: I couldn't agree more Your Worship
>
> REPEAT AD INFINITUM'

In 1977, an RLC case came before Justice Yeldham, NSW Supreme Court.[231] While presiding on a tenancy matter, Justice Yeldham thought the operations of the Centre so extraordinary that he found it necessary to report his concern to the Law Society. A barrister acting on behalf of the Centre had taken instructions from a client without an instructing solicitor being present. The Judge referred aspects of RLCs practice to the Law Society being:

1. Whether a relationship of solicitor and client can and should exist between a client and a body corporate

2. The nature of the trust account at the Centre
3. Who held a practising certificate
4. Were unqualified practitioners operating at RLC?

Justice Yeldham's letter gave rise to a meeting between John Kirkwood (UNSW) and Don McKay, Vice President of the Law Society, at which McKay suggested again that the Society have a committee member attend at RLC Management Committee. The proposal was 'spiritedly rejected by the RLC contingent.'[232]

Some judges were on side though. High Court Justice Lionel Murphy's visit to the Centre on 8 November 1977 was followed by a lunch at restaurant Dilinas, which was described as most convivial. The RLC News[233] commented that 'John Terry's and John Kirkwood's respective faith in lawyers has been partially restored by the visit and they have graciously agreed to be available for any such lunches in the future.' It was also noted that 'Nobody was sure who had paid for the lunch.'[234]

The group involved in establishing the Centre differentiated their aims for a legal service from that of the more traditional approach of the legal profession as enunciated by the Law Society and the Bar Association. They were aware of the profession's previous hostility to the government's Australian Legal Aid Office and reform of the profession generally[235] and that, as Kevin Bell points out, community legal centres represented an even 'more fundamental challenge to the dominance of private practice.'[236] There was a general belief in Basten's claim that 'Any legal centre worthy of the name will be attempting to upset the status quo to some extent.'[237] Weisbrot notes that the centres attacked (or ignored) traditional notions of professionalism by advertising, using paralegals and blurring the distinction between solicitors and barrister.'[238]

Several months after the opening of the Centre, the Council of the Law Society made inquiries of the Law School and arranged a visit to the Centre. On being shown around the Centre, one senior member was heard to remark that 'it is just like a legal practice, really.'[239]

George Zdenkowski remembers:

> I do recall there were issues with the Law Society at the beginning around the sort of activities that were going on—issues such as supervision and the whole notion of volunteers and students. It was dressed up as concern for standards of professionalism but in some ways they were very conservative about that. I don't know if they saw it as a threat but it took a long time for the profession to realise the incredibly important role that CLCs had as a complementary part of the system.[240]

Virginia Bell adds:

> We had difficulties with the Law Society over letters on Redfern Legal Centre letterhead. They were concerned that Redfern Legal Centre was a company limited by guarantee and not under a name of the Principal. I remember going to talk to the President of the Law Society, Rod McGeoch. These things were new, and new for the Law Society. I think we had a siege mentality in the sense that, outside a few barristers that were sympathetic, we tended not to call on the Bar and started off assuming the professional bodies were not in favour of the Centre. We saw ourselves as outsiders. I think we were apprehensive and felt that we were not treated well.[241]

Volunteer lawyer Paul Farrugia explains:

> The legal profession definitely had a bit of antagonism to the Centre because we were taking work away from the private profession but I would say the kind of work we are doing would not be taken on by the private profession and the clients were not ones that private lawyers wanted. We didn't do

conveyancing or personal injury. We had panels of lawyers later on we referred matters to.[242]

Debbie Whitmont remembers, though, that local lawyers were generally welcoming and that the Centre had good relationships with them.[243] But the profession's fears were slow to dissipate. In 1984, the President of St George/Sutherland Law Society raised his concerns about the Centre in a newsletter. 'I have statistics of the Redfern Legal Centre. They open an average of 341 files per month, 4,086 files in 1983 and granted 7,958 interviews in 1983. Want to know where all the clients are going?'[244] This concern by the private profession that they were missing out on clients, and therefore income, was common in the early years of community legal centres and legal aid bodies[245] but evaporated after the profession realised that clients taken on by CLCs and legal aid were in almost all cases clients who could not pay private fees and in fact referrals from CLCs to the private profession actually increased work for private lawyers.

## REDFERN COURT

The Redfern Court House was designed by the Government Architect WL Vernon in 1896. A report in the *Sydney Morning Herald* on 25 August 1897 described the buildings as 'one of the most commodious and best fitted Police courts outside the city of Sydney.'[246] It was not opened until March in 1898 when the *Daily Telegraph* reported that 'At Redfern yesterday morning several prisoners earned the rather unenviable distinction of being the first to receive sentence in the new courthouse, and were probably the only interested persons present who did not appreciate the comfort and conveniences of the building.'[247]

## MAGISTRATES

Andy Haesler recalls some of the magistrates sitting at Redfern Court in the 1980s and 1990s. "Reasonable Doubt" Jones SM—a lovely inoffensive man, who actually knew what beyond reasonable doubt meant. Kevin Anderson SM—who when he sat would occasionally come over for morning tea/lunch and often as not helped out at the counter! He was a gem—unless you were prosecuting a DV case in front of him.[248] He and police prosecutor Sergeant Ray Hood worked hand in hand and didn't like the newfangled legal aid lawyers across the road.'[249]

Magistrate Sue Schreiner was at Redfern Court for about eight years from 1980 to 1988. In 1962, she was the first woman in the ACT to be admitted to practice, signing the High Court roll as a barrister and solicitor and was also the first woman to appear in the ACT Supreme Court.[250] She was a larger than life figure at the court in the 1980s and well known by all the RLC and ALS staff at the time. She had an unusual way of dealing with matters in the court saying 'You were dealing with the people in front of you and you had to look at how to deal with drug problems, and how to deal with drink driving. I started a number of ways of dealing with those sort of things other than fining people who had no money, or sending them to jail because there was no point.'[251]

Haesler remembers she could be intimidating particularly to young women in court. 'I had words to her once or twice about her stern demeanour, particularly to young women. She said she was trying to help (old style feministas were like that!) She advised me to get them to see her in chambers before their first appearance. It didn't work, she was still too demanding. She told me once "before I come on the bench I promise myself I'll be nice, BUT then I see the prosecutor and all you lot and well…" It could be a circus at times… she once loudly invited me to the bar table ahead of turn to "restore some sanity to the proceedings" much to the embarrassment of the ALS solicitor who was then appearing. When I appeared for Brian Huckstepp the prosecutor said "Not known to the court." Sue responded "Well he's known to me and Mr Haesler!" She had a toy box for any kids in court.'[252]

Goddard recalls: 'I vividly remember my first ever cross examination of a witness. She rolled her eyes and told me point blank that my questions were totally irrelevant. Either she was trying to toughen me up or my questions were in fact totally irrelevant and I deserved it. Either way, having been scarred for life, it was also my last ever cross examination of a witness…I did like the way she wore ugh boots though, long before they were fashionable.'[253] The author recalls an occasion in court when Magistrate Schreiner was dealing with a man convicted of drink driving. Bypassing his barrister, she asked the man to tell the court exactly what was wrong with drinking and driving. As his response was only that one could get caught and get a fine she decided to make it a compulsory part of his sentence that he write an 1000 word essay on the dangers of drink driving. At the Bar table his barrister sighed deeply and muttered sotto voce "I suppose I'll have to write that for him now as well." She was particularly interested in the welfare of Aboriginal people who came before the court and would always try to assist them in a constructive manner.

One incident occurred when a representation of Aboriginal men in custody, taped to the wall in front of the prosecutor's desk in court, had been rescribed to say 'I Went to the ALS, and now l ended up in here' was brought to the attention of the ALS. The upshot was that Magistrate Schreiner, upon hearing an application that the Prosecutor's leave to appear be withdrawn, declared that she would hear no matters involving Aboriginal people that day, whilst the matter was examined. The Sergeant, whose occupation of the relevant desk was intimate and long-term, denied having even seen the item until it was drawn to the court's attention."

Barrister, Angus Webb adds: 'I rode a motor bike in those days, which was always tucked in next to the front steps during the day. On one occasion I asked her [Schreiner] to stand a matter in the list as a regular had failed to appear. I went off on the bike and brought my client back, to avoid the issue of a warrant for his arrest. She loved telling the story over the years, but also the success of the venture meant that it was repeated a number of times!'[254]

Other magistrates at the court during this period include Greg Glass who had been State Coroner. The Centre invited him for a morning tea one day which was the custom with all new magistrates. As he was leaving the room, Gordon Renouf famously exclaimed "He's got the concentration span of a gnat." As Goddard recalls 'Gordon's inability to whisper and the cavernous nature of the Town Hall' ensured he must have heard the comment.[255]

In 2004, the NSW government announced that 'the historic Redfern courthouse will be shut down by early next year because it is unworkable, lacks security and is too expensive to upgrade.'[256] The court was closed on 20 May 2005 and the records were transferred to Local Court at the Downing Centre.[257]

## MANAGEMENT AND COMMUNITY CONTROL

The first Redfern Legal Centre management committee meeting was held at the seriously committed time of 10am on a Sunday morning on 20 March 1977. Kathy Pierce was the Chairperson and ten others attended. Nitty gritty matters were dealt with—details of services to be provided, statistics, file procedures, the all-important Diary and File Book. Stephen Catt was the treasurer, the bank account contained $1310 from the Law School Notes Fund and the Student Law Society. Lindy Jones was doing publicity and arranging promotion in ethnic newspapers and information for radio. John Basten was to chase the Council for information about the promised Council social worker/Coordinator position.[258] By April 1977 a management committee meeting noted that things were clearly moving ahead. It was minuted that Stephen Catt was authorised to 'obtain twelve porcelain mugs, detergent, two tea towels, half a dozen tea spoons, a sugar tin and a scrubber'…The significance of this item of business was noted at several stages of the meeting.'[259] Terry Buddin comments that for many years, apart from the core group, basically the management committee was open to anyone who wished to turn up. Once the full-time people were employed they drove the management committee. 'That is the astonishing thing about it—there were so many superb human beings who were incredibly dedicated and really believed in what was happening and devoted an enormous amount of time to achieving change.'[260] Funding was a constant issue. 'We were in survival mode a lot.'[261]

Once Roger West came to the Centre, he became involved with the management and took over a lot of the management issues together with Clare Petre.[262] West had come from Melbourne and studied law at Melbourne University finishing in 1975. He joined a commercial firm in Melbourne and went to Fitzroy Legal Service as a volunteer lawyer. He decided he wanted to leave Melbourne, took up an offer from law firm, Dawson Waldron and en route to Sydney he read in a newspaper in Canberra that Redfern Legal Centre had opened that week.[263] 'I started to go to RLC at night. It was said that that Dawson Waldron were a bit lefty—the pink lawyers but when I tried to talk to other young lawyers at the firm about coming out to the Centre they were excited by the idea but some of them found that the partners who they worked to were not the least bit impressed by the fact they would want to do this. To the point where a few of those lawyers did come and volunteer at Redfern Legal Centre they would walk out of the firm at 6pm which was very early for a young lawyer to leave in the evening…they would carry a squash racket to pretend that was why they are leaving… I was taken aside by a partner: 'If you don't show that you're committed to our firm and its interests and you have divided interests with poverty law… then people will be questioning your commitment.'[264]

Lansdowne recalls: 'I remember the day Roger West arrived. He had driven up from Melbourne and arrived in his pick up truck. He came in fresh faced and wanted to be part of it.'[265] 'We noticed a number of changes when Roger arrived in 1979. Roger put a bit more rigour into the system as a practice but there had always been an expectation that we had to be better than the private practice. Given they didn't want us, then we had to show that we could provide a service they weren't providing. We had to be the equivalent at least in terms of legal advice that you could get from the big end of town'.

West comments, 'One thing I noticed …I think I was the first salaried solicitor who had come out of a large law firm and the thing that I noticed was that some of the lawyers would operate outside usual practice administration terms. It never occurred to most of the lawyers to have a formal file review system for instance. Files would be left in the offices or they would rely on their memory. I introduced a formal file review system… People were not very aware of legal practice law rules whereas I had been trained in those things due to my work in the law firm. I was very conscious of that to the point of probably being a bit anal about it. This may have annoyed some people but most accepted these ideas and over the next five years, the legal centres became more conscious of these practices and more professional and conscientious about how they did things.'[266] People tell jokes still about Roger's attention to detail.[267]

West went onto the management committee straight away. Two years later, in 1979, he left his firm and became full-time Principal Solicitor at RLC. 'We used to say it's really important we are not here in 20 years from now on. We consciously knew we would not make a career out of this. Later they [staff of RLC] all wanted us to be on the management committee but we said "No, we don't want to rule from the grave"—we didn't want the old people telling the young people what to do. Often now people don't leave—they are very experienced people. I just know the atmosphere is different. I would not have had the freedom in those legal centres to do anything I wanted to do I would have had to meet their approval. It doesn't mean it's not a better legal centre.'[268] Cathy Kerr[269] remembers: 'I remember a speech by Virginia Bell where she said they thought if they were doing their job well there would be no reason for them as what they were doing was empowering people to do their own stuff.'[270]

The Centre was not a grassroots community organisation. There were always tensions between the needs of the local community and the wider population, and debates as to what extent the Centre should be community controlled. Community control was a topic of much discussion in the 1970s in Australia, the UK and the USA in relation to human services.[271] Arguments in favour of community control present the demand for vesting governmental authority at the neighbourhood level in terms of the liberal democratic tradition. According to this model, individuals become alienated from government and society unless they can effectively participate in the determination of public policy as it affects them most directly.[272] Law Centres in the USA endorsed a model whereby community control was in part a means of negating control by the organised bar which they felt would be opposed to a more aggressive form of advocacy, one that would seek to use the law as an instrument of social change. The lawyers were also committed to altering the conventional power relation between the poor and the agencies that purport to serve them. Community control would create new opportunities for the poor to participate in determining agency policy and decisions, and this principle should also apply to legal service programs for the poor, or so it was felt.[273]

Many of those influential at Redfern Legal Centre's beginning wanted what they termed community focus, not community control, possibly developing a new and more accurate description of the community involvement that was to become the standard in Australian legal centres. This can be contrasted with the rhetoric at Fitzroy and other Victorian community legal centres.[274] In a paper on community control, Basten wrote 'I remain to be convinced however that "community control", as a principle of general application, is any more than a catch cry based on an anachronistic view of society and appealing to the guilt felt by privileged but concerned professionals working with disadvantaged people.'[275] In papers written by RLC staff and volunteers the issues were canvassed. As Lansdowne pointed out 'Redfern Legal Centre was not set up in response to a cry from the heart of Redfern—it was largely a matter of contingencies that the legal centre was sited in Redfern rather than somewhere else.'[276] The varying arguments raised in RLC papers about community involvement were in summary that:

 a) the Centre should be arming the poor to fight their own legal and political battles, not making middle class professionals such as Centre staff indispensable;

 b) the Centre should be working to overcome the powerlessness of the clients, and responding to the real needs of the clients by enabling clients themselves to identify their needs and priorities;

c) there should be accountability to the community for expenditure of funds and decisions about service provision to clients;

d) community involvement would build political support in the community and maintain the vitality of the Centre;

e) it took considerable time and effort and resources to get members of the local community on the management committee together with concerns that people may be out of their depth or bored and, given that middle-class members may overpower others, may not be worthwhile;

f) a concern that other people would change the culture of the Centre if their involvement was anything other than token;

g) it would be better for workers at the Centre to get involved in already existing community groups or formalising control to have places for local residents on the committee to allow community input.

These issues about the role of community members in the Centre were to have an important role in Centre discussions for the next 40 years.[277] Community involvement as a concept was of national concern to CLCs and was the subject of a session at the Second National Conference of community legal centres in March 1980.[278] The conclusion adopted by the RLC team was in the end 'that the concept of "community control" is vague and even in its most practical sense it will be difficult to achieve.'[279] 'We were a bit cynical about community control as it didn't really seem to be about the punters on the street but community organisations.'[280] The Centre was set up as a company limited by guarantee however the directors of the company in practice delegated decision-making power to the Management Committee. Workers at the Centre such as West believed that efforts to adopt 'community control' would end up with members of community organisations being represented on the RLC management rather than any real representation from local individuals.[281]

Centre workers decided that legal aid agencies should provide legal services to disadvantaged individuals and groups in a way that consumer powerlessness is lessened and sense of reliance on professional help minimised. The Centre should have close links with the neighbourhood in which it operates. This was to come about without vesting control of Centre policy to local residents. Examples given of how this could occur is that staff could live in the local area, staff can assist in local organisations, drink in local pubs, members of local organisations may attend Centre meetings, etc.[282] At the beginning of the Centre's operations, Basten observed that although the Centre:

> Never had any local residents on its management committee, that committee actively sought comment and criticism from local social agencies. The management committee never had a fixed membership and was open to anyone working at or interested in the operations of the Centre. [283]

The basic operations of the Centre—evening advice services and general casework—continued mostly unchanged through the 1980s and 1990s. Relationships with the profession and government though changed over the years. As Noone points out, by the 1990s government support and funding had increased. CLCs were no longer on the fringe of the legal aid system but were considered to be an essential element of the system by both government and the legal profession.[284]

## CONSOLIDATION: 1980S AND 1990S

'There was a view that the place should have been closed down by 1984. All the things we wanted to achieve had been achieved by 1984. We had shown that laws could be changed by groups of volunteers and that there was another way of doing legal practice. When I came back in 1985, we kept working on establishing it as a professional and lasting legal office... It had lost its mad edge or its cutting edge and became more of an institution that governments and other agencies turned to expecting a professional service. We became mainstream... Maybe we shouldn't have—maybe we should have stayed a voluntary service.'[285]

*Andy Haesler*

### Simon Rice, solicitor and volunteer at the Centre remembers:

I was 22 or 23, and these were intensely confronting personal experiences and when you think of the autonomy we were given to do this...I thrived on it. I learnt a great deal and I wasn't ever frightened by it which is why working on insurance cases at Sly and Russell was never going to capture my imagination... We used to go into people's homes—going into the housing commission or going in terraces living in beautiful neat poverty or complete squalor.

The first case I ran—I acted for a pregnant woman who was attending a family clinic in Surry Hills where they also did terminations. While there, a mad woman who used to permanently protest terminations outside the clinic photographed her—screaming at her and so my client pushed that woman out of the way. The woman called the police and I ended up defending my client against an assault charge. She didn't have a defence. I ran what I suspect was a fairly incoherent case. The magistrate though was so appalled by the conduct my client was subjected to. He separated battery from assault and came to a finding in her favour. An example of justice transcending the law as I tell my students...I remember going to Redfern Court with Andy [Haesler]. We would do the tenancy list. This was where I learnt from Andy and Roger, the strength of attention to detail. We would constantly defer evictions by finding technical faults with notices issues under the *Landlord and Tenant Act 1989*.... It was a great game and a lot of fun. But it was keeping people in their homes...That casework directly led to the work RLC did and Andy principally did to lead to the repeal of the 1989 Act and the enactment of new tenancy legislation...We used to go and do apprehended violence work. There was no special legislation and we would get breach of the peace orders and complain when the peace was breached... I used to do some work for kids at the Children's Court. Bidura. I ended up running a neglect case representing a grandmother who had been caring for her grandson and Community Services wanted to take the child away from her and the mother. I represented her in front of [magistrate] Barbara Holboro. That was at the edge of my experience. I was struggling.'[286]

Management structure and governance did change slightly in the late 1980s. At the beginning RLC had a flat management structure. All staff were equal and decisions were made collectively. Meetings were held once a month and anyone who showed up was part of the Committee. 'Sometimes 12 people would turn up and sometimes 45. It worked pretty well. There was robust discussion … You had the sense of a community. It was a bunch of people with more or less values aligned, teasing out difficult problems, working out what the priorities should be but also on a collective mission to achieve something.'[287] In January 1988 after a management consultant's report following an industrial dispute, the management structure changed to have a fixed membership which included staff, volunteer and community representatives.[288] Not everyone was in favour of these changes. Basten: 'The whole thing became more established… There was less room for the informal activity…it was always intended to have a political focus and to be involved in political campaigns... I thought community people would never understand how that could be done as they weren't part of the legal system and we would get the wrong people...we got people who were used to being on committees...it was never our idea that we would be community run.'[289]

The Management Committee would decide the area of work people would focus on. When Gordon Renouf arrived in the mid-1980s he quickly got involved in the Management Committee. "Sometimes people would get irritated when people went on too much. From memory people were respectful. A lot of staff attended meetings. The role of chairing and taking minutes was always a bit vague. One day I volunteered to take minutes and people liked the way I took minutes and as a wet behind the ears volunteer I was very chuffed by this.'[290]

Sarah Crawford was a volunteer representative on the Management Committee during the 1990s. She described the work as 'a mix of policy and organisational issues...It always seemed to be about the balance between casework and high policy work and whether we ran a community service or a law reform service—that was the main flavour that permeated throughout... Redfern should be an essential part of every law student's study... this is the real face of what you are doing—just to get a concrete picture of how the law can affect people...'[291]

Staff meetings at the Centre at this time were the focus of decision making. Steve Bolt recalls the 'Hour of Power' at staff meetings—a democratic initiative to allow people who might not have other matters on the agenda to raise any issues they wished to. Staff meetings discussed staffing matters, work issues on different projects, arrangements for leave. Topics at staff meetings and management discussions overlapped. 'Staff meetings were more jokey—more laughs were had.'[292]

Matters were discussed in great detail at management meetings. Katherine Biber recalls that everything was discussed even pest control. The Intellectual Disability Rights Service, when they were upstairs, had a running battle with a pigeon infestation. 'At one point the Centre was infested with cockroaches and a proposal to spray them was advanced. Someone did some research and said that pesticide is really dangerous—one of its side effects is that it could "feminise" men and someone else said what's the problem with that?… I can't believe we even had to discuss getting rid of the cockroaches… They would even crawl out of the handset of the telephone you were using. We had this discussion which went for a long time and eventually ended up using some natural type of pyrethrum or something.'[293]

Helen Campbell recalls: 'Redfern Legal Centre was a member of a group of community legal centres in those days known as the Combined Community Legal Centres Group and we had monthly meetings. We used to meet in the Media Arts Alliance Building on Redfern Street. I used to have contact through that meeting when I was working with Womens' Legal Centre or Blue Mountains Legal Centre with Redfern Legal Centre staff. We would all sit around in a circle. The Redfern people were so bossy. The tyranny of structuralness. Basically, my impression with that group was that nothing would get done unless Redfern Legal Centre wanted it done… I don't know why—It's the oldest and was probably the largest legal centre. It had a reputation and the other community legal centres were not there yet. Many of the other CLCs had developed out of Redfern Legal Centre. It was like Redfern was a parent'.[294]

In 1983, Roger West went off to work at the Welfare Rights Centre.[295] When he came back in 1984, he and Virginia [Bell] became joint Principal Solicitors. In 1984, Andy Haesler went to work at CAALAS (Central Australian Aboriginal Legal Aid Service).

Dominic Gibson recalls: 'All of us were just waiting to get a job in legal aid. I applied for the consumer credit job at RLC about March 1983…When I was waiting for my interview, Crash Craddock was being interviewed before me. He came down the stairs out of the interview room with the remains of a six-pack of beer that he had just shared with the interview committee.'[296] When Dominic Gibson went for his next interview at RLC around June 1983, he took a bottle of red wine in. I thought I'd go one better than Crash.' [297] The interview panel happily shared the offering.

Ben Slade recalls his luck in getting a job interview at RLC in August 1984 despite spelling the word Centre wrongly in the first draft of his application.[298] At the interview he was asked by Nan Rogers[299] if he would consider working for the Prosecution. He knew that if he had answered this question in the affirmative, and said he could see no difference in value in working for the defence as compared to the Prosecution, he would have failed in his demonstration of his social justice credentials.[300]

Within three months of Slade starting, at the end of 1984/1985 Virginia Bell, Roger West and Clare Petre came out to the volunteers' front desk and made the announcement that they were all resigning. West and Bell decided they were going to the Bar. Petre was going to work in TV. Slade recalls: 'Bill Dickens who had been there a year said to me 'Oh god. You've just started and we've inherited a legal centre.' 'It was really frightening. I didn't know how to do anything and Bill Dickens was a baby.' Slade recalls: 'It was really shocking. They were Mum and Dad and we were all the kids who drank too much and partied too much and had no responsibility and didn't feel we could run the bloody place. It was like Mum and Dad were leaving without talking to us.'[301]

RLC advertised for a Principal Solicitor and didn't find anyone suitable. There were difficulties at CAALAS in Alice Springs. Haesler got a number of calls asking him to apply for the job. He decided to return as Coordinator and Principal Solicitor. He was back by mid-1985 and stayed till 1989. Then Simon Rice and (following his departure) Frances Gibson were employed.[302]

When Haesler came back he had a policy that the Centre should be in the media every week. He realised that this was an effective way of getting noticed and getting the law changed. 'Important people' were encouraged to drop into the Centre. Lionel Bowen was the local member. Clover Moore would come in. The Centre had a reasonable relationship with Council. Outreach legal advice services were run at Department of Housing tower blocks and various women's services.

Mick Hillman studied social work at the University of Sydney in the late 1970s. Clare Petre came out to the university and did a talk on the legal aid system. "She was a breath of fresh air".[303] In the early 1980s, he coordinated a Family and Children's Centre in Botany and had some contact with the Centre referring clients to RLC.

He described the RLC *Legal Resources Book* (later *Law Handbook*) as a "bible sitting on the shelf at the time."[304] Hillman started work in the social worker position at RLC in 1987. He understood that every social worker who had been there had been 'an entirely different kind of social worker which was to some extent confusing for the solicitors there.'[305]

> It was a chance to be in an organisation that was very politically active and to mix up the range of social work jobs that I was interested in. There was a very steep learning curve and it was very much full on... there were lots of people coming in all the time... it was full on in the variety of issues that came in and the people that came in... a wide range of different ethnic groups and

> the extra rigour if you want to call it that—that lawyers brought to a place. I was the fall back person for a lot of things that the lawyers probably saw as not their role... I felt on the negative side at times that a social work role was defined as being everything that wasn't legal and I was worried how the collaboration would come in... but that was just something we had to work through...I had quite a lot of autonomy... I split it up into areas casework... advocacy rather than just counselling, supervision of volunteer shifts, community education... juvenile justice and community development role and policy work.[306]

Hillman worked on immigration cases including for Fijian Indians wanting assistance after the coup in Fiji and domestic violence and social security cases. He also appeared at the Residential Tenancies Tribunal occasionally. He was quite involved with Department of Housing cases where the Department was taking action about cases where they thought premises were underoccupied. He organised a roster of people on call to assist young people being interviewed by the police. Hillman notes there was an all open staff model of management where everyone had their say inherited from the original idea of Redfern Legal Centre but when Mary Perkins was appointed as a Coordinator it was easier for staff to know where they fitted in. It was he says, though rare, if a staff member really wanted to do something that the staff meeting would say no.[307] 'We all used to repair to the Cricketers Rest and quite a lot of ideas came through that...I think the level of stress was quite high…it came in waves when deadlines came up or on occasions where funding was threatened'.[308] Hillman says 'I regret leaving—it was probably the best job I had.'[309]

Mary Perkins had been involved in many activist movements in the 1970s stemming from the Vietnam War. She worked with the Aquarius Youth Service in Kings Cross with homeless youth in the late 1970s and notes that there was very little legal assistance for young people until Redfern Legal Centre appeared to provide assistance. She then worked on setting up the Tenants Union. 'This was also in Redfern in Botany Road in the old Church in 1980s. Redfern had a lot of innovative community organisations at this stage. The whole social welfare organisation had adopted a more participatory and activist approach to service delivery. I suspect this came out of the Whitlam era and the notion we could have a more participatory democracy.'[310] Perkins worked with Roger West in these times and the community lawyer. The TU would also work with Andy Haesler on tenants' campaigns such as the Camperdown tenants' campaign in the early 1980s.

Perkins notes:

> RLC was originally a boiling pot of ideas...then it stopped being a brand new organisation and consolidated into an organisation with a place in the legal system rather than being on the fringe yelling at the legal system... I was interviewed for the position of Coordinator. It was made very clear to me that they wanted to move away from a collective model of organisation into one where it was more delineated in terms of roles and responsibilities....I remember thinking it was a tall order...Redfern was breaking new ground on significant case work—The State Bank case, the Nicholson housing case and Home Fund cases were kicked off by Redfern.[311]

## HIV/AIDS

Australia's first case of Acquired Immunodeficiency Syndrome (AIDS) was publicly reported in May 1983.[312] This new disease provoked a phobic reaction which caused the professions, the media, and the public to treat it as much more dangerous and infectious than it was.[313] The Federal Labor government invited the gay community and other at risk groups to be part of devising the official government response which built on activist work to raise awareness. Their expertise ensured Australia had an outstanding response to this disease and infections peaked in Australia in 1983 and had dropped by 1987, though, the effects of the disease in relation to legal problems continues. Redfern Legal Centre acted for a number of clients with AIDS in different areas of the law during this period.

The Centre ran victim's compensation cases involving people whose HIV status had worsened as a result of the attack on them and ran housing cases of various types for clients with AIDS.[314] There was a great deal of fear in the community and inappropriate responses by the bureaucracy. The author recalls appearing at Redfern Local Court for a client who was HIV positive only to find all the police officers attending the court dressed in head to toe white protective suits. In 1988, the Australian Federation of AIDS Organisations (AFAO), with help from Redfern Legal Centre Publishing, published a pamphlet 'AIDS and Your Rights' which channelled inquiries to the community legal centres 'because many people affected are unable to afford legal advice and representation; because of the experience of the community legal centre movement in anti-discrimination law and public law issues; and because of the role of legal centres in cases where the cause is novel and the facts are challenging.'[315] The Intellectual Disability Rights Service (IDRS) produced a policy document on AIDS and Intellectual Disability.[316]

During these years RLC also played a significant role in assisting new services develop. Campbelltown Legal Centre (now Macarthur Legal Centre) was set up in 1987, Illawarra Legal Centre was set up, IDRS became independent. At one point Andy Haesler while Principal Solicitor of RLC was also Principal Solicitor for the Welfare Rights Centre, IDRS and Illawarra and Campbelltown.

# STAFF, STUDENTS IN LEGAL AID CENTRE

Mr Michael Berg (Arts/Law II), Mr Terry Buddin, Lecturer in Law, and Mr Romano Di Donato (Arts/Law III) are among those involved in the new Legal Centre at Redfern Town Hall.

Students and staff in the University's Faculty of Law are the prime movers in a community legal aid service which opened on 14 March on the ground floor of the Redfern Town Hall in Pitt St, Redfern. The premises have been made available by South Sydney Municipal Council, which is also helping to meet the Centre's running expenses.

The Redfern Legal Centre is operated by a committee of lawyers and volunteer members of staff and students from the Faculty. Actual legal advice and assistance is given by legal practitioners who attend the Centre on a roster basis. Volunteer Law students are also regularly rostered and, although they do not give advice, they help in interviews and follow-up action.

The Centre is open to all comers on Mondays to Fridays from 6pm - 9.30pm and on Tuesdays and Thursdays from 2 - 6pm. Students man it at other times on weekdays to take telephone calls and make initial contact with people seeking legal help.

Mr Rick Raftos, a Tutor in Law who is closely associated with the Centre, says that it was established particularly for people whose legal needs were not being met by private solicitors or by existing legal aid services. As well as offering legal advice from solicitors and barristers, the Centre will undertake follow-up action, such as telephone calls, the writing of letters or the conducting of negotiations on behalf of a client. If appropriate, matters will be referred to a private solicitor or an existing legal aid scheme, but efforts will be made to see that the referral adequately satisfies the client's needs.

Mr Raftos says that the Centre will identify closely with the inner city neighbourhood in which it works. "It will be responsive to community needs and is in close contact with social welfare agencies working in the area," he says.

Although there is no official connection between the Centre and the Law Faculty, Mr Raftos believes that the Centre could give UNSW Law students valuable experience in the procedures of a solicitor's office and in dealing with clients. Mr Raftos says, "It is a tremendous opportunity for students to apply the theoretical knowledge in a way that is valuable both to them and to the community at large."

The Centre will offer the services of solicitors and barristers to appear in court for clients in tenancy matters, matrimonial matters in petty sessions where there is no legal aid available, minor traffic matters and criminal charges. It will not engage in conveyancing, probate, commercial matters or personal injuries or workers' compensation claims. It plans to build up a specialisation in conducting negotiations with landlords and government bodies, as well as in representing people in social security appeals and consumer claims. Community agencies can phone for advice on the legal problems of people they are helping.

THE UNIVERSITY OF NEW SOUTH WALES

FILE NUMBER
29 November 1976
MP/SC Secretariat

SUBJECT: LEGAL AID CLINIC

At the meeting of the Faculty of Law held on 26 October 1976 it was resolved (76/45):-

i. That approval in principle be given for the setting up of a legal aid clinic as soon as practicable;

ii. That an ad hoc committee be established to consider various models for such a clinic, the means of operating and financing it and its relationship to the teaching programme of the Faculty including the Clinical Legal Experience programme;

iii. That the ad hoc committee report to the Curriculum Committee as soon as practicable;

iv. That the membership of the ad hoc committee be

J. Basten　　　　K. Swan
P. Burgess　　　R. Lansdowne
T.L. Buddin　　S. Churchman
J. Disney

with power to co-opt.

Forwarded for your information.

K.L. JENNINGS,
Registrar

## Legal aid restored for most cases

**By SIGRID KIRK**

The Legal Aid Commission, caving in to enormous public pressure, will restore legal aid for most civil cases.

The managing director of the commission, Mr Colin Neave, said last night that aid would now be available for consumer protection cases, civil liberties and all inquests in which the public interest would be advanced. It will also be available for inquests in which representation is a preliminary step in other proceedings where aid is available. The commission decided earlier to restore legal aid for victim compensation cases.

However, legal aid will still not be available for environmental cases or those concerning professional negligence or personal injury.

Cutbacks were imposed last December after the commission told the State Government that it could not carry on with civil matters unless it got $5.9 million community legal centres claimed that justice would be denied to many in need of help.

Mr Neave said the reversal of the original decision was decided by the commission "after careful consideration of the needs of the community".

A lawyer with the Redfern Legal Centre, Ms Fran Gibson, welcomed the move and said that the denial of legal aid had made many people suffer in the face of an expensive, complex legal system.

"We now call on the Government to allocate adequate funding to the commission to meet its commitment to ensuring access to justice for all," she said.

Ms Gibson also called on the commission to restore aid for professional negligence matters, personal injury and environmental cases.

"It does not cost much to fund meritorious actions," she said. "Most environmental matters recover full cost awards

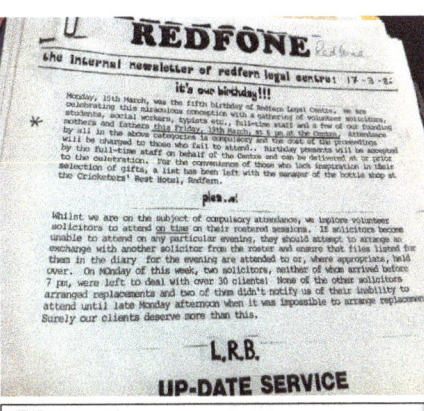

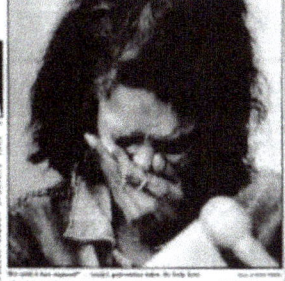
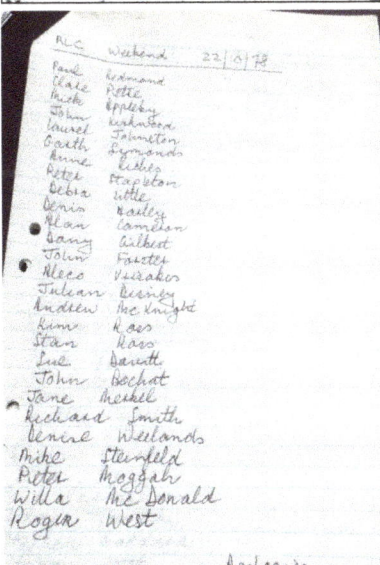

1. Sue Schreiner, Magistrate, Redfern Court.
2. Cheque for costs awarded in the State Bank case.
3. *Sydney Morning Herald*, 14 October 1993
4. Article on David Gundy, Indigeneous man killed by police 1980s. RLC appeared at the inquest.
5. Anik Shapiro: Anik adopted RLC and RLC adopted Anik. Anik's life has been chronicled by Clare Petre.

## CLIENTS

**R**LC has of course assisted thousands of clients. RLC's Principal Solicitor, Alexis Goodstone started work at the Centre in 2017. The clients 'come from a range of cultural and socio-economic backgrounds, age groups, geographical areas and abilities. They have diverse experiences and perspectives, and a wealth of different stories. Many have suffered childhood sexual abuse or other trauma, removal from family and community, dislocation, systemic discrimination and family violence. Despite this, they show amazing resilience and tenacity.'[317] Special mention though must be made of Anik Shapiro and Mr Santalab.

### ANIK SHAPIRO

Anik came to one of the first meetings and was a regular feature at the Centre in the early years.[318] He was a client who formed a deep friendship with RLC staff and became very important to the Centre. Clare Petre is publishing the story of his life, as he was so much a part of the Centre. Debbie Whitmont remembers him: Long term client Anik was at the Centre all the time …He had a special bond with Clare [Petre] and Clare was wonderful to Anik. Anik always stunk of metho and wasn't always that good to have around… He always had a radio on and slept god knows where… He was a big feature of the Centre.'[319]

Anik was regularly imprisoned in Long Bay and it would be known he came from Redfern and knew people at Redfern Legal Centre. A bloke called Connolly charged with murder looked after Anik in the gaol as he knew he was from Redfern Legal Centre. Crash Craddock often had to take Anik home. 'That meant actually trying to find where he was living at the time. That could be a mattress hidden behind a building. 'He would have his radio, one time he had a jar absolutely full of thousands of brightly coloured pills and medications. He didn't like taking his medications. I remember one Friday night late and he was very drunk… and he was reasonably strong despite his age etc. On this occasion I had to get him out and get him home…he was between me and the door and he had a large knife and I didn't. He was pissed and very aggressive and I didn't want to ring the cops. He was waving the knife around and I was trying to reason with him… He spoke very little English. That's the sort of thing that would happen every now and then… Anik would be locked up as an inebriate and he'd find himself in a hospital. And he didn't like hospitals.'[320]

## MR SANTALAB

'There were some great characters like Mr Santalab. He would go past his neighbours gardens and pick the flowers and then present them to us….I think he liked the company…He was borderline homeless and certainly alcoholic…People would listen to him'[321] 'Mr Santalab was usually there not for a legal reason…He had badges on his jacket, a bottle opener, safety pins…but also he would come every week and borrow money from the staff and then he would come every week and then repay it. Staff would keep $20 in their desk to lend to him.'[322] 'Mr Santalab loved us all…he was a beautiful man…there were a few people who would just drop in cause they wanted a chat.'[323]

Tamara Sims remembers 'one very memorable client—Mr Santalab. He was hilarious. It would be fair to say he had a bit of a drinking problem but was a genuine character within the Redfern area. He lived in one of the Departments of Housing blocks but he always had problems or didn't have any money and he really would just come in for a chat but every now and then he would get himself into trouble might have debt issues or beaten up or whatever, so we would help him out and sort out the legal problem if there was one or just be there for him. He was my favourite client. He always used to like to access the toilets as well.

He could come in and just go to the bathroom and I'd be like 'what are you doing!' and he would say 'I need to go to the toilet!' and I'd say 'OK' There was a front desk and he would try and hide so I couldn't see I was there, he would walk past me but as he walked he would get lower until he was crouching and I'd be like 'Mr Santalab what are you doing! He also wore a lot of jewellery, heavy chains and you name it, he was quite the character.'[324]

## WORKING WITH NON-LAWYERS

> In an ideal world, the role of nonprofessional advocates would not be determined by examining what legal tasks could be delegated to a person with less or different training, but by a broader functional view, including consideration of all of the possible ways to handle, manage or solve a problem and then identification of those groups of people who might best be able to perform those functions.[325]
>
> *Carrie Menkel-Meadow*

The use of non-lawyers in providing legal services was and still is, controversial.[326] Law Societies and the Law Council have generally been opposed to use of non-lawyers to perform legal tasks.[327] In most legal offices, lawyers, in theory at least, do the legal work and other administrative staff do the other work though law students may act as paralegals undertaking legal tasks under supervision of a lawyer.

Arguments relating to private legal practice in favour of using non-lawyers include breaking down the monopoly that lawyers hold on providing certain services and thus reducing costs for clients. Concerns include fears that certain sections of the community, that is poor people, will be denied lawyers in favour of paralegals while richer people would get lawyers.[328]

From the 1970s onwards there was increasing interest in the use of paralegal services and non-lawyers in relation to access to justice work.[329] Advocacy groups in the USA such as HALT (founded in 1978) called for change in the lawyers' monopoly. The *Wall Street Journal* described their work:

> The advocacy group, whose acronym stands for Help Abolish Legal Tyranny, is waging a sophisticated state-by-state campaign to chip away at lawyers' monopoly on the legal system. Its activists lobby bar organisations and state legislatures to persuade them to open lawyer disciplinary proceedings to the public and the practice of law to trained non-lawyers … It would allow legal technicians (non-lawyers like paralegals) to provide out-of-court legal services for 14 non-criminal matters, such as uncontested divorces, simple bankruptcies, name changes, housing and estate planning that often require nothing more than filing the correct documents. The technicians would be required to use written contracts, give estimates of fees and inform clients that they aren't lawyers.[330]

Early on CLCs recognised the important role that non-lawyers can play. At an Australian conference discussing 'Access to Law' in 1978, there was a call for the increased utilisation of paralegals both in the traditional sense and more innovatively in providing advice and advocacy.[331] Of course, CLCs also took the view that services such as education and law reform activity often conducted by non-lawyers at the centres are as important for clients as direct legal advice and casework.

The innovation by CLCs was to have lawyers and non-lawyers working together to provide services to clients. As we have seen Fitzroy Legal Service had started with non-lawyer workers and the first employee of Redfern Legal Centre was a social worker. Part of the role of the non-lawyer was to interpret what lawyers were saying—this role was prominent in the positions of field officers employed at the ALS.[332]

Menkel-Meadow pointed out in 1985 in the US context that there were dilemmas in using non-lawyers for specific legal tasks in the delivery of legal services in that separation of tasks may thwart legal services goals; in that by making certain tasks routine, neither lawyer nor non-lawyer was encouraged to approach the issue from a broader perspective.[333]

This concern arose from situations where non-lawyers were simply allocated specific tasks in casework under a lawyer's supervision. Noone noted that the experience both overseas and in Australia indicate that paralegals in the private profession acted as subordinates to the supervising solicitor whereas the legal aid paralegal 'is more often developed as a preferred alternative to a solicitor in areas of the law not normally serviced by the private profession.'[334] CLCs, of course, often delivered legal services with non-lawyers or paralegals such as law students and social work students.

In addition, however, centres employed in the legal office legal publishers such as at RLCP, community/social workers such as the first position at RLC, legal educators as at IDRS and policy workers all delivering services to the community of a legal/advocacy nature. Thus, all workers at RLC were contributing to a broad advocacy service aimed at achieving structural change in the legal system by education, lobbying or casework and advocacy tasks could be assigned to those with the relevant skills. This was very different approach from the position at private legal offices or even the government legal aid services where paralegals were really seen as an adjunct to solicitors rather than legal service professionals in their own right.[335]

## VOLUNTEERS

The Centre from its inception depended on volunteers. It is difficult to estimate the number of students, lawyers and other volunteers that have worked at RLC but it must be over 6,000.

# A BEGINNING

Volunteers are the backbone of the Centre's services and it would have been a very different and less effective service without them. The Centre also had a big effect on many volunteers' lives.

Bill Dickens started at RLC as a volunteer student and remembers: 'RLC kept me sane and I don't think I would have finished law unless I had Redfern. I was working with a whole lot of inspirational people and there was a good social life.'[336]

Dominic Gibson describes his first day as a volunteer at the Centre in September 1979. 'I turned up there on a beautiful Sydney summer day with the sun shining through the frosted windows… The first job I was given was to go to the Rozelle psychiatric hospital to get some information from a patient. …I had never interviewed a client…there was no induction program…It was a Damascus experience – I loved it… Later on, I used to take work from the Centre back to my private firm I was working at during the day and they were ok with that.'[337]

Helen Campbell was part of the students' legal service set up at ANU where the Legal Resource book put out by Redfern Legal Centre was used as the basis for advice. To some extent then as now, she believes that 'Redfern Legal Centre is like the generic term for a legal Centre. You come across people who think Redfern Legal Centre is the only one.'[338] 'While she was completing her College of Law she joined the volunteer roster at Redfern Legal Centre. She was working on Monday night with Ben Slade.

> It was a whole lot of fun. We beavered away talking to clients then we all went to the Lebanese restaurant… In those days there was no front counter—there were just table and chairs. Clients would just come in and wander around. There were no barriers. It was pretty relaxed or chaotic depending on which way you want to look at it… The whole place felt like a rabbit warren… But it was also really strikingly open to the public. So If you wanted to talk about access to justice and what that feels like in a built environment … the contrast with what you got between Redfern Legal Centre

and any private legal service or government department was just noticeably different. It had a great feeling of commitment to a style which was acknowledging and valuing every human and not setting up a distinction between the expert and the needy... ... I remember the guy who came in and had torched his car and was being done for insurance fraud. ...We gave him some advice about how to deal with the criminal charges. He listened politely to all this and then said but 'When do I get the money?'... It was a fun gang.

Ben Slade and Gordon Renouf, Crash Craddock and Will Stubbs and others... I remember a client coming who said "I rented out a flat and the Council has said it's not fit for habitation and my tenant's stopped paying rent. I am just an old pensioner and I can't afford to fix the place up". I was a student and took the story to Ben. Ben said 'We don't give advice to landlords. I said but he's an old pensioner with no money but Ben said it doesn't matter. We don't give advice to landlords. Ben must have seen my face cause he said but it's ok. I will go and tell him. This was the first time I realised the limits on community services and the need for policies...[339]

## Katherine Biber[340] started as a volunteer in 1992.

I was looking for ways to make my legal education connected to the world...My first shift was on a Friday afternoon with Pat McDonough on duty. Quite soon after I arrived Mr Santalab [client] came in and he said he'd been assaulted and he wanted someone to go with him to the police station so Pat sent me with him to go to the police station. I didn't know who he was...I thought he probably seemed a little bit drunk but that was OK. I took him to the police station and some very young constable, probably the same age as me, took a statement.

Mr Santalab said he was assaulted by his friend but he didn't know his friend's name and he didn't remember what his friend looked like or anything about anything. He had brought along another friend as an eyewitness, and when the cop asked him what he had seen, he said he hadn't seen anything as he was myopic. That was the day I learned the word 'myopic.' This police constable kept looking at me...it was clear that there was really very little to advance any investigation. We were there for some time and then we left the station and he parted with me on a street corner—very happy—he was happy with the service that I had provided. I went back to the Centre and told Pat what had happened…she kind of laughed and then she showed me how to find a file in the cabinet where all the files were. I was down on the ground opening the bottom drawer of the filing cabinet and someone came up behind me and opened the top drawer and the whole filing cabinet fell down on top of me… Pat said "oh, you aren't having a good day—why don't you go into the kitchen and take a break."

I went into the kitchen and there was a huge pile of dirty dishes. So I thought I'd just wash the dishes. People kept walking in and commending me on my initiative. I remember Andrew Miles came in and offered me a joint. I remember thinking this place is really not like the life I have ever led to date. That was my first shift.[341]

Biber stayed at the Centre for a number of years until about 2002 during her university studies on Friday afternoons and then Wednesday nights. "This was the start of the gentrification of Redfern and we started to see those people coming in. This was a change among the clientele."[342] She got involved in the domestic violence work of the Centre and took a six-week job working on the domestic violence cases.

I remember DV clients who were in a persistently violent relationship and how traumatic some of the victims compensation clients cases were…I was probably only 18 when I started there and I was given a lot of responsibility and I needed to rise to the challenge…I was given responsibilities that I wasn't given in other areas of my life.

When I was on the afternoon shift I used to get calls from the volunteer solicitors from the evening shift apologising for not attending their shift. I remember thinking how irresponsible that was…I felt it was a responsibility… that was why I kept going… the Centre introduced me to a cohort of people that I hadn't previously known…and they were all people who were not motivated by money and I definitely realised that these were people who were definitely as intellectually capable as all the law students who go on to corporate jobs…I remember being very impressed by that.[343]

Pat McDonough was employed at RLC in 1991 as the SRC (Students Representative Council) solicitor. The Centre had an officer at Sydney University and the SRC solicitor represented students in a very wide range of matters—insurance, criminal, domestic violence, car accidents, and problems with the university such as plagiarism.[344]

McDonough worked three days at the university and two at the Centre including a night shift. She remembers the stress of the evening advice rosters. 'At 5 o'clock, I used to have a pain in my stomach. They [volunteer solicitors] would always all turn up or no one would turn up…I thought the structure of the Centre was amazing.' There were about 100 volunteers including the solicitors going through the Centre in a week. 'For that time it was amazing—the filing system, the client card system… For a small organisation running large cases such as the State Bank.'[345]

Steve Bolt liked the Centre immediately: 'I thought it was groovy. I liked the idea it was like all the other shared households I used to frequent and sometimes live in—the kitchen was just like a shared house kitchen. I really felt comfortable with that. I enjoyed the ramblingness of it.'[346]

Cathy Kerr remembers this time:

> I became aware that you could volunteer at Redfern Legal Centre when I moved to Sydney. I lived in Newtown with Helen Campbell and Phillip Kellow. I worked on Monday nights which were credit and debt nights. I can't remember any induction. I did a bit of observing. Then the next thing I knew I was sitting by myself with a client and taking instructions. I would get the information then go and discuss the matter with a solicitor. I don't think there were any appointments. People would come in and put their name down and be seen in order. I thought the purpose was providing free legal

> services to people in a geographical area. The clientele seemed very local—mainly social welfare dependent migrants. RLC had been successful representing debtors in consumer credit actions. I saw how the law could change things My volunteer work at RLC prepared me for employment including my first job with legal aid in Alice Springs. I remember Andy Haesler put me in contact with an Aboriginal Legal Aid lawyer in Alice Springs and this being a great introduction to the town and the type of work I would be doing.[347]

Sarah Crawford starting volunteering at the Centre in 1989 while a student at UNSW.[348] After attending an induction, she started at the Centre. 'There were three, four volunteers with the duty person looking after us—sitting round the big table in the middle of the room…it was organised, we knew what we were doing, we knew where to get information …it was relaxed… it really helped me when I started work.'[349] When she started work as a tenancy advisor in 1993 she volunteered at night at RLC and worked with RLC staff on funding of tenancy services and joined the Management Committee until 1999. 'At night the phones would always run hot… a lot of the lawyers were from the big city law firms who wanted to get a dose of reality…I think they had a feeling of responsibility and wanted to give back… Redfern was really lucky and had its pick of volunteers…We were in a very fortunate position to have the best… it was fun we developed a great sense of teamwork, always went for drinks to the Tudor afterwards…and Pron Prohm [Thai restaurant in Redfern Street] and Wilsons.'[350]

Irene Baghoomians was looking to find kindred spirits when she called the Centre and enrolled as a volunteer while a law student in about April 1992.

> Andrew Miles was the volunteer coordinator. He was very welcoming to volunteers. I was placed on a night shift. We had sessions on how to interact with clients and conflicts of interest which you never heard anything about at Law School. Ben Slade was my supervisor and could be quite intimidating if you met him

as a law student. The staple had to be in exactly the right place on the file. At the beginning we were scared stiff. He used to shout at us but it was shouting collectively. We used to laugh a lot behind his back. But as he warmed to us he seemed really lovely. The whole thing was really revelatory to me as a law student, I was so happy that day when I did my first interview. It was a simple assault matter and I needed to check the *Crimes Act* to see the elements of the crime.

## Mehera San Roque and Katherine Biber started volunteering around this time.

We developed a real camaraderie. We used to have hilarious discussions about the staff. Ben was working on the State Bank case. When John Basten would call he would never say hello or anything. He would just say "Basten—Slade". And we had to read between the lines. We would laugh and say to each other 'Couldn't he at least say hello or something!'

We had such positive impressions of all of the staff. Everyone was friendly. We could ask questions and get involved in things such as I remember a great workshop on how to interview clients from NESB backgrounds. These lessons are still useful to this day. No matter how many scholarly articles I read, I still use these experiences in my teaching of law students…I remember the transition from the card system to computer system to the early model of Macs.[351]

## Tamara Sims remembers;

When I did start volunteering there, I loved it both from a practical way to apply the stuff I was learning in law school and seeing how legislation says one thing but how that impacts on the reality of people's lives in another way. I also met some incredibly funny, amazing clients who would come through that door who became quite regular drop ins not necessarily having a legal problem, more so for a chat, the doors were always open, and everyone was welcome and whilst you have work to do, part of what you're also doing is making connections with the community. The many wonderfully funny incredibly complicated characters that would come past as well I particularly enjoyed.[352]

As Redfern became more affluent as a suburb and become more gentrified, a whole kind of other different people were accessing the service who did have a bit more money than previous clients and a younger student population particularly with the tenancy advice service who were accessing Redfern for assistance with their tenancy disputes. Amy Munro volunteered at RLC before going on to being elected to the board in 2010 and serving as chair from 2011 to 2020. Here she considers one part of the value of RLC for volunteers:

When I was going to the Bar, one of the things you have to do is to line up someone to mentor you at the start. I didn't know any barristers, really, other than a few and I certainly had no personal connection to them.

Anyway, so I ended up contacting Jeremy Kirk, a very well-known barrister. And he wrote back to me and said words to the effect of anyone that has volunteered at Redfern for as long time as you have is someone I want to meet. It was quite amazing that it had opened up that door to someone that obviously recognised the value of the centre. Jeremy had done a lot of public law work, so understood it. So that's a very direct impact.

Redfern equips you with so many skills that are so critical, whatever the type of work you do, particularly in terms of dealing with clients. But what is critical at working at Redfern is being able to distill the multiplicity of problems that people are having to the legal question and being able to assist them with that part of what has brought them into the centre.[353]

## TEMPORARY RELOCATION AND ABOLISHING OF THE MANAGEMENT COMMITTEE

Around 1998–99, the Centre was relocated to an old house near Waterloo Green while the Council was renovating the Town Hall. The Centre was based there for about a year and a half, in substandard accommodation with five flights of stairs and damp offices to deal with. It was a difficult period for the workers. Clients had difficulty finding the Centre and in this period the Council decided they would no longer fund the social worker position which had been the first funded position at the Centre.[354]

During this time there were serious problems between staff at the Centre. This relocation may have exacerbated staff issues and accounts differ as to the causes of the discontent but it eventuated in the Board taking over control of the Centre and abolishing the Management Committee.[355] The Board no longer had staff representatives or volunteer solicitors involved in Centre management and the Centre changed from a flat structure to a more hierarchical structure. This was a significant change.

Elizabeth Morley:

> In the 1990s, the time of competition reform started. Government agendas about competitive tendering and the start of the rise of the big charities tendering for services. It became clear if you are too small you will get trampled on. Instead of farming things out you have to grow to be able to be competitive. Perhaps we were not so ideologically driven at that time. In the 1980s, funding available for a mental health advocacy service was with Macquarie. The question came up as to whether the funding should stay with MLS or go to Legal Aid Commission.
>
> I was one of the people who believed that one of our roles is to identify a gap, address it and then get it mainstreamed... of course what happens is we see it go off, it's a great service but at a legal

## A BEGINNING

centre we deal with casework and systemic reform....but then it becomes mainstreamed we see what becomes a duty solicitor scheme with limitations about who accesses it and little systemic reform.[356]

CHAPTER 3
# THE WORK OF THE CENTRE

The sheer variety of work at the Centre from its inception, is illustrated by an entry in a policy paper for a Centre meeting in February 1980. Some of the recent work of the Centre was outlined including being instrumental in getting an inquiry into Goulburn gaol up and running, the Greek social security cases, an Australian Law Reform Commission (ALRC) inquiry into class actions, work on legal services for children, assisting tenants in Chippendale (leading to the development of the first tenants cooperative in Sydney), ALRC inquiry into debtors, CLE including radio tapes on law for migrants, activities in local paper 'The Guardian', creation of a video tape on RLC, a video tape on defending yourself and articles on legal issues for prisoners magazine *Imprint*.[357]

## PRO BONO ALLIANCES

In the early 1980s, as Principal Solicitor, Roger West had enough good friends in his old firm, Blakes, to form an allegiance with that firm so that they would take cases as part of a formal pro bono program. This was probably the first formal connection of a firm with a legal centre in Australia.

The Centre's work has been assisted by a number of long standing pro bono arrangements over the years. Private solicitor Paul Farrugia started giving advice on evening advice nights in 1978 and later left his private practice to do advice on afternoons for

Redfern Legal Centre workers and volunteers demonstrating outside Liverpool Street Magistrates Court about the so-called Greek Social Security Conspiracy.

20–25 years as well as spending time working on the Management Committee and the Board.[358] In 1988, the Centre was approached by law firm Clayton Utz to develop a pro bono partnership whereby the firm agreed to take on 50 cases a year. The Centre also had an arrangement with Frederick Jordan Chambers whereby barristers would act pro bono on matters referred by the Centre.[359] These, and similar partnerships developed over the years, enabled the Centre to help many clients who could not otherwise have accessed legal assistance.

Giddings and Noone describe the growing interest in the formation of partnerships between large legal firms and community legal centres reflecting the increased focus on pro bono activities within the legal profession, limited government funding and the ethos of 'partnerships' or 'social coalitions'[360] that now pervade commercial activities. This is reflected at RLC. Large law firms work with each specialist area that the Centre runs. In 2011, RLC expanded the long-standing partnership with Clayton Utz to assist in employment matters, underpayments, unfair dismissals and discrimination.[361] Gilbert and Tobin are pro bono partner for the domestic violence service, Mallesons assists the tenants' service, Ashurst assists the Credit and Debt Team, McCabes is partner for the international students' service, and Fragomen partners with RLC on migration matters. The Gandevia Foundation partly funds the outreach to Indigenous clients.[362]

## SPECIALIST AREAS OF WORK AT RLC

A feature of RLC's work has been responding to community demand by the development of specialist areas. The concentration of effort and commitment by staff and volunteers in certain areas led to many of the new organisations developed by RLC. It is also, though, an integral part of the way the Centre worked. Allowing staff to follow areas of interest and allowing them autonomy in the choice of matters led to notable successes, involvement in high profile legal matters and campaigns for reform. Areas of work that led to significant innovations in practice such as completely new services or products or new modes of providing legal assistance including family violence, intellectual disability, welfare rights, prison work, aged care and publishing will be described later. Other areas of specialisation detailed below have been in coronial inquests, consumer credit, drug reform policy, housing and legal aid funding campaigning.

## INQUESTS

Deficiencies in coronial law and practice received considerable attention during the 1980s and 1990s in NSW and to some extent this was a result of the involvement of the Centre in providing legal assistance in an area where there was little free legal assistance available.[363] There were concerns relating to the status and resourcing of the Coroners Court, the accountability and transparency of the coronial process and the Court's ability to carry out its research and educative function. RLC generally focused on inquests where there was an element of public interest such as systemic problems in the justice or policing systems. There was no one else providing legal assistance to the families of the deceased.[364] Haesler comments 'we did it [appear in inquests] if we thought we could make a difference and raise matters that would have been swept under the carpet, particularly matters involving potential police conflicts or where having the State "assist" the coroner in a matter involving state agency, didn't seem right, given the number of cover-ups occurring or being alleged at the time.'[365]

This work started in conjunction with the Centre's early work on police issues such as verballing and prisons work, and continues today. The Centre appeared at such inquests as:

a) for the family of Warren Lanfranchi into the inquest into his death in 1981 in Dangar Place, Chippendale at the hands of the police officer Roger Rogerson;[366]

b) for Sasha Huckstepp and Brian Huckstepp, (daughter and ex-husband respectively) into the death of Sallie-Anne Huckstepp. Huckstepp, 26, was found floating in Sydney's Busby Pond, Centennial Park, on February 7, 1986 by a man walking his dog. Ms Huckstepp was in a relationship with a man named Warren Lanfranchi who was a drug dealer. She went public after his death and accused Rogerson of executing Lanfranchi. No one has ever been convicted of her murder despite it resulting in one of the longest running inquests of its kind in Australia, from 1987 to 1991.[367]

c) into the death of Catherine Dale Payne, a police informant;[368]

d) for the brothers and sisters of David Gundy, an Aboriginal man shot dead by police in Marrickville. Mr Gundy was killed when police raided his home before dawn on 27 April 1989 by members of the Special Weapons and Operations Squad (SWOS), searching for another person.[369] The raid was looking for another Aboriginal man wanted over the shooting of a police officer. Commissioner Hal Wooten found that the basis of the information was on a "nonsensical statement" by an informant that the shooter may have been in David Gundy's house. David Gundy was shot in the room near where his small son Bradley Gundy was sleeping.

e) in 2013 in the Le Marseny inquest which highlighted the issue of medical staff not being available for people in police custody after 10pm on Friday and Saturday nights;[370]

f) in 2015 into the death of Dylan Maher who died in a car involved in a police pursuit.[371]

## CONSUMER CREDIT

The Centre had undertaken work on credit and debt matters since its inception but it was in the 1980s and 1990s this specialty came to the fore, and developed into what was probably to be RLC's most significant area of major litigation. From the 1990s, people were encouraged to assume responsibility for the enforcement of economic rights and interests in an increasingly diverse and complex legal regulatory system.[372] Consumer and financial rights were areas previously unexplored to any great extent by legal aid services and RLC and other CLC lawyers saw possibilities to achieve change that could benefit disadvantaged consumers through both policy work and litigation.

In 1978, RLC obtained funding for a financial counselling service[373] and led representations to government for funding for increased financial counselling services.[374] Most cases were individuals seeking minor assistance. An RLC solicitor described one case:

> I remember an Aboriginal client coming in and he had received a notice from the tax office saying he hadn't paid his tax bill. I looked at him and said 'So why haven't you paid your tax then? He said, "I'm an old age pensioner, I'm illiterate, I'm Aboriginal and I'm drunk all the time." I said, "that sounds reasonable" and I wrote that down and sent them a letter. He never heard from them again.[375]

Penny Quarry recalls:

> I applied for a job at RLC as a credit and debt solicitor. I was interviewed by Simon Cleary and Beth Jewell. At the end of the interview I was asked how much alcohol I drank. They gave me a list of questions which were quite difficult but I had studied up for the interview. I fought banks, car yards and finance companies on behalf of disadvantaged people. It was hard to get them out of contracts except by using the Contracts Review Act. I decided to start looking at the bigger picture.
>
> I started working with credit lawyers all over Australia...I took a case on against the Aboriginal Housing company for an Indigenous bloke, I had a female Aboriginal client who had 14 fines from all over the State we contested, I had a client who died of old age in the middle of a case. I had to take instructions from him at his house in Botany. The case was about a faulty water tank. One client ran after me in a shopping centre and called me a saint.[376]

In 1984, it was decided to set up Monday night advice sessions as a specialist credit and debt service. This led to the establishment of a credit group who aimed to develop expertise in this area.[377] The Centre's work in this area included casework, research, education, policy and campaigns. Many years of lobbying by RLC and Macquarie Legal Centre with other groups led to the establishment of the specialist Consumer Credit Legal Centre in 1986.[378] Work on credit issues was a collaborative process and RLC worked closely with the consumer credit legal centres in Victoria and NSW as well as the peak body of financial counsellors—the Australian Financial Counselling and Credit Reform Association (AFCCRA). Work was undertaken on issues such as what came to be known as as 'sexually transmitted debt'.[379] The Centre produced a number of reports relating to credit matters, including: *Need or Greed* (1987), a comprehensive guide to credit and debt law for financial counsellors, community workers, lawyers and consumer;[380] the *Debt Survival Guide* (1987);[381] *Financial*

*Over Commitment—the Consumer View* (1988);[382] *More More More*, on financial over commitment and credit assessment (1988);[383] and *31c in the Dollar* about consumer credit insurance. These reports had public impact and were seen by one politician as part of 'a disturbing and well-orchestrated attack on credit providers in Australia.'[384] The Centre's work was raising consumer issues that lawyers in New South Wales had rarely if ever addressed.

Policy and campaign work included media events such as the AVCO dump.[385] In 1984, clients whose few household possessions were secured by AVCO (a finance company) under a Bill of Sale,[386] were encouraged to 'dump' those broken possessions, or those they did not need, on the steps of AVCO's head office in Sydney and Melbourne. Financial counsellors then set them alight. The press gave this stunt significant coverage and AVCO agreed not to execute on household furniture. This was followed by an agreement by the Australian Finance Conference locking in their member companies to the same agreement.[387] The Centre ran a Bank Bashing Day, utilising volunteers to answer calls from people who had problems with their banks. But it was in 1984 with the advent of the *Credit Act 1984* (NSW) that the Centre's casework in this area expanded significantly. A solicitor from the Consumer Credit Legal Centre had worked out there was a provision in the *Credit Act* section 32—a disclosure requirement, which, if not complied with, meant there was a sudden death provision that any credit charges had to be refunded or couldn't be charged.[388]

After this, RLC initiated the *State Bank* case.[389] The *State Bank* case was an application under section 86 of the *Credit Act* asserting breaches of the Act by the State Bank of NSW. Over 300,000 borrowers were involved. The solicitor responsible at RLC, Ben Slade, recalls:

> The material was so dense even the bank lawyers had trouble with it ... It was two–three years before I really understood the *Credit Act*. It was complicated and really hard law. One document in evidence in the State Bank case had a note by the in-house counsel for the State Bank which said "Ben Slade has rung again about the *Credit Act*. It's so boring I can't bear reading it." But we had instructed John Basten, Mark Ierace and others—we had such incredibly brilliant barristers.[390]

Simon Cleary[391] started volunteering at RLC in 1992 on evening advice sessions after previously volunteering at Caxton Legal Centre in Brisbane.

> Buildings are really important places... walking into the space of Redfern Legal Centre—the old Town Hall—it was an old institutional building... something felt right and interesting about it... I was wanting to understand how the law could address poverty. Redfern had a reputation...and had a history behind it and credibility... The Centre was conducting a large piece of litigation—the State Bank case and Ben [Slade] needed someone to take witness statements and I was employed to do this. The State Bank had contravened the Credit legislation in a number of ways including by failing to disclose various pieces of information they should have disclosed. The bank then had to bring an application to the Commercial Tribunal to recover interest on the loans ...The litigation then had to be commenced by the lender in a risk free way to the borrowers. The Centre was aiming to put as many consumer experiences as possible to the Tribunal. The case went on for years and when the Commercial Tribunal handed down its decision it was the largest civil penalty given against a Bank at the time.[392] The hearing was a week long. John Basten and Janet Manuel were the counsel involved. These type of cases really elevated in the minds of policy makers the importance of disclosure to consumers.'[393] Cleary left the Centre to take up a position with Queensland Legal Aid to establish a consumer protection unit that was established on similar principles as RLC and still exists today.[394]

The Centre saw itself as engaged in a David and Goliath struggle against the banks. David Vaile comments:

> The *NSW Credit Act* was in effect self-enforcing. As soon as you showed that there was a systematic breach of the Act on the standard contracts, they were in trouble ... Ben [Slade] had encouraged me to see Redfern's role as being in systemic matters, test cases, class actions, influence on regulations, and policy. No one was going to be able to provide representation for every single client, we had to have large scale impact and to take on systemic problems... The opponents were powerful organisations that were totally screwing the interests of borrowers. Ben would say "We are so fucking pure ... They should be scared of you." Where they were vulnerable was in their reputation ... Ben said "Never show them the inside of Redfern Legal Centre. If they see how small and weak we are they will realise they can cripple us by just writing us a letter every day."[395]

Another major case was taken against Garendon Investments, a timeshare company. Two thousand, three hundred people borrowed money from Garendon to buy timeshare units in a resort.[396] RLC successfully acted for Serena Afa, a secretary who had obtained finance for a time share.[397] The case concerned allegations the company was providing credit without a licence and engaged in high pressure selling tactics.[398]

The Centre (with the Public Interest Advocacy Centre) was also involved in the *HomeFund* case.[399] HomeFund was a NSW Government-sponsored home loans scheme which provided home loans to 57,000 low-income borrowers between 1986 and 1993. As Yates points out[400] the HomeFund experiences in NSW highlighted the difficulties faced by many marginal borrowers.

> Deferral of interest payments contributed to negative amortisation of the mortgage outstanding and this, in combination with low initial equity and a slow down or

reduction in house prices, meant that many households had negative equity in their homes. Regardless of whether they had suffered income loss, they were unable to refinance and so take advantage of reductions in interest rates because of the reduced value of their security.[401]

The matter went to the High Court. Those who benefited from the Centre's work were the 3,700 borrowers who still had HomeFund loans and became entitled to reduced interest rates which were dramatically less than their contract rate. In addition, over two thousand borrowers who had had their home sold up but still owed money on their loan due to the ballooning nature of the loan, had that debt waived and their credit records amended.[402]

The effect of these major successes was to demonstrate the power of strategic casework combined with media and lobbying skills, even in situations where RLC was opposing companies or law firms with considerable resources. Apart from the demonstration of the Centre's legal ability, the size of the cases meant there were large financial rewards for the Centre on wins or favourable settlements that could be beneficially used for other unfunded projects providing practical resourcing for innovative ideas.[403] Funding for credit and debt matters dried up post 2010 and it is now funded through funding channelled through LAC.[404]

In 2019, a new statewide service for people experiencing financial abuse in intimate partner relationships was launched as well as a new statewide Migrant Employment Legal Service in partnership with Marrickville Legal Centre, Inner City Legal Centre and Kingsford Legal Centre.[405]

Laura Bianchi describes the creation of the new Financial Abuse Service which in its use of pro bono partners and philanthropic services has a very different approach from past methods of funding a new service:[406]

> I remember mentioning it [the concept] in my interview, I knew that Redfern had done a little bit of work with the solicitor that was in the Credit and Debt role prior to me and I was aware that that was a policy issue. It was fairly new but gaining some momentum in that area of law and it was an area of interest of mine. I remember mentioning that in the interview and when I started out at the time it was Jacqui Swinburne who was acting CEO, I remember Jacqui and then Joe saying that it was obviously an interest of mine and interest of the centre. We started thinking of ways that we could do more in that space and we were also an auspice at the time of the Sydney women's domestic court advocacy service, and they were seeing a lot of financial abuse coming through… So, I connected with them, and I started getting referrals for financial abuse matters from them and I was also starting to identify it coming through our local catchment as well. Then we did a bit of scoping to see is it a local issue or a much broader issue? What's the legal need here? It was much greater than the Redfern local catchment area, so we went about seeking funding to be able to set up a state-wide service.
>
> So, the strategy behind that was to engage corporate partners which was somewhat of a new funding direction for Redfern at the time. We were strategic about that because we knew that there would be financial institutions that had foundations or philanthropic type support for various community projects and that this one being financial abuse would be quite relevant to them and their work. It would also be an opportunity to create partnerships where we could almost work from within so we were in partnership with a financial institution, and they became more aware of financial abuse issues then it was also more likely that they would address them within their organisation as well. So, we went about setting up partnerships and trying to bring them on board for both funding and for some pro-bono support

from their in-house lawyers. We managed to secure enough foundation supporters to get the state-wide service off the ground in June of 2019. We launched the legal service in June and then we grew with some additional philanthropic funding for policy and law reform work over the next few months and launched formally the service roughly as it is now in December of 2019.

So initially we were really focusing on Credit Debt and Consumer Law issues as that was the expertise that was born out of the Credit & Debt practise. It was just me in the practice to begin with, one solicitor and we grew in that six months from June to December 2019 and brought in a second solicitor, I went into the team leader role but I was still very focused on Credit Debt and Consumer Law issues but we also hired a full time policy and capacity building officer so we were able to do more in terms of the systemic issues and using the legal service as the evidence base to inform the sorts of work that we wanted to do to both prevent and respond to financial abuse.

Still again at that stage focusing on Credit Debt and Consumer Law issues but then we identified that clients had a lot of intersecting family law issues particularly clients who had/could potentially access property from the relationship so we brought in a pro-bono partner who had expertise in family law to help us very ad-hoc delivery of advice to clients who had no other option to get family law advice or if it was very interconnected with the Credit Debt and Consumer Law issue. We would do what we now call co-advice where we have an expert solicitor with Credit and Debt experience with an expert in family law meet with the clients together and take instructions and deliver the advice together so that they can hear each other's advice and come up with a strategy that might be in the best interests of the client but perhaps from both areas of law. We introduced that in 2019 but we didn't have the funding for a position until later in 2020 we managed to bring on Commonwealth Bank as an additional funder and we hired an in-house family lawyer who is still working with us. That was when we expanded into doing more family law and we also in that first year of operation identified that there were a lot of people who'd experienced financial abuse who also had company law issues so they've been signed up as a director to a company that their partner controlled and that there were potential directors liabilities issues, business debts and guarantees and also potential tax liabilities that flow from that. Which is an area that frankly almost no CLC's have expertise in and legal aid won't touch.

So, we identified that we needed to update our intake criteria for financial abuse to upskill and try and provide some of that advice in house because literally no one else other than private solicitors would do it and none of our clients could afford it. So, we're still not all the way there for getting funding for an expert in that role but that's the next stage in terms of expanding our legal expertise little further in the practice will be to bring on a solicitor who can really advise on those issues in a more fulsome way than what we are currently doing.

## CIVIL LEGAL AID CAMPAIGN 1992

In 1992, the State government legal aid body, the Legal Aid Commission of NSW conducted a review of its services.[407] Although the ensuing report made no recommendation about civil legal aid services specifically, on 17 December 1992 a decision was made to drastically curtail the availability of legal aid in civil matters in NSW.[408] This left disadvantaged people in NSW with little recourse to the courts in civil matters. In response, the NSW Combined Community Legal Centres[409] decided that all NSW legal Centres be levied to employ a campaign coordinator to run a campaign to get legal aid for civil matters reinstated. Though some Centres were concerned about using funds for what they saw as 'political purposes' and thought that the Commission was unlikely to change its decision, Centres agreed to fund a worker one day a week for six months to run the campaign. A solicitor at RLC was employed to coordinate this campaign.[410] Coordinated activities occurred continually over ten months, including a Fund Legal Aid cakestall run outside the NSW Parliament House and appearances on current affairs programs on TV including a segment run on ABC's *7.30 Report* designed to be watched by Legal Aid Commissioners present at a Board meeting held at the same time. There was a letter-writing campaign from community organisations, the Lawyers Reform Association, local MPs, and private lawyers all over the State. A complaint was made to the Sex Discrimination Commissioner on the basis that a cut to civil legal aid was discriminatory to women, and this all led up to a planned Day of Action set for 27 October 1993. This Day of Action was supported by the Law Society, politicians, and community organisations, and a large protest in Martin Place was planned. Media were lined up to report the event, when two weeks before the planned Day of Action, the Legal Aid Commission reversed its decision and reinstated legal aid for many civil matters from 1 November 1993.[411] This was seen as a significant victory and allowed many people to gain access to legal assistance in ensuing decades.[412]

In 1994, RLC with other Centres successfully lobbied against legislation that would have seen them lose their direct representation on the governing body of the Legal Aid Commission.[413] Loss of this representation in other states meant that the innovations in the delivery of legal services developed by CLCs could take longer to penetrate the broader delivery of legal aid services.[414]

## COMPUTERS AND THE INTERNET AGE

The late 1980s into the 1990s saw the advent of computers and then email. Julie Bishop, who had been the convenor of a major expert systems group inside Telstra and was interested in the IT area, became head of the National CLC office in 2001 after working with RLC as a consultant on their computing systems in the early 1990s. David Vaile recalls:

> Julie inspired me to see that technology could be used for social justice purposes. At that stage it was controversial to use Macs. Julie's view was that where you had a usability problem, it was easier to train people on Macs. It was controversial as it wasn't what all the law firms were doing and it was thought to be more expensive. Julie's view was that there wouldn't be secretaries at RLC who would do "the typing", and learn how to wrestle with clunky early PC interface foibles, so benefits in terms of easier training, more obvious interface design, and thus lower support costs would more than offset any hardware difference ... Later many other CLCs used Macs due to Redfern's enthusiasm about Macs and RLCP's [Redfern Legal Centre Publishing] pioneering use of desktop publishing to create cheap, fast and accessible community legal information and professional development material.[415]

As a result of Bishop's approach, RLC became an early adopter of the new technology including desktop publishing and computers on lawyers' desks.

David Vaile noted:

> In 1992, you got onto the internet through a dial up modem. It was all text based and very slow. The World Wide Web was yet to really get going, it had just been invented, there were no web browsers in use yet. The internet wasn't publicly available. In the community and social justice centres they would use bulletin board systems. The cost of access was very high ...[416]

Vaile demonstrated to the Centre staff the potential uses of Pegasus—a social justice ISP based in Byron Bay (part of a global network running in parallel to the internet based in universities). Commencing in June 1989 this was one of the first services of its type in Australia.[417] 'Some people realised how amazing it was. It was a really powerful direct technology for activists.'[418] These inspirations persuaded some at RLC to push for the new systems of communication and soon RLC staff were adept at computer use. Later developments such as email, the legal centres' secure national bulletin board system—First Class Law (hosted by the Law Foundation), and the internet were championed by the more forward thinking members of staff and quickly incorporated into the Centre's practice due to this early adoption of breakthrough technology.

Katherine Biber remembers 'I remember when we first had a management committee meeting about the website many of us thinking what a waste of money it was to have a website....It seemed really expensive. No one really knew what the internet was and poor people wouldn't use the internet anyway.'[419] Some staff had a similar attitude to early email systems but soon adapted.

## LEGAL EXPERT SYSTEMS

**DIVORCE FORMS:** In the late 1980s, RLC recognised that many clients attended the office seeking assistance to complete the paperwork for a simple divorce. Legal Aid had been available for this when the Australian Legal Aid Office was first set up but had been discontinued during the 1980s as legal aid sought to manage its budget.

In 1990–91 the Centre commenced a project to automate the completion of divorce forms. The idea was to produce what would later be called a document assembly system whereby people could complete their own divorce forms by entering relevant information into a computer. This project commenced well before the world wide web was widely available (it was only invented in 1989) and decades before the idea of online form generation tools became more widespread.

Gordon Renouf started the project in his own time and when it was showing promise applied for the grant from the Law Foundation. The project unfortunately however ran into difficulties. Vaile explains: 'The software was a bit too simple for what we needed. It got to the point where we had done most of the work but not the hardest bits and that proved to be much harder than we thought. Big IT systems fail because you want to appear to make progress by doing the easy bits first… We thought we would get to the end of the project when we had the prototype but as was explained by Steve McConnell Rapid Application Development, the first few iterations should be throw away prototypes. You should produce disposable prototypes in order to work out what the hard problem is and fix that first or you'll burn up all your money and time and not have a solution. We had a prototype but what it revealed was that some of the hard questions were not answered. There were many too complications in 'just filling out a divorce application' that it turned out could not be easily mapped in a basic decision tree"[420] The funding ran out and the project faltered. The Centre was to return to this type of work with the international students app in 2018.

## STUDENTS

RLC has been assisting students for many decades. In 1991 a branch office was set up at the University of Sydney to provide advice to students of the university.[421] Currently the RLC branch office at the Sydney University Postgraduate Representative Association is funded by SUPRA, via the compulsory Student Services Amenities Fee paid by University of Sydney students.[422] This service provides free legal services to postgraduate students from any of the university of Sydney's campuses. There is also legal assistance provided at eight Sydney TAFE campuses.

Commenced in 2016, the Centre also runs a UTS student clinic currently run online.

In recent years, there has been increased demand on legal services from international students facing a wide variety of legal problems. The COVID-19 pandemic has exacerbated these unique vulnerabilities, including wage theft, insecure housing and tenancies, education fee issues and, more recently, migration concerns brought on by closed borders.

Redfern Legal Centre's International Student Legal Service NSW (ISLS) is available to the 200,000 international students usually enrolled to study in NSW (onshore and offshore). Sean Stimson, who heads up ISLS, joined RLC in 2015, after leaving private legal practice. Stimson was pleased to get the job. 'It is difficult to get a foot in the door of such a highly-regarded community legal centre as RLC…I was lucky that my time at Inner City [Legal Centre] allowed me to start at RLC with some locum work. It seemed like many people I meet know about Redfern Legal Centre.'[423]

Prior to Stimson's arrival at ISLS, the international student practice had been running for four years, but was only funded by the NSW Department of Education on an annual basis. This led to a high turnover of staff and an inability to carry on any major systemic or law reform work. Wanting to ensure sustainability for the international students' practice, Stimson came up with the idea of creating an app that would be sold to education providers on a subscription basis, which would allow their international students to access the app free of charge. This concept was presented to RLC's Board and became My Legal Mate (MLM).

Created for international students in NSW, MLM is a video-based legal information resource that is interactive and available in seven languages. Users are asked a series of "yes" and "no" questions about their legal issue, and are provided with individualised referrals, information and advice based on the answers they provide. Despite MLM's obvious advantages to NSW's international student community, the 'big problem is that we initially had few resources, which made it very hard to realise the idea… conservatively, you need about $100,000 to build the content itself and design the app's pathways. You need to go through a testing phase to ensure it relates to the user and performs to their expectations, while also delivering accurate legal information through its pathways. Someone has to write and code the technology. It's a big project, especially for a CLC.'[424] Stimson explained, 'so international students are given a legal information resource with answers to the most common problems that they face, I felt it was important to include the information in the languages most commonly spoken by international students in NSW.' [425]

After more than two years of development, MLM was launched on-campus at Macquarie University in October 2019[426] and was made available to thousands of Macquarie University students. However, shortly after its launch, the world was impacted by the COVID-19 pandemic and education providers' priorities shifted as revenue streams tightened. RLC's priority remained that of ensuring international students had access to information. COVID-19 specific information was able to be easily added, and constantly updated, to inform the international student community enrolled to study in NSW of resources and information as circumstances changed. A Western Australian adaptation of MLM is currently in its final stages of development, with additional information streams created especially for the needs of WA's international students.

In 2021, Stimson says, 'it is hoped that MLM will be made available to all international students enrolled to study in

Australia in the future, with each state or territory having its own version of MLM, together with a dedicated community legal centre providing free, on-the-ground advice for international students, all funded by the sustainability model of MLM.'[427]

## HOUSING

Housing has always been a major part of RLC's work with workers representing tenants in eviction, repairs and general tenancy matters since the Centre opened.

> One early RLC case in August, 1978 related to housing in Glebe Point Road—one of the 700-odd houses that the Federal Government owned in Glebe, as part of an experiment in community oriented low cost housing. In August 1978, the NSW Supreme Court found the Fraser Government at a loss to explain why it had thrown a group of tenants out on the street and ordered the residents to leave within 15 minutes or they would be arrested under the Commonwealth *Crimes Act* as 'trespassers'. When the residents queried this order, the police said they had 14 minutes left to leave so, unwillingly and feeling intimidated and threatened, the residents left, the doors and windows were barricaded. The residents' clothes, food, furniture, and even their pet cat, were locked inside. Stencilled signs were sprayed over the building, saying: 'COMMONWEALTH LAND: TRESPASSERS WILL BE PROSECUTED'. The residents immediately sought legal advice from Redfern Legal Centre —they were advised that if they held a lease on the premises that was still current, they could not be arrested as 'trespassers' (and hence they should not have left). They could only be dealt with under the NSW Landlord and Tenants Act. Accordingly, the next day several of the residents and friends re-occupied their home. They sprayed signs on the

> front walls saying that they were tenants not trespassers, and sat on the front roof, waiting for the Project Office and the police to arrive. The police dragged seven people back in off the roof, charging all of them with trespass and resisting arrest. A lawyer who was present was not allowed to talk to the arrested.[428]

RLC solicitors were often engaged with housing cases in the Local Court, tenancy tribunals and in Supreme Court challenges to Department of Housing policies The Centre also focused on law reform in residential tenancy and on regulation of boarding houses, often with serious opposition from real estate interests and developers. Principal Solicitor in the 1980s, Andy Haesler was a recognised Sydney expert on tenancies including protected tenancies for tenants and was involved in assisting in drafting new tenancy legislation in the late 1980s.

RLC ran test cases against the then Department of Housing on a number of issues including the concept of no fault eviction. The issue was eventually litigated in *Nicholson v NSW Land and Housing Corporation*, where Stoddard J held that the Department of Housing could not evict a tenant without grounds, as the principles of natural justice applied to prevent the Department depriving tenants of the right to a fair hearing.[429]

Education initiatives developed by the Centre were not always well received. In the 1990s, 'The tenancy service made stickers saying *"don't go mental over rental."* There was a complaint from a mental health agency—on management we all went 'oh fuck, what have we done'.[430] There were also differing views in the Centre as to appropriate policy stances to take on housing issues. 'There was an Aboriginal liaison officer for a while—Trevor Bates. He was very angry that the tenancy service had taken a view about the Block. They wanted to preserve the Block as an Aboriginal housing area and he represented another voice in the

Aboriginal community who thought the Block was a disgrace to human rights and Aboriginal people should get out of there.'[431]

Beth Jewell had studied in Canberra and was working in the Sydney Tenants Advice Service and worked with the Centre on tenancy matters. 'RLC had a really good reputation and a vibe of being run by young people. It used cases to change the law and Redfern would take risks and do radical work to try and change the law and make it fairer. Redfern had a different reputation than the other legal centres. The history had a folklore around it. Other community legal centres paled in its reputation. Back then before social media, you only had media and word of mouth.'[432]

Jewell got a job at the Centre when the tenants' services were all defunded starting as the new tenants service worker there in 1993. Then in about 1994, Andrew Miles the social worker left and then Jewell applied for the job. In 1995 she became an employee at Council as the social worker with tenancy as the main focus of the job. The Council had a very hands off approach with the job and were happy with Jewell's proposal to focus on housing. The Council left it up to RLC to define the role. This was at a time when there were no tenancy services.

I remember Ben Slade saying:

> God you've only been here a month and you're holding mass meetings in the Boardroom with 30 tenants'… That was the case about the hot water system that was the boiler in two five-storey tenants blocks in Glebe. There was only one boiler for all the tenants. By the time, tenants in the far blocks got their hot water it had travelled for five minutes so they were getting these huge bills for gas. I took 30 people to the Tribunal in their wheelchairs and with interpreters. I got a bus and took them to the Residential Tenancies Tribunal. You couldn't have class actions. I got them all heard on the same day. We did a lot of work. Me and the tenancy workers—Sue Robinson and Kylie Kilgour or Polly Porteous. We interviewed everyone, negotiated

## THE WORK OF THE CENTRE

with the gas company, and I went to Energy Ombudsman. The Department of Housing commissioned an independent assessor report that said the boiler was adequate and there were no problems. But the night before the hearing the independent who had done the report rang me up at home and said "it's all lies and I am going to be your witness tomorrow. I have had a conscience attack."

When we arrived at the Tribunal I talked to the Department of Housing's lawyer and introduced him to the assessor who was going to change his evidence. We negotiated that each tenant would have their own heater put in each flat. And then another group of tenants from another building rang up and I negotiated with the Department of Housing and they all got their own individual hot water heaters too. It cost an incredible amount of money for the Department. The tenants were very pleased. We rid Sydney of big boilers![433]

Emma Golledge, tenancy worker at the Centre noted the nature of RLC's clients in the 1990s. 'We had many old vulnerable people getting evicted. We had the most drug-addicted and mentally-ill clients I have ever seen.'[434] Leading up to the Olympics, RLC produced a website (very unusual at the time)[435] and the potential detrimental effects of the Olympics were used in the media to demand measures to protect people in boarding houses and to monitor and protest unfair rent increases. General protests about the housing situation were held.[436]

In the months before the Olympics, 'all the boarding houses in Darlinghurst and Kings Cross were being converted into units. All the boarders had nowhere to go. Rents were rising. We formed the group Rentwatchers and produced a tenancy kit. *"Through the Roof. How to fight Rental Increases and Evictions."* Closer to the Olympics, we had a 24-hour homeless helpline where people could record if they were having trouble with police. Students took the calls to help people get accommodation in

Parramatta and further away from the Olympic sites. Father Bill Crews helped us and nine government organisations. We had a lot of media.'[437] Jewell went overseas to talk to the Housing Committee of the United Nations with help from the Law Foundation in 1999.

> That was a fantastic experience—I had all these pictures of housing, and homelessness but then you meet people in much worse situations from round the world. The UN wrote to the Australian and State governments about the issue which was useful in lobbying politicians. The ABC news did stories, Today Tonight, the commercial news…That was so good. No one but Redfern Legal Centre would have let me talk out against the Olympics. I got some vague death threats from callers etc and abuse from radio commentators. That is the value of a place like community legal centres. You can say things that are not popular. This was very unpopular stuff. That experience sort of put me off doing media. I haven't done any since.
>
> We were always working on tenancy law reform, We worked with Clover Moore putting up boarding house and tenancy reform. It's a long term thing. There is boarding house legislation now which is a huge thing. Years and years after we started… '.[438] 'I did my best work at RLC. From the beginning I was encouraged. All staff were encouraging. There was passion for credit and debt law which was great. No other organisation—legal aid or tenancy service would ever have allowed me to do what I did.[439]

When Jacqui Swinburne was a university student in 1995 she and her flatmates were hit with three rent increases in a short amount of time. Towards the end of her Bachelor of Arts degree, Swinburne went to her local tenancy service to get some advice. Impressed by the service, she volunteered at the Eastern Area Tenants Service and was offered a job. After that she worked at the Tenants Union and worked with RLC on the Rentwatchers campaign.[440] She started work at RLC in September 2001 as a tenants advocate with a focus on public housing evictions, repairs, bonds. Deciding to study law (after observing the limited capacity of some of the law student volunteers and realising she could do better) she completed the course and stayed on at RLC as the Centre's longest lasting employee. Jacqui has frequently acted as CEO in the absence of Jo Shulman and believes her acting as CEO has given tenancy more credibility in the Centre and more focus.[441] Tenancy advice has become more complex as basic tenancy information is on the internet so the queries the Centre receives are more complex.

New South Wales Government and Law Foundation and other funding allowed the Centre to develop housing publications and to put them on the internet when that form of publication was available. As the NSW Attorney–General Jeff Shaw noted in Hansard in 1998 the Centre 'has an outstanding reputation in educating consumers about the law.'[442] In 2011, RLC launched The Boarders and Lodgers Legal Information Kit. In February 2012, the Housing NSW Repair Kit, a guide for public tenants on how to get repairs done and Guides to Share housing [443] are other publications.

The Inner Sydney Tenants' Advice and Advocacy Service (ISTAAS) is now part of RLC and provides free, confidential legal information, advice and advocacy to tenants living in public and private residential housing. In March 2014, the NSW government announced its intention to sell all its public housing properties in Millers Point, Dawes Point and the Rocks, and to relocate all tenants living in the area. The decision impacted at least 400 households. A large proportion of the tenants affected were over the age of 65, and relied on neighbours, as well as hospitals, doctors, public transport and other support services close to the city. Many had strong ties in the area, having lived there for decades, or even their whole lives. RLC ran an advice and advocacy service for tenants affected by the relocation since May 2014. RLC continued to operate the Waterloo Tenants' Advice Service in 2020 in anticipation of the proposed redevelopment of the Waterloo public housing estate.

## DRUG LAW POLICY REFORM AND POLICE POWERS

In the 1990s, in conjunction with the continuing police powers work of the Centre, the Centre ran an active drug policy program, and in the mid-1990s funded a drug policy reform program from the costs won on successful casework in other areas of law. This was a first for legal centres in Australia. A solicitor, Steve Bolt, was employed to do drug casework and spend two days a week on drug policy. He had previously worked as a general solicitor, tenants advocate and in other positions at the Centre from 1991. In 1995 the Centre published a report advocating harm reduction policy on controlled drugs[444] and in 1996 another report, *Beyond Prohibition*.[445] The project lobbied parliamentarians, promoted community discussion on the issue and produced facts sheets, bumper stickers, etc. (Biber remembers: 'The Drug Law Reform project released some stickers and the stickers said "Break the crime cycle"—and some other words like drug law reform and I remember seeing kids around Redfern who'd cut the sticker in half and stuck "The cri cycle" on their bikes.')[446]

The positions argued in these papers are, as their author Steve Bolt notes, 'still relevant today sadly.'[447] The work resulted in publication of a legal text[448] and has had an impact on debates in Parliament about the issue.[449] 'In a way there is direct line … the policies developed in the mid-1990s about injecting rooms etc could be presented to Bob Carr who to his credit was open to them.' The NSW Drug Summit was held in the NSW Parliament from 17–21 May 1999 and brought together members of the

Parliament, experts and professionals, community representatives, families, and people who have had drug problems, to find ways to deal with drugs in the community. It involved all members of the new Parliament and 70 invited delegates.[450]

After Bolt left, Tim Moore was employed to work as Drug Policy Project Officer with the Centre, collaborating with others on a range of influential publications on drug law reform and harm minimisation issues.

Tim was a strong advocate for human rights and civil liberties, leading a campaign questioning the use of sniffer dogs and hard-line tactics against drug users by police and advocating against unlawful discrimination against marginalised communities. Tim's policy work was widely published in a range of sources from academic journals and professional publications to online forums. During his time at the Centre he also co-authored a book entitled 'Modernising Australia's Drug Policy' with Alex Wodak, then Director of the Alcohol and Drug Service at St Vincent's Hospital in Sydney. This book advocated a change in approach to drug policy in Australia and outlined a ten-point plan to reduce the death, disease, crime and corruption associated with current approaches to drug policy and law enforcement. Sadly, Tim died in 2014.[451]

In the late 1990s, the NSW government trained sniffer dogs for the Olympics and after the event retrained them to search out and identify drugs in public places. The *Police Powers (Drug Detection Dogs) Act 2001* (NSW), which came into force in February 2002, gave police the power to use sniffer dogs without any 'reasonable suspicion' of drug activity in places like pubs, entertainment centres and public transport stations. RLC lawyer Polly Porteous recalls: 'This was a time when a lot of people around Redfern were on heroin. They [the police] put sniffer dogs at Redfern station. We ran a big campaign with dog sniffer T-shirts etc.'[452]

An issue which also gained much media attention at the time was the establishment of the safe injecting room at Kings Cross. In November 2001, six months after the injecting room opened, the New South Wales Parliament enacted new laws which would allow use of the sniffer dogs and tougher policing in other drug hot-spots. On May 21 2002 the Redfern Legal Centre's website, which sent SMS messages to registered members with the precise movements of the sniffer dogs, crashed due to the demand for information.[453] The Centre campaign against the sniffer dogs was controversial and opposed by many including Parliamentarians.[454]

Solicitor, David Porter bult up a policing practice at RLC 2010–2016. The RLC Police Powers Clinic is an educational program that was set up in conjunction with the University of New South Wales after discussions by academic Vicki Sentas, Frances Gibson and the Faculty of Law whereby UNSW students spend one day a week at RLC over a semester, putting their legal knowledge into practice working on police issues. The Centre operates the only specialised police complaints advice service in NSW, assists in formal complaints and acts in civil litigation against the state of NSW for false imprisonment, assault, battery, and malicious prosecution.

Sophie Parker started work at RLC as police powers solicitor in 2016. Samantha Lee, solicitor, focused the Centre's work on strip searches. From 2016 to 2017, strip searches conducted after the use of drug dogs have doubled in NSW. RLC was contacted by many people who have been subjected to humiliating full-body strip searches at festivals and other public places. Teenagers and children as young as ten had been subjected to a full-body strip search. In some circumstances, they were asked to squat and cough.[455] The *Rethinking Strip Searches by NSW Police* report, commissioned by Redfern Legal Centre (RLC), revealed the number of strip searches conducted in NSW has increased almost twenty-fold over the past 12 years. This work received considerable publicity and a report by the New South Wales police watchdog cast significant doubt on the use of strip-search powers by officers in the state, arguing common practices including forcing people to squat or move their genitals are not legal.[456]

The Centre continues work on policing and strip searches particularly of children in conjunction with UNSW through the police powers clinical legal education program run at RLC, and this work continues to be controversial.[457] The Centre is working towards a test case with Senior Counsel and DLA Piper seeking to confirm whether police have the power to search mobile phones and delete mobile phone content.[458] Concerns have been raised on issues such as use of footage by police of body worn cameras in NSW, and access to this footage by defendants.[459] The Centre is also speaking out on handling of complaints about police—particularly where the police officer is alleged to have been a domestic violence perpetrator.[460]

## CHAPTER 4
# A NEW CENTURY 2000-2022

Redfern has always been seen as the innovative centre and it's part of our role. It's a culture and a history and you need an certain level of ...umm ...ego—a track record to be able to do that. There is an expectation now that that what RLC is and that tradition carries on.

*Joanna Shulman*

I'm awfully fond of the place—It is a shopfront; it's a corner shop full of lawyers—you can pop in and get help. People would just come in if they got a letter and they couldn't read. Or cause they needed to use the phone... Despite the gentrification, it's still the largest public housing estate in the Southern hemisphere.[461]

*Helen Campbell*

Hilary Chesworth started at RLC as Administrator in 2001 (was there for 20 years) taking over from Deneale Crozier. The position involved managing the Centre's somewhat complex finances—paying bills, organising cost centres for projects and other administration tasks including front desk shifts.

There were a lot of problems between the Board and the staff at the time. Beth Jewell noted:

The way that RLC ran depended on the relationships between staff and the Coordinator and the Board. When we had planning days we looked at cases and law reform but we didn't look at how we could make the place function better. All NGOs have the same issues—personalities, people who were employed who

Redfern Legal Centre staff and volunteers, 2000s, including Jacqui Swinburne, Will Dwyer (credit and debt lawyer), Jo Shulman (CEO), Nick Manning (Intake and CLE Manager), Hilary Chesworth (finance and administration) and Wendy Wang (administration and data entry).

shouldn't have been. I have seen it in any size of organisation. No one knows how to fix a problem when it first starts. People find it hard to talk to people who aren't performing. Volunteer boards go through huge ups and down. They either are too involved or not involved enough.[462]

These issues within the Centre continued in 2002. The Board of Directors decided to take over the management committee and staff/volunteer positions on the Board were abolished.[463] The structure of the organisation changed from a flatter structure to more hierarchical. A position of Director of the Centre was established after a review by Gordon Renouf.[464] The Board appointed Helen Campbell to this position. This was a big change in the Centre's management processes. Campbell observes:

> The management committee had been pretty much run by the staff up to this point. The Board felt this was no longer appropriate. There was a real structural problem there ... managing a community legal centre is a great deal more difficult than it used to be. The capturing and storage of information is easier and governments require much more accountability and there is a lot more competitiveness for funding. There are much higher standards of OHS, human resources etc. Management has become a professionalised role. Staffing structures have become more hierarchical. Management committees are more like Boards and on the whole not that representative of the communities they are serving.[465]

Elizabeth Morley was part of a group in the late 1970s working on setting up a Womens' Legal Service and was a solicitor at Marrickville Legal Centre from 1983–1988, later working at the Disability Discrimination Legal Centre. She became Principal Solicitor at RLC in 2003.

> Marrickville was a flat structure—more of a collective than Redfern. Everyone was paid the same no matter what their job. There was a real drive to be responsible and taking your turn to do all the

necessary jobs and model a society where you were responsible for all your own work. Why should a lawyer be paid more because of a historic context where lawyers are valued more when admin staff are working same hours with the same commitment... We burnt through a lot of workers in the early days—repetitive strain injuries, stress etc. I think we take more care of our workers now. It means we miss those days when people worked 80 hours week but there were people who that approach took a toll on... We had workshops where everyone talked about their jobs and often we would have a facilitator to plan.[466]

At one point [at RLC], there were serious problems within the staff team. There were a lot of staff changes. Jewell comments:

The morale was just terrible. Toxic. There were different views about how the work should be done. We didn't have the structure to repair the issues. There was a review. Suddenly people arrived from the past. Gordon Renouf was hired to do a review and Mary Perkins came on the management committee. We turned up to the Management Committee meeting and staff were told there was to be a review. Staff weren't consulted about what was to happen... Some staff members were more focused on individual casework. Others thought the place should be run differently. There were questions about how much power the Management Committee should have. There were perceptions of secrecy about the place. At one point staff weren't allowed to go to meetings. We kept the service going and did some great work but it was stressful.[467]

RLC had been through a rather tumultuous time. Morley comments:

People had been burnt out and taken it out on one another. There had been Workcover complaints etc. The brief that Helen Campbell and I had was to help to rebuild the Centre. Helen arrived in 2002... There was to be a new hierarchical decision making structure under the new regime. There was to be a clear line of decision making... Each worker brings strengths and weaknesses. And quite often what makes people an incredible advocate also makes them incredibly hard to manage. They are idiosyncratic, they take quirky looks at things from left field, they have an energy and trying to marshall them to work in a team is difficult.' You have to find ways to make this work.[468]

In the new century the Centre was larger and operated under more constraints from funders and government.

For a small centre the advantages are you have a small group of committed people. Like Francis Drake against the Armada. You can be fast and pick up issues and doing very meaningful work if it's working well. Everyone owns the work they are doing and it's a great place to work. But there are issues about consistent quality and range of expertise and it's always vulnerable to implosion if something goes wrong. In a bigger centre you have more bureaucracy and you have a more hierarchical structure. You have to because you just have more people doing things and ...decisions have to be made in a timely way and everyone can't be across every issue... In small centres the autonomy of various workers is very high but you could come back and talk about it as everyone had a high level of awareness about what everyone was doing – a high level of consensus existed. In bigger centres it's similar but you get workers who don't have the sense of responsibility for administration. They are consistent workers but they don't see the way the centre runs as their responsibility—not the same sense of ownership—that has to be in a way—you don't have time to do everything. You don't have that same feeling of ownership and joint responsibility and feeling of going forward like in the early days for the work of the centre.[469]

Morley continues:

At the start Board members wanted to track every client and their passage through the Centre and make sure they got outcomes. A lot of resources went into that. In 2010 we had a major review then the focus shifted to systemic advocacy. This wasn't really always a happy process. Judith Stubbs was brought into do strategic planning. The Board instigated it... Helen left and Jo [Shulman] arrived to drive that process. We have restructured. We lost some of our organic relationship with the community as we were putting a message out that RLC knows best. There is less time to be part of local community groups. We have to monetize stuff like CLE as well. RLCP was a monetising organisation but we are not out talking to community groups as much...The sense of competitive tendering has created a loss of sharing of ideas and information and collegiate work has been less as centres are more mindful of intellectual property and ideas. They are less likely to put ideas forward for discussion in case someone else takes the idea and also Legal Aid don't seem themselves as collegiately aligned with CLCs as part of the legal aid sector. It was a small world back in the '70s and '80s –we all knew one another – we went to the same wine cask and cheese and jatz parties—We had planning days when volunteers, management committee and staff would all be together in some small cottage... Those things do not happen now.[470]

RLC kept innovating though and taking on new projects though not all were long running. The Centre played a part in the Redfern Waterloo partnership project which was set up in 2001 and was a joint government community approach to combat serious long term problems in the area. In 2006 an animal rights project was set up at the Centre funded by Voiceless – named the Pro Bono Animal Law Service (PALS). This was a short term project. Marianne Maguire was selected to run the project. PALS organised pro bono assistance for some interesting cases on such areas as activists entering commercial piggeries and publicising film of the conditions they saw there. Helen Campbell comments though: 'It didn't rate as much of a priority for us—The cases that came in were not relevant to our clients—one was about retired Clydesdales in rural NSW—I mean what do we know about horses?... But we were always looking for money. I was running seven different services with nine different sources of funding-all of which required reporting etc… There was an expectation that the Director would bring in more money to the Centre—we were able to look beyond our neighbourhood—we got funding for a project to support sugar cane farmers. The credit and debt team provided a state wide legal service to financial counsellors—we said we will help the sugar cane industry—we made a DVD and took it up north and training for financial counsellors about crop liens etc.'[471]

Jo Shulman started law as a student at UNSW. She did a Kingsford Legal Centre placement and volunteered at DDLC.

> Once you start down the CLC path it was like a whole new world—I never looked back—it was the first time that law actually made sense and gave me a reason to keep studying. The legal centre movement allowed me to understand the power of the law as an agent of change. Dealing with clients and feeling as if you could make a difference in peoples' lives. It was a huge turning point for me. I did a summer clerkship at Phillips Fox and then got offered a graduate position. It was a time when they had graduate offers they couldn't fill so they gave me $5000 and I went travelling. When I came back I finally got a job at Inner City Legal Centre in early 2000. I remember resigning from my role at DLA Piper and a partner said "I'm so happy for you I wish I had done that but it's too late now." Another said they guaranteed I'd be back within three months. While I was at ICLC, I was in awe of the whole CLC movement—this collaborative movement that pushed the boundaries—I was doing amazing discrimination cases around sex change. Then I went to DDLC and started as Principal Solicitor. That was intense – no resources – and state wide service operations. Then I went to PIAC. In about 2011, I came to Redfern Legal Centre. It has a history of being a leader in the sector. Also I became a bit disillusioned with direct practice of law…discrimination law seemed like a toothless tiger. I was ready for a new role. The job was CEO. I was brought on with a definite set of instructions from the Board to boost strategic work. There was a feeling that RLC wasn't as strategic as it could be. They had

hired consultants before it started who produced a report. My job was to implement the recommendations of that review. And also repair the damage the review had done. Some staff were offended by the way the review was positioned and felt judged by the review process.[472]

So in the first decade of the new century the Centre moved to different work arrangements under another restructure. A new Chair of the Board, Nick Patrick was interested in large scale litigation as well as day to day local legal problems and most of the members of the Board at this point were lawyers from private law firms. After these changes, RLC was no longer a strictly generalist centre but had strategic focus areas which continue today. There are six major practice areas: tenancy, employment and discrimination, international students, policing, domestic violence, credit and debt. CEO, Jo Shulman notes:

> The areas selected came from community consultation, analysis of legal need and looking at what we were already doing. We put one team on each area and a pro bono partner and an advice night so we created centres of excellence in those areas and pushed for development of different skills sets so everyone does media work, policy, legal education and direct client and test case work. There are huge expectations.[473]

This process, as described by CEO Jo Shulman, was an attempt to rethink why CLCs exist and how they are different from legal aid. The management system of the Centre changed, incorporating corporate practices such as 'key performance indicators' which staff must report to, monthly meetings with the CEO and each practice leader. She notes

> It feels quite corporate but it constantly reminds us of what we are trying to achieve. Overall it seems really successful in redirecting our work to focus on strategic outcomes. There were some things lost [in the change process]. We became much less accessible

to the community. Less "just drop in and talk to anyone anytime", so we have made an effort to keep a generalist service for vulnerable people. We hadn't thought through our connections etc. Some other CLCs thought they might be left with extra clients. We have tried to be quite responsive and if someone is very disadvantaged we try and make appointments.[474]

The growth in size of the Centre (from around 7–10 workers in the 1980s and 1990s to around 23 today) has meant that the management systems have had to change. Noone noted in 1992 that

a number of the features that have made CLCs unique in the past relate to internal practices and structure. Unless Centres wish to become replicas of private practice or a regional legal aid commission office, they will have to strive to ensure that the internal work practices remain unique. This means maintaining a non-hierarchical approach based on a team approach; lawyers and non-lawyers working together.[475]

It would seem that a strict non-hierarchical approach may have gone forever. However, the collegiate nature of the work and team approach remains.

In 2011, Sophie Farrell became the Centre's first communications and volunteer manager. 'The website was a shambles, so we started from the beginning, building a new website to tell the story of our work—we didn't really have strong relationships with journalists—we had our branding being one of the oldest legal centres in the country but not a huge number of media inquiries coming through… Communications is essential for all of the advocacy work the Centre does.' [476] Farrell did a lot of work in the local media and focused on particular client groups such as international students.[477] Farrell comments, 'I emphasised Redfern's role as a centre of excellence that is leading the sector.' [478] She sees the Centre's history as relevant to current volunteers. For the law students, the history of the Centre is important, that legal students started it from nothing and that became a movement, and that so many famous and influential lawyers started here.'[479]

In 2014, a hospital-based Health Justice partnership with Sydney Local Health District was set up focusing on Indigenous clients. The service trained over 300 health workers on identifying legal issues and developed a referral pad containing a checklist of issues. An evaluation of the service showed that the clients that are seen are clients RLC would never have seen without the service.[480] The HJP works in close collaboration with Aboriginal health focused service sites at Sydney Dental Hospital, the Royal Prince Alfred Hospital (RPA Hospital), Redfern Aboriginal Medical Service, Redfern Community Health Centre, Men's Cave, RedLink, and the Women's Cave.

The Glebe Legal Outreach and Advice Service first launched as a pilot program in July 2016. It operated out of the 'Have a Chat Cafe' in Glebe's old Fire Station on Mitchell Street. The legal clinic provided confidential legal services, alongside legal information sessions on issues identified as relevant by the local community. RLC and Legal Aid NSW decided not to continue the legal clinic beyond July 2018, due to budget constraints and low numbers of client attendance.

Former staff member Haesler comments:

> With the exception of maybe EDO or PIAC the [Government Legal Aid] Commissions are running the big cases not CLCs in terms of prisoners, detention. The days of the big test cases run by CLCs are gone. But they may now be run by big firms taking pro bono cases from CLC's. Legal Centres have become a service providing legal advice to people in their communities who cannot get legal assistance. By the end of the 1990s staff at RLC focus had moved away from litigation to community work.[481]

Centre staff feel that there may be some truth in this claim but with the Centre's restructure they are now conducting more litigation. Cases in tenancy in the 2000s led to changes in the law. Police powers litigation through the law of torts is ongoing.

Kingsford Legal Centre Director Emma Golledge says:

> Test cases in the '70s are really different from test cases now. I think it's hard for CLCs to run test cases now and when you do win the gain is often legislated away. RLC has a really strong reputation. I think it always will be the leading CLC—the history, the idea of what a CLC means.[482]

# FUNDING

Funding remains a constant issue for RLC as for other legal aid services. Staff are on rolling contracts because of uncertain funding.[483] The Centre has adopted an entrepreneurial stance to seek out funding, is very proactive in exploring opportunities and is often successful. These funding sources have led the Centre to taking up work which would not have been envisaged in previous decades—either in geographic areas well outside the Centre's traditional catchment or for new types of clients or areas of the law.

In 1997 Noone prophesied:

> As the economic imperative of the market takes hold in the legal aid arena, CLCs will have to compete with the private profession to provide services, particularly as the National Competition Strategy is applied to the legal profession ... A local private practitioner could compete to provide legal aid services to a geographic area. More disturbingly, CLCs will compete against other CLCs or welfare organisations. The basis of the CLC community involvement may well be undermined.[484]

These concerns[485] are reflected in relationships between the Centre and other organisations. As Noone and Giddings point out 'the Federal government now often makes policy and decisions about CLCs without input from the LACs. The tender process creates an environment of competition between CLCs, LACs and the private profession rather than one of working together to improve access to justice.'[486]

Morley notes:

> In some ways as well we are victims of our own success. We have convinced LAC that civil law is important, that they need to go out to where people are rather than just offer central services but in doing that they are waltzing into areas where we are already operating. In Redfern, the LAC are doing quite a lot of outreach but why don't we work together to get pro bono services. Instead of saying there are too many CLCs in inner cities why don't they move paid staff out to western NSW etc. [487]

The Centre's longstanding good relationships with other organisations can be affected by the funding issues and the Centre's actions to secure funding for its activities. Helen Campbell, former Director of the Centre recalls one example in which, as a result of competitive funding processes for domestic violence services, what were 'comfortable collaborative sharing relationships turned to shit. Marrickville Legal Centre put a complaint about Redfern Legal Centre to Legal Aid but Redfern received the funding.'[488]

The community and volunteer sector have long been acknowledged as a conduit to government regarding information on society's unmet needs and preferences.[489] Their value to government is established. The move to a contracting environment for funding, however, has caused many issues for centres such as RLC. Research in New Zealand has found that the contract environment for NGOs:

has led to heightened fears surrounding several issues: funding being cut; difficulties in maintaining independence while taking government contract funding; restrictions on what services they can provide to whom, and how these will be provided; and the redirection of their labour to meet the efficiency and accountability demands of government funders.[490]

## Jacqui Swinburne, acting CEO of RLC says:

There are gag clauses in government contacts—we are not supposed to do advocacy services —i.e., speak out against government ... The Environmental Defenders Office and the Refugee Advice and Casework Service were partly defunded as a result of their advocacy work. ... Being able to get independent money that's not from the government gives huge advantages. We do feel restricted about speaking out under the current government. We are careful about what we say. We are quite careful about social media. If you are in the *Sydney Morning Herald* there is more security than just tweeting about it. We used to march in the streets about employment law changes with RLC T-shirts on. We wouldn't do that anymore ... The policy is now, we are just careful. We do speak to the media but we make sure we only speak in areas where we have case studies. There is a media policy which prescribes who can speak and who has to authorise it.[491]

With the move by Legal Aid Commission to more control of community legal centre funding there is a perceived conflict of interest, As Swinburne points out:

They [LAC] are managing our funds as they are expanding—for example they are opening up health justice partnerships every few weeks. In theory this is good, but it's at the same time that CLCs are facing a lack of funds. Legal aid is not based in the community. They are not part of the community—they have 15-minute appointments, the solicitors are on a roster etc. CLCs are really unhappy. It feels like a takeover. They give us money but they have to approve the qualifications of the solicitor etc.

> We have more demand on services, as people can find us now. We have a higher turnover of students. We spend a lot of time on policies and procedures. We are becoming more and more bureaucratic. The Centre has grown, but not huge amounts ... but we are always taking on extra projects.[492]

In fact, in the current funding climate, the Centre is facing major challenges due to the changed demographics of the community it serves. Former Director of the peak body Community Legal Centres NSW CEO, Polly Porteous comments:

> Legal Aid has looked at indicia about disadvantage from ABS. Weightings are given to try and identify the poorest households. Legal Aid mapped this looking at the catchment area for RLC, and across the State. The catchment area for RLC isn't very big in terms of disadvantaged people—there is still public housing but a lot of people in the area are not disadvantaged. They haven't revised the catchment area for 20 years.[493]

Hitter (LAC) notes, however, that there is still real legal need in the area.

> There are still huge pockets of disadvantage in RLC's region for example, the Northcott flats in Surry Hills. It's a huge housing development and chock-a-block full of people with mental health and addiction issues. Massive disadvantage. There is still quite a large Aboriginal community in that area. And in the CBD there is a huge homeless community. The key thing is getting out there and getting in contact.[494]

Shulman notes that Legal Aid's services now take a more CLC approach. This forces CLCs to question what their place and role is. There is still conflict as LAC manages CLC finances.[495]

The Centre hired a full-time fundraising officer in 2016 and charges full fees for its community legal education program including webinars.[496] This position lapsed but discussions are now in train to bring something similar back. As Chesworth says about RLC's funding situation 'it never stops changing; our CEO is constantly involved in negotiations with current and potential funders.'[497]

In 2020, the Centre expanded its premises. Amy Munro:

> This happened just before I left—the expansion of our premises. That might sound for most organisations a relatively minor decision, but anyone that's been involved with Redfern will know that the image that immediately comes to mind is Redfern Town Hall because that's where the centre has been for so long. But those premises no longer fitted its purpose as the centre had outgrown it. And just before I left, we expanded by having offices, a short walk away from the town hall in Redfern with with more fit for purpose office spaces for solicitors and staff. That was a really significant achievement at cost, but it was an expense the Centre decided it was time to pay for.[498]

In developments that would not have been anticipated 30 years before, the Centre has now developed corporate partnerships with AMEX and CBA. 'We wanted to see financial institutions changing the way they responded to their clients' experience of financial abuse and in particular ensure they weren't facilitating it.'[499] The CBA has provided funds to the centre to do research on financial abuse issues. 'It has been a very different way of working. But it has increased our income... 30–40 per cent of our overall budget is non-government funding and this is a major component of it.'[500]

In its forty-fourth year, the Centre carries on. Rice argues that if ever CLCs pursued a radical agenda, wholly independent of— and in contest with—the State, they long ago gave up that role. Instead the independence claimed by CLCs is compromised, the inevitable result not merely of choices they made, but of choices that the State made them make. Decisions about funding relationships that CLCs made in the 1990s and since have rendered them, effectively, outreach service providers for government.[501]

Current staff are convinced of the Centre's continuing worth.

> Everyone who works at Redfern works here because you never know what the next day will bring you, you are often involved at a high level. You have the chance to influence outcomes. RLC get consulted on a lot more things than other CLCs. We love the building. We don't have enough space. But the lack of space does facilitate collaboration. People meet in the hallway. But I don't think anyone would want to move in a hurry. It's a special place with a special meaning.[502]

★

## CHAPTER 5
# 2020: A PANDEMIC

As a result of the pandemic RLC's physical doors were closed for the first time since 1977. Staff and volunteers serviced clients by phone, email and videoconferencing facilities. This did not work for everyone though. Principal Solicitor Alexis Goodstone notes 'it has been very challenging meeting the needs of our most vulnerable clients, for example those without phones.' The Centre has taken new premises but uses the Town Hall for advice. It's much quieter. "the world is more stressed, our clients are more stressed…everything is a lot more compartmentalised than it used to be.'[503]

The Centre's international students' service saw an increase in students in need. A typical example was an international student who was about to commence a new course of studies when COVID-19 struck. She was stood down from her job as a result of the pandemic. As she was not eligible for government assistance, she decided to put her studies on hold and return home. Airfares were suddenly far more expensive due to COVID-19, and she had to use the last of her savings to book a flight. Her flight was rescheduled twice, only to be ultimately cancelled, with the airline refusing to refund the cost of the airfare.

Having already arranged with her landlord to vacate her property before booking her fight home, this last-minute cancellation left the student without a place to live. She was stranded in Australia, homeless, unemployed and financially

destitute. As she had withdrawn from her studies, she was also placed on a bridging visa. While she was grateful to be able to remain legally in Australia, this visa type precluded her from accessing many COVID-19 relief packages. ISLS helped her with a short-term accommodation solution and worked on looking for longer-term solutions to help her. RLC's Credit and Debt practice provided her with advice and commenced engagement with the airline in an attempt to recover the airfare.

ISLS' pro bono partner provided visa advice, and she was able to regain her international student visa and re-enrol in a course of studies. This then allowed ISLS to have her accepted for the early access list for the NSW Government COVID-19 crisis accommodation scheme for international students and her accommodation was secure for a number of months, while she got back on her feet.

A new employment law service has been developed with other CLCs (Inner City and Kingsford Legal Centre). Zelie Appel, a volunteer at the Centre noted the effects of the pandemic. 'Definitely I think it's affected a lot of the clients that come in just because, on the employment team obviously it's about your rights at work and whether employers can mandate vaccines and employees being stood down because they refused to get a vaccine or being stood down because there's no more work, for instance in the hospitality industry.'[504] Centre lawyers continue to inspire the next generation of students. Appel undertook her Practical Legal Training at the Centre during the pandemic.

> Usually I would be in-person, but I started, and I got a couple of days in person and then it's been pretty much online. So, I've mainly just been interacting with the two people on my team; Sharmilla [Bargon] and Regina [Featherstone] but they have both been really incredible mentors and I've learnt so much from them. They've given me a lot of one-on-one mentorship and

advice and feedback. But then I think also just the fact that I'm able to observe their work so closely has been helpful. They're both really amazing and inspiring people.[505]

As Finn O'Keefe[506] (RLC Volunteer coordinator) comments:

RLC is well known for the quality and care it takes with service delivery and because of our history, we are in quite a privileged position where we are well recognised and well-regarded and people want to be part of that, people really respect the work that the centre does and we attract people that have the same values that our staff do.

People really, really care and I see that so much when you see the work, time and energy that our volunteers put into things. They do it because they really believe in legal help to make a difference in people lives and they deliver that every day.

When asked if the pandemic has affected the the Financial Abuse Service, Laura Bianchi comments:

Yes massively, so up until March of 2020 we were delivering most of our services face to face so our volunteer solicitors would attend the office and be supervised by one of our staff members to give advice, we are state-wide service, so we have a lot of clients that are not living locally, and we do a lot of telephone advice anyway, but we were still seeing quite a few clients face to face. When we had to close the office and lockdown, due to covid, we had about a week to try and transition our service to remotely being able to work with volunteers and being able to deliver an appropriate service to clients which was very difficult for a family violence service.

As you can imagine because when people were isolating with their partner their safety situation changed significantly so we had to be very mindful of being able to advise clients and communicate with them in a safe way while they might be locked down with their partner or otherwise just having difficulties because of the pressures of the world at the time.

So, what we ended up doing was finding IT solutions to be able to work with the volunteers remotely and it was a rather complicated system at that time. It's certainly been refined and improved over the last 18 months but basically, we tried to provide the same level of supervision to the volunteers through video meetings and working with them calling clients and doing telephone advice for clients and offering if the client wanted a video meeting with the solicitor.

The good thing was that we managed to get it all set up and we didn't miss any clinics or appointments so from a client's perspective it was seamless. From our perspective at the office, it was hectic and now over the last 18 months with improvements in technology and improvements just gently understanding how to work remotely, we've really refined that and now it works really well now. To the point that a lot of our clients and volunteers have that as their preference and I think we will continue to work in a bit of a hybrid way even beyond covid and lockdowns.

## Shulman identifies some positives in pandemic practices.

We have really rethought how we provide our services. Advice service are now provided by volunteers. The centre just calls back clients when the volunteer is ready and there are no advice services as such…We know that some clients experiencing extreme vulnerability just disappear…Technology doesn't supply a good solution for them… The centre is currently rethinking how it will provide its services in the future. The connection between volunteers is more difficult. There are online chat forums with other volunteers. But it's not the same as sitting around the front office with cold pizza and being able to chat through stuff.[507]

## Tamara Sims:

RLC has some core focus areas where it has identified the different need within the catchment. The pandemic has increased access to those services by different communities such as international students which has a higher uptake in people with issues in tenancy and education provision because people have paid for a certain course that they don't "get what they pay for" and more employment/discrimination matters… Everything has changed to telephone advice, there is no face-to face, front desk or triaging of people walking in off the street.

The Centre has had to change the way it operates where people call the centre then get called back or if people need legal service, they need to access the website and put in a request for assistance. This falls through the cracks for some people like for example if I was an elderly person from a CALD background, I am probably unlikely to have a computer or necessarily know how to navigate that system to get assistance which is why the telephone still exists and everyone can leave a message and get a call back, but I do think access has become an issue throughout the pandemic.[508]

COVID-19 health regulations have brought a new set of issues relating to police powers. Redfern Legal Centre's police accountability solicitor Samantha Lee is concerned police were using COVID-19 health orders as a form of anti-protest legislation. 'The purpose of the COVID-19 public health law is to prevent the spread of disease, not to prevent the public's right to protest.'[509]

Concerns have also been raised by the Centre about police discretion in issuing fines for breach of regulations. After figures showed that NSW Police handed out more than $1 million in fines amid the coronavirus pandemic in just over five weeks, with $50,000 in fines given to children, the Centre set up a free COVID-19 fines advice service.[510]

Staff member Jacqui Swinburne is still at the Centre:

I just love the way it's so flexible and so much autonomy, Law reform work is exciting. One moment you are up at Parliament House in front of a committee then the next day out talking to the community. It's just the best job in the world…I think in the last 19 years we have a higher demand on services, there's a higher turnover of students—we are becoming far more bureaucratic—it has grown …we are working together better now—DV, housing—it all overlaps and we do a lot of law reform work and publications together.[511]

## Laura Bianchi:

I think having Jo, Jacqui, and Alexis in the three senior leadership positions since I've been at Redfern has been incredible because they all offer me something different. When I went into the team leader role, I didn't have any formal management or leadership experience and so I've been able to learn so much from them and they've been so available to me. The way that they lead the organisation is so clearly by putting people first both staff and clients.

I think that's probably what I've learned the most from Redfern that if you've got the right culture amongst your staff and the way that you deliver services is quite client focused then you're going to have collaboration, you're going to be listening to the community and you'll have all the elements that I think make for an incredible place to work but also a place that people really want to work hard for. It really translates to the quality of the work because the people that work there really want to work for you.

## Amy Munro:

I was inspired as a very young law student. And that really motivated me to just entrench myself within the organisation, so they couldn't get rid of me! But it also continued right through to my time as Chair of the Board. One of the wonderful things that I was able to see as Chair, was staff from one of the areas of the Centre providing us with a report on what they were doing. Every time there was a presentation, I was overwhelmed with inspiration and pride as to the activities that that solicitor and their team, were doing and the outcomes they were able to achieve with the resources that they had. So, I was constantly inspired by the organisation. That is really why I stuck with the organisation for so long was because it really gave me so much. And ultimately, I decided in the end that I was probably getting more out of it than they were getting from me. It was time for them for a change in that way. But it's very inspiring institution.[512]

This is a common theme in discussion about Redfern Legal Centre—the strength of its reputation which is Australia wide. Laura Bianchi, solicitor at the Centre was previously working in Western Australia and comments:

> I was aware of Redfern before I even moved to NSW it had such a national reputation and I was very aware of their work particularly having worked at the Aboriginal Legal Service in WA and doing a lot of that criminal and police powers work. I was aware of the police powers work at Redfern and the specialist work they did also the law reform and policy work that they did more broadly… I think from my experience going from Credit and Debt which is the very local community to doing a state-wide service has been positive in that I can see that Redfern's reputation and the kind of value that people see in this service isn't just in the local community.
>
> When I connect with people outside of the Sydney–Metro area they still have amazing things to say about Redfern and really appreciate the community legal education, the policy work, and the state-wide services that we offer. I think through leadership there's been a positive way of getting our services out to the broader community.[513]

The Centre has assisted well over 200,000 clients in its long history.[514] Hansard records Alex Greenwich MP stating 'For 40 years the Redfern Legal Centre has been a beacon of justice for disadvantaged and marginalised people across inner Sydney'[515] and the Centre continues to innovate. It is possible however that the external context, changes in Centre structure and the nature of the relationships with other organisations affects the Centre's ability to innovate, and the rate of innovation. As Stapleton notes: 'The early days of any organisation are great challenging days—a lot of fun. The importance is maintaining that and make sure the organisation keeps running which Redfern has.'[516]

Redfern Legal Centre is still a vital part of the community. Current solicitor Laura Bianchi:

> Redfern Town Hall is so iconic and accessible to people that they really see Redfern as being the place to go if they need help. So I remember when I first started working at Redfern I would do shifts on the front desk as a front desk supervisor and that's really where you get to see the way that particularly our recurring and returning clients and our engagement with community at that very front desk level, I think you get to see that at its best because you can see that there are certain clients that you end up knowing by name and you know are such an iconic part of what Redford Legal Centre is and what services we provide to the community and that they feel like they can come to us no matter what their issue is and even if we can't help them we'll find a way of finding someone who can. I think that they know that they're not just going to get turned away like someone's going to try to find a referral or find a way of helping them. I think that gives people the kind of certainty and comfort that they want when they go to a community service.[517]

> Redfern Legal Centre was a hothouse for training the radicals of future generations, and I don't think that it should ever feel it has to apologise for the progressive nature of its activities. The law itself is such a conservative and status quo organisation that a push for law reform has to come from somewhere, and its only by the actions of places like Redfern that this will ever happen.
>
> *Meredith Burgman, Redfern Legal Centre*
> *30 Anniversary speech, 2007*

1. *Legal Resources Book* (the precurser to *The Law Handbook*) was printed in Melbourne and there was a pilots' strike the day of the launch. Michael Mobbs persuaded everybody to go ahead with the launch and managed to get the books brought down in a small plane.

26.1.83

The Hon. F. Walker
Minister for Youth & Community Services
Parliament House
Macquarie Street
Sydney    2000

Dear Frank,

Congratulations on your new portfolios.    It's nice to see that
you chose something easy, so you can have a bit of rest..........

Thank you for all the support and assistance you've given to Redfern
and the other legal centres during your years as Attorney-General.
We hope that our relationship with the new Attorney will be as positive.

We look forward to working with you in your new areas of welfare and
housing.

Best wishes,
REDFERN LEGAL CENTRE
per:

.........................        .........................        .........................
Virginia Bell                    Clare Petre                      Andrew Haesler
Legal Coordinator                Social Worker                    Casework Supervisor

## Jackson did the wrong thing: lawyer

*S.M.H. 4/9/82 P.3*

Virginia Bell, the solicitor with the Redfern Legal Centre, yesterday accused the Minister for Corrective Services, Mr Jackson, of "acting with contempt" towards the Ombudsman's Office.

She was commenting on Mr Jackson's revelation to the Herald on Friday that he had filed "in the wastepaper basket" a report by the Assistant Ombudsman, Susan Armstrong, on Goulburn Jail.

Miss Bell said the condition in which prisoners were kept in the notorious "tiger cages" — or front yards — at Goulburn Jail were so atrocious that "it is very likely we are in breach of our international obligations to provide minimum standards of care and treatment."

"For the responsible minister to file the report on these cells in the wastepaper basket is a matter of grave public concern.

"We pose as an enlightened nation on the international scene, yet Mr Jackson admits that he hasn't even read the report."

Miss Bell, who lodged the complaint which led to Miss Armstrong making the investigation, said the report was factual and its recommendations moderate.

MEDIA RELEASE          27 February 1992

## WHITLAM OPENS CENTRE IN REDFERN

Mr Gough Whitlam will be the main speaker at Redfern Legal Centre's 15th Anniversary Open Day celebrations to be held on Tuesday 10 March 1992.

The proceedings will commence at 10 am with official speeches and then the cutting of the cake by Mr Whitlam, Clare Petre, (the first employee of the Centre) and a colourful local resident, Mr Santalab.

"The purpose of the day is to celebrate, inform and promote the work of the Centre" said Frances Gibson, principal solicitor.

Redfern Legal Centre was the first community legal centre in New South Wales and opened its doors to the public in March 1977, staffed by volunteer law students and young lawyers. The aim was and still is to provide a free and alternative service to that offered by the traditional legal practice. 15 years later the centre is still housed in rooms at Redfern Town Hall, given to them by South Sydney Council. The busy atmosphere reflects the dedication and commitment of staff and volunteers to the service.

The Centre stresses the importance of working with and for the local community particularly those residents disadvantaged by the mainstream legal system. "An organisation can't and shouldn't be a community legal centre without a policy/law reform component in its work." says Mary Perkins, Co-ordinator of the Centre.

Past and present staff and volunteers, politicians, community organisations and the local residents will join together in celebrating the commitment that Redfern Legal Centre has to providing an innovative community legal service to those in need.

For further information, contact:
Maureen Nash or Frances Gibson on (02) 698 7277.

1. Jane Goddard and Frances Gibson, late 1980s, party at Redfern Legal Centre.
2. Redfern Legal Centre 20th birthday celebration invitation/poster.

1. Wilsons Lebanese restaurant, Pitt Street in Redfern – the first Lebanese restaurant in Sydney and Redfern Legal Centre favourite.
2. Cricketers Rest Hotel (now Tudor Hall Hotel), another Redfern Legal Centre favourite (courtesy Australian National University, Noel Butlin Archives.
3. Ex-Redfern Legal Centre staffers at Wilson's, 2010. Left-to-right: Gordon Renouf, Jane Goddard, David Vaile, Ben Slade, Louise Blazejowska, Mary Perkins, Clare Farnan.
4. Mutant Death's *Police Verbals/RLC Blues* song.

## CHAPTER 6
# SOCIAL INNOVATION AT REDFERN LEGAL CENTRE

If Centres ever lose their sense of political purpose and their innovative tendencies they will die and probably deserve to.[518]

*John Basten*

We always thought of ourselves as gadflies stinging other people into action.[519]

*John Basten*

The early legal centres illustrate David Donnison's definition of innovation as "springing from the collision between traditional assumptions and changing realities, between theory and practice, in a creatively irreverent mind capable of perceiving how poorly conventional wisdom fits the evolving world.[520]

*David Neal*

One way in which community legal centres are distinguished from other legal service providers in Australia is by the nature and extent of new services they have developed for clients and the methods of providing those services. Innovation was always seen as important to the survival and growth of law centres. Julian Gardner (former coordinator of Fitzroy Legal Service) of the Commonwealth Legal Aid Commission made this clear at the first National Conference of Community Legal

Prime Minister Gough Whitlam, Clare Petre and favourite client, Mr Santalab, at Redfern Legal Centre's 15th birthday celebration in 1992.

Centres in 1979.[521] These new services and methods were social innovations, implemented novel solutions to a problem—in the form of services, ways of organising work, or a product—that met a social need and improved the quality of life for individuals or communities.

In this section a selection of innovations at RLC in the early years will be examined as examples of the Centre's innovative approach. During the first 20 years of the Centre's existence, community legal centres were based on a community development model. As Noone and Tomsen point out, 'After 1994... the Federal Government began to purchase community legal services rather than to grant funds to community legal centres as such.'[522]

An integral part of the burgeoning legal centre movement was that it forged a path that stood apart and separate from traditional legal practice. The Centre expanded the concept of legal services, who received legal services and for what types of problems. It was to play a part in creating a new approach to provision of legal services nationally, particularly to disadvantaged communities and clients. The areas of innovation of Redfern Legal Centre in this period to be examined are examples of all these:

a. Innovation in ways of determining legal need;
b. Innovation in new services and products and;
c. Innovation in the methods of providing services.

## METHODS OF IDENTIFYING LEGAL NEED

The ethos of the Centre in the early decades was that it was the Centre's role to demonstrate legal need in sectors of the community. Once the government accepted that this need existed, the Centre could hand over responsibility for providing the service to the government and move on to work on other areas of need.[523] As Basten states, 'we always thought of ourselves as gadflies stinging other people into action.'[524]

Identification of legal need is a notion that only came to prominence in the legal profession in the late twentieth century. Historically, as indeed is the case today, the private legal profession would provide services to those who made their needs known and could afford to pay for services. There was no need or requirement for private lawyers to explore legal need except where they had an interest in expanding their services into new potentially financially rewarding areas of law. There was also a prohibition on advertising by lawyers only relaxed in 1991 by the NSW Law Society allowing advertising as long as it could not 'reasonably be expected to bring the profession into disrepute.'[525] The UK Royal Commission into Legal Services noted in 1979 that in adapting to the changes of the twentieth century in the spheres of commerce and property the profession 'has done well.'[526]

The same might not have been said in the realm of provision of legal services to disadvantaged communities. The criterion for legal assistance to the poor historically was 'neither the most efficient use of available resources nor a recognition of a right of access to the legal system for all poor persons, but rather a concern that funds not be used to support clients or causes that were in some sense unworthy.'[527] It was no role of the private legal profession to seek out previously undetermined legal needs for people who could not pay to have those legal needs met.

In the 1990s there was a shift in the approach to legal needs studies[528] with work which looked at the occurrence of 'justiciable' problems in the community and how people respond. In the 21st century there are numerous examples of increasingly significant and sophisticated work on measuring and determining legal need both in Australia and overseas.[529] This was quite different from studies in the 1960s and 1970s. The techniques used by RLC and other CLCs pre-empted this approach recognising that people do not always realise they have a 'legal' problem rather just a problem. The innovatory approaches by CLCs took different forms but focused on actively seeking out information on legal need in selected communities of interest.

Two examples of this in the 1970s and 1980s were the use of community legal education/outreach and phone-ins. This was possibly the first time practising lawyers in Australia had taken pro-active steps to discover specific needs for their services. Approaching potential clients had long been forbidden to lawyers. All Bar Associations and Law Societies in Australia had previously imposed restrictions on the means by which their members could attract business[530] and until about 1980, solicitors in all parts of Australia were prohibited by professional rules from advertising.[531]

By 1982, in a discussion about a relaxing of these rules, the NSW Law Reform Commission had recognised that advertising 'can stimulate innovation and improve efficiency within the profession'[532] though even today there are still rules about advertising particularly in personal injury matters.[533]

## COMMUNITY LEGAL EDUCATION

Giddings notes that:

> In keeping with their commitment to demystify the law and break down the traditional lawyer-client relationship, CLCs developed initiatives designed to educate the community regarding their rights and responsibilities. This type of community legal education was not seen as an end in itself, but rather a means to empower people to make informed choices about what further law-related actions they might take. It was designed to promote 'legal literacy' and to raise the profile of poverty law

issues rather than providing a way to resolve specific immediate problems.[534]

One example of the earliest steps that RLC took to ascertain legal need was the use of outreach services including community legal education to prisoners in the 1970s. As Petre says of the Centre's services:

> The legal advice was locally focused—that's where the need was, but I think that the other characteristic of RLC right from the start is that they would identify a need relevant to the local area—and prisoners was one of the first. Volunteers would go out to prisons, Long Bay particularly and provide legal services and advice out there.[535]

Zdenkowski, a legal academic at UNSW involved with the Centre notes:

> The Parramatta debating society was a Saturday morning group which a small group of prisoners organised and which was an opportunity to have a speaker come out and talk on a topic. People would go out to Parramatta gaol and sometimes the talks would involve legal issues. It was about contact and expanding horizons.[536]

This new approach of conducting community legal education (CLE) and outreach services in the gaols was a method of ascertaining the legal needs of prisoners which had not previously been seen in Australia. The Centre has focused on CLE initiatives throughout its existence – both in the form of measures such as in podcasts, websites, radio and TV programs, media work and an entire offshoot publications section to become known as Redfern Legal Centre Publishing.

In the early 1990s, the Centre was responsible for initiating a document containing details of all CLE publications and resources produced across Australia by CLCs in the then new

Filemaker format thereby reducing duplication in work and informing Centre workers across the country of CLE projects.

## PHONE-INS

Another tool used for shedding light on legal need in the early days of CLCs was the phone-in. A phone-in is a tool which allows members of the public to call an organisation and raise concerns about certain pre-designated issues. While phone-ins had been used from the 1960s in researching social issues[537] and in some cases for political advocacy, notably by the environmental movement,[538] it appears that the Centre was the first legal organisation to use this method as a tool for determining legal needs in a selected area of law.

In 1982, the Centre ran a phone-in for people to raise concerns about social security matters. Roger West, a solicitor with the Centre who helped organise the phone-in, said: 'I was devastated by the results. Episode after episode of quite frightening stories of a very tough administration and bureaucracy was very serious.'[539] This reaction and other social security cases run by the Centre brought attention to the legal need in this area and was a catalyst for proposals to set up the country's first Welfare Rights Legal Centre (WRC) as described below.

In March the same year, Redfern Legal Centre joined the Social Welfare Action Group and others to conduct a phone-in survey of abuse of elderly people. On the weekend of the survey, 466 complaints were recorded. Many abuses mentioned in the phone-in, such as denial of appropriate attention, victimisation and lack of freedom, could be seen as part of a total legal framework which did little to protect the rights of elderly people in retirement villages, hostels and nursing homes.[540] A Report entitled *Prisoners of Neglect: A Study of Abuse of Elderly People* was produced out of this phone-in.[541] Later the Centre ran phone-ins on insurance issues[542] and in 1984, the Centre ran a 'Bank Bashing Day' phone in—using numerous volunteers to answer calls from people who had problems with their banks.

This method of discovering and exposing legal need in a community has been used by government organisations and researchers since that time, in areas of law such as domestic violence.[543] Phone-ins were an effective innovation in demonstrating legal need and bringing attention to an issue being both inexpensive (staffed by volunteers in the case of CLCs) and allowing anonymity from participants. Staff of the legal centre analysed the data collected and compiled the information incorporating it into reports that could be used to raise attention to issues and lobby government for change.

The claim that the Centre engaged in innovation must be viewed not only against the general political and historical climate at the time but also against the background of the legal profession and changes to the legal system in Australia as previously discussed. As Disney *et al* note, 'before the period of innovation that occurred in legal aid[544] in Australia in the 1970s, to practice law was almost inevitably to engage in private legal practice.'[545] The role of most lawyers in the twentieth century was to provide legal advice and representation to individual clients, including corporations, and other groups. The lawyer's role was frequently that of 'an interpreter to a lay audience of the body of laws.'[546] Practising lawyers in non-appearance roles focused on established markets such as conveyancing, commercial and company law, car accidents, estates, tax, family law and workers compensation.[547] Most of their time was spent in direct provision of services to middle and high income groups in the community.[548]

For the first time in Australia in the 1970s there were lawyers engaged in collaborative projects designed to achieve a fairer basis to direct provision of services, policy development and law reform for disadvantaged people and groups in the community. As stated in 1986, the Centres 'have had a positive impact on the legal aid system out of all proportion to their actual size.'[549] The lawyers and other workers in these centres had a focus not only on disadvantaged clients but on ways of empowering people to understand and use the law.

The early CLCs had a distinctly different approach to the way they provided legal advice to clients from the services provided by the private legal profession or other legal aid providers[550] in that free legal assistance was provided to anyone who walked in the door; Centres were staffed by both lawyer and non-lawyer volunteers working on an equal footing; Centres were open out of normal office hours, usually in the evenings; the physical surrounds of the offices and the clothing of the lawyers were informal; there were often no formal organisational or administrative systems; clear explanations of their legal situation were given to clients; and clients were involved in their own problem solving.[551]

Redfern Legal Centre was one community legal centre that developed a tradition of innovation which led to dedicated services never been seen before in Australia. Though there were many developments in legal aid in the 1970s and 1980s[552] and in pro bono assistance from the private profession, the Centre's services were novel in being provided for new categories of clients (e.g. prisoners), or in areas of law (welfare rights, intellectual disability) that had not been systematically addressed by legal aid offices or the private legal profession.[553]

Redfern's offshoot services would include:
a) Prisoners Legal Service (PLS): a service that provided legal assistance including legal advice and representation to people serving gaol sentences in NSW gaols;

b) Intellectual Disability Rights Service (UDRS): a legal service addressing the legal needs of people with an intellectual disability and their families and carers which took an innovative approach of providing services through education and involving people with an intellectual disability in the service's management;
c) Redfern Legal Centre Publishing (RLCP)/Lawyers Practice Manual/Streetwize Comics: a self-funding legal publisher aimed at providing community legal education;
d) Women's Domestic Violence Court Advocacy Service (WDVCAS): a multidisciplinary legal and welfare service for women suffering domestic violence;
e) The Accommodation Rights Service (TARS): Australia's first legal advocacy service for older people in nursing homes and retirement villages, and;
f) Welfare Rights Centre (WRC): a specialist centre focusing on welfare rights issues.

## GOVERNMENT FUNDING: FRANK WALKER

NSW Attorney–General Frank Walker is an example of an individual who was instrumental in the success of the Centre's work. Without Walker's support many of the new services developed by the Centre may not have come to fruition. The Hon. (Frank) Francis John Walker, QC was a member of the Legislative Assembly from 1970 to 1988 and Attorney–General from 1978 to 1983. At his funeral in 2012, High Court Judge Mary Gaudron said that 'A lot of people have had, and many others will have, a much better life than otherwise because of Frank Walker.'[554]

Bruce Hawker,[555] who was an advisor to Walker, had been a volunteer at the Centre and was an important connection between the Centre and Walker. Hawker notes Walker's introducing the first state-based land rights legislation in Australia and says, 'In all my years in politics, I cannot recall another state politician with such a consistently strong record of empowering the powerless.'[556] His list of accomplishments in reform in NSW is quite outstanding.[557]

While Walker was Attorney–General and in the Ministry, funding was provided for a number of the Centre initiatives described above as innovations. In 1982 the NSW Government provided funding for the Prisoners Legal Service within the Legal Aid Commission.[558] On 28 September 1982, the NSW government announced funding for the Welfare Rights Centre. By 1984, Walker had moved to the portfolio of Minister for Youth and Community Services and Minister for Housing and it was in 1985 that Department gave the Centre $60,000 and IDRS was established at RLC in one of the rooms upstairs in Redfern Town Hall.

It is clear that the role Walker played was crucial in the development of a number of the Centre's innovations and is an example of the role that an individual can play in innovation.

Opposite page:
1. Joyce Ingram Aboriginal Elder and community leader. The last protected tenant on The Block and finally left 78 Eveleigh Street in 2004.
2. Joyce Ingram.
3. Tony Pooley, Mayor of South Sydney and Redfern Legal Centre volunteers.
4. Redfern Legal Centre Christmas party, upstairs at Gusto's on Abercrombie Street, Darlington.
5. Redfern Legal Centre's Domestic Violence team: Lyndal Gowland, Dixie Link-Gordan, Susan Smith.

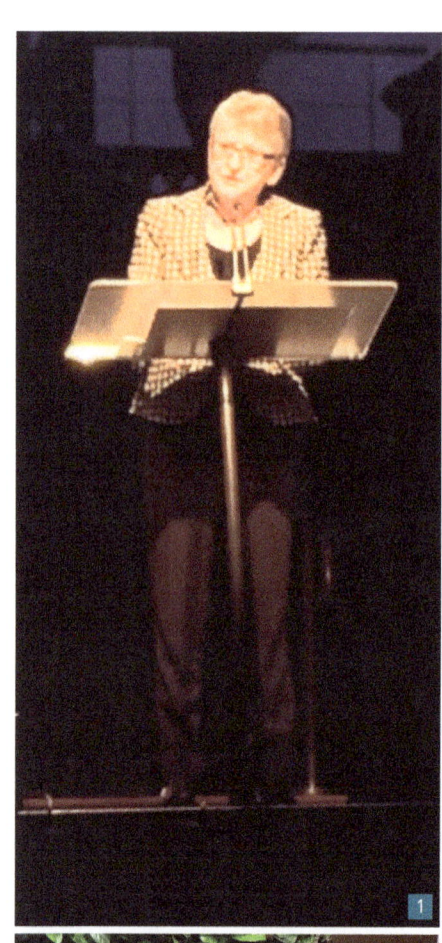

1. Virginia Bell.
2. Jacqui Swinburne, Redfern Legal Centre's longest employed staff member.
3. John Basten.
4. Peter Stapleton, Terry Buddin.
5. Paul Farrugia, Roger West.
6. Alan Cameron, Virginia Bell, Peter Stapleton, Sue Davitt, Clare Petre, Terry Buddin.
7. Selena Choo, Craig Lenehan, Beth Jewell, Ben Slade, Matthew Hazard, Kylie Kilgour.
8. Frances Gibson, Harriet Grahame, Simon Rice, Polly Porteus.

# CHAPTER 7
# 'THE BABIES': SPECIALIST SERVICES DEVELOPED AT RLC

## THE PRISONERS LEGAL SERVICE

In February 1984, a man rang RLC early one weekday to say that only five minutes previously he had been driving along Anzac Parade behind a police paddy wagon. When both vehicles stopped at lights he became aware of shouting from the rear of the van. The motorist wound down his window and made out a voice calling 'Ring the Redfern Legal Centre, I'm being taken from Long Bay to Maroubra to be interviewed about a murder. Get hold of Redfern Legal Centre' After some intensive investigation the Centre tracked down the client after driving to Maroubra police station.[559]

*RLC News*

Prison work started early in the Centre's history. Historically there had been little, if any, legal assistance for prisoners in NSW, who often faced harsh conditions and judicial indifference.[560] Brutality in NSW prisons in the early 1970s led to major prison riots erupting at Bathurst gaol in 1974. Lobbying by prison activists, NSW parliamentarians, legal academics and lawyers was successful in getting mainstream press attention to the issue. This led to a Royal Commission into NSW Prisons beginning in 1976, conducted by then Justice of the NSW

Supreme Court, John Nagle.[561] One of the first Centre lawyers, Virginia Bell, remembers:

> I had followed the Nagle Royal Commission and the revelations were quite shocking ... I saw quite a bit of the hearings ... There had been an institutional approach to the infliction of physical beatings on prisoners described as intractable. That had resulted in one case in a man becoming a paraplegic. The beatings were officially administered and were savage. When that material came to light, I think it was a shock to people ... At the time the Report was tabled my recollection is that there was a lot of press coverage about the shocking revelations and the Premier Neville Wran made statements that this would not happen again.[562]

In 1978, a loose group of legal academics, lawyers and prison activists formed the Prisoners Legal Service (PLS), based at the Centre. Zdenkowski, a legal academic at UNSW involved with the Centre, notes:

> We did a lot of legal visits to the gaols and there was some litigation that took place. It grew out of that ... [The Centre] received a lot of letters and individuals received letters from prisoners. The PLS provided an opportunity to educate prisoners about their rights and we made regular visits to prisons ... I used to take out a group of law students weekly to Long Bay Gaol. That was mutually beneficial.[563]

Those working in the PLS consisted of Centre staff lawyers, barristers briefed by the Centre, and also volunteer lawyers. The Centre solicitors were well known in the gaols and word-of-mouth brought the PLS many clients. John Basten went to the Bar in 1981 and was briefed by the Centre on many prisoner cases.[564] The Centre ran appeals for prisoners challenging disciplinary convictions. This work led to the government legal aid service extending legal aid funding for those matters.[565] The Centre

## 'THE BABIES': SPECIALIST SERVICES DEVELOPED AT RLC

also ran many cases about prisoners' remission entitlements[566] and was instrumental in the establishment of the Visiting Justice system in the late 1970s (independent magistrates dealing with disciplinary charges in prisons).[567] 'Before that internal discipline was entirely run by the Governors of respective gaols and there really was no outside input…The moving force behind that was Kevin Anderson, Deputy Chief Magistrate.'[568]

Work done at the Centre for prisoners was undertaken in loose coalitions with other organisations. One of these, the Prisoners Action Group (PAG), had been formed in 1973 and 'was committed to abolition (not reform), to activism (not passivity), and ex-prisoners were to have the final say on policy and activities.'[569] Prisoners would make complaints about their treatment in gaols,[570] and the PAG would arrange for solicitors from the Centre to take instructions from them. As Genovese notes, PAG was:

> a unique alliance that would be hard to imagine in our own regulated and politically demarcated times. It included ex-prisoners, UNSW legal academics such as George Zdenkowski and David Brown, libertarians and civil liberties members—all committed to exposing the horrendous conditions in NSW jails. They wanted to transform the criminal justice system itself, with a long-term goal of abolishing jails altogether, and employed the intellectual framework and street performativeness of situationism to great effect in the politics surrounding the Bathurst Jail riots and Nagle Royal Commission into the NSW prison system in the 1970s.[571]

The lawyers working for Redfern Legal Centre's Prisoners Legal Service worked with activist community workers on a number of campaigns and for particular clients. There are many examples of this. One was the campaign for the closure of Katingal, a notorious NSW gaol. It had opened in 1975, billed by the NSW government as 'the country's first modern, purpose-built extreme maximum security prison.'[572] It was built to house the worst killers and intractable offenders. A moat was built as an anti-tank trap, in case anyone resorted to such measures to engineer a break-out. Prisoners were confined to cells 1.5 metres wide by just over three metres long on two levels. They had little visual or physical contact with guards, who watched their movements through a peep hole.[573] Within three years of its opening the Nagle Royal Commission into NSW Prisons expressed the opinion that it should be shut down. The Report stated that 'it is clear that the cost of Katingal is too high in human terms. It was ill-conceived in the first place, was surrounded by secrecy and defensiveness at a time when public discussion should have been encouraged. Its inmates are now suffering the consequences.'[574] Initially the government claimed there was no alternative place for these prisoners to go and refused to close the prison. The recommendation that Katingal be closed was finally accepted, but only after a hard-fought campaign over a period of months.[575] Barrister Helen Golding, who was working for the Centre, was very involved with the campaign run by a number of organisations. Campaign action included burning a model of Katingal outside the District Court, halting traffic for a demonstration on Sydney Harbour Bridge and setting up a tent vigil outside Long Bay where Katingal was.[576] She worked on other prisoners' rights campaigns and was assisting prisoners from Katingal on a regular basis in the courts. In June 1978, Katingal was closed.[577]

Media organisations were involved. Radio Skid Row, in the basement of the Wentworth building at the University of Sydney, conducted interviews on prison issues with the lawyers from RLC.[578] Nick Franklin at ABC Radio 2JJ began broadcasting *The Prisoners Program* in 1979,[579] and there were other prisoners'

## 'THE BABIES': SPECIALIST SERVICES DEVELOPED AT RLC

programs on community radio stations in Sydney. These collaborations and close ties were instrumental in assisting the Centre not only in the establishment of the Prisoners Legal Service but increasing its effectiveness by making it responsive to prisoners needs and interests in a way that distinguished the service from traditional private legal practice.

While the PLS mainly focused on prisoners in male gaols, another organisation, Women Behind Bars ('WBB') concentrated on providing legal assistance and advocacy for women prisoners. Staff of the Centre were involved with activists in WBB.[580] In 1979, Robyn Lansdowne was working with the Feminist Legal Action Group (FLAG) and WBB[581] to assist clients Violet and Bruce Roberts. Violet Roberts and her son were convicted of murdering her violent husband, Eric in 1976.[582] Lansdowne recalls:

> I interviewed Violet Roberts who had been convicted of murder and had been given a life sentence. Her case was very tragic and through WBB there was a movement to have her and her son released. In 1980, there was a street campaign —sit-ins, marches etc and public meetings at Redfern Town Hall. There was a formal process when I was the solicitor for Violet at RLC making an application for Violet's release on licence and a campaign through the media including *60 Minutes* episodes etc.[583]

Lansdowne was employed by the law firm Freehills and, in another innovation, was the first pro bono lawyer to be employed by a law firm to work in a community legal centre. 'The terms of my employment were that I worked one day a week for the Centre and four for Freehills and Freehills paid me five days a week.'[584] At the Centre, Lansdowne worked on Violet's case. Ultimately Violet and her son were released on 15 October 1980.[585] Their release ended a vigil outside the Department of

Corrective Services and then Parliament House begun 99 days before. By that time over 20,000 signatures had been collected on the petition calling on the government to set them free. There was extensive press coverage of the case and the issues it raised, virtually all of which was sympathetic, and public calls from all sections of the community for release of the Roberts (culminating in a half page advertisement in the *Sydney Morning Herald* on Monday 13 October 1980). The Attorney-General, Frank Walker took the responsibility for the decision and indicated that he was prepared to make a public recommendation that a licence be recommended on legal grounds because the Roberts had suffered a 'serious miscarriage of justice'.[586]

There was strong support amongst prisoners for Redfern Legal Centre, to the extent that one of the demands by prisoners in a sit-in at Parramatta Jail on 13 January 1979 was that 'jail authorities organise among prisoners a collection of money to aid the Redfern Legal Centre'.[587] The Centre undertook casework for prisoners but also took an activist approach to prison issues. In 1979, the Centre organised lawyers to go to Goulburn Gaol to take statutory declarations from prisoners detailing their treatment in prison. This work formed the basis for the terms of reference in the Goulburn Gaol inquiry into warder bashings and other offences.[588] The inquiry led to Public Service Board charges against five prison officers.[589]

Well-known prison activist Brett Collins finished a prison sentence in 1980 and was keen to make a difference in NSW prisons.[590] 'Redfern was the only Centre [in NSW] following through on prisoners' issues. It was a Centre linking the Prisoners Action Group with other activists and lawyers—a safe place and a place of networking.'[591] Collins and other prison activists used the Centre as a resource and the Centre lawyers and volunteer

## 'THE BABIES': SPECIALIST SERVICES DEVELOPED AT RLC

lawyers were involved in all aspects of prison work, including the management of a halfway house for prisoners in Glebe.[592]

Anne Healey, a Centre staff member, recalls:

> The prisoners were getting a voice they hadn't had before and my impression was that the armed hold up squad didn't like it at all ... There was a palpable hostility from the Redfern police ... I remember thinking particularly Virginia [Bell] and Nanette [Rogers] [RLC Solicitors] were really brave ... They never thought of changing their behaviour as a result of the police hostility.[593]

In 1979 and 1980 the Centre had discussions with the State Government's legal aid body, the Legal Services Commission, with a view to setting up a funded, independent Prisoners Legal Service. RLC 'never wanted to run duty solicitor services or provide bulk legal services to the population…and when it became apparent that there was a need for an ongoing service for people in prisons…we just thought this was something we couldn't do…it really required an institutional base.'[594] On 27 May 1981, the Legal Services Commission resolved to recommend to the Attorney–General that a separate division of the Commission be established to create a comprehensive Prisoners Legal Service.[595]

The government contracted the PLS services to RLC and other community legal centres. Redfern, Marrickville and Macquarie Legal Centres participated in the Legal Services Commission's Prisoners Legal Service by providing solicitors to attend at Long Bay, Parramatta, Silverwater and Mulawa Jails on a regular basis to give general legal advice to prisoners.[596] An in-house service at the Legal Aid Commission was established in February 1986 staffed by three solicitors and three support staff. The service was responsible for provision of an advisory service to prisoners in all metropolitan prisons; representation of prisoners charged before the Visiting Justice in all metropolitan prisons; coordination of similar services provided by the Service to prisoners in country gaols by rostered private solicitors; and, coordination of a roster of private solicitors to appear for prisoners before the Parole Board at revocation and review hearings.[597]

The legal regime in prisons was arcane and little was known about it. The Centre's work led to the first Australian consolidation of prison law in *Halsbury's Laws of Australia*.[598] Previously, prisoners had been almost always unrepresented. Cases were run by the Centre, such as *Riley v Parole Board of New South Wales*,[599] where Mr Riley had been refused release by the Parole Board for years with no reasons given. The case was taken on as an issue of natural justice and its successful conclusion assisted not only Mr Riley but also many other prisoners.

Centre staff lawyers represented prisoners at Visiting Justice hearings for which the Centre had received specific funding. Andrew Haesler, a solicitor at the Centre notes:

> We engaged in strategic thinking about the work being done. In the PLS work for instance, we asked, 'if we run this case will we change the remission system?' We forced changes which got lots of people released. We would send someone down to the gaol with a particular facts situation in mind and try and find someone who fitted that case. We didn't want to be just a duty solicitor.[600]

### Prisons solicitor Bill Dickens recalls work in the 1980s.

> We used to do a lot of sentence calculation work ... At the Department of Corrective Services, there was an employee whose sad responsibility it was to calculate the sentences. These were done on handwritten cards which had all the arithmetic on them. And it was complex because of the nature of the remissions system ... We used to get the cards and would check the release dates and inevitably the Department would get it wrong and we would then commence extensive litigation

## 'THE BABIES': SPECIALIST SERVICES DEVELOPED AT RLC

to calculate the proper sentences. This was a good source of income from costs for RLC for a while.

Dickens relished the opportunity to challenge the inefficiencies and inequities of the system, describing his work here as 'a lot of fun'. He adds:

> I remember one time when the prison released a person and he said to them, 'I am not meant to be released now' and they said, 'yes you are, on your way' and about a week later they contacted him and said, 'please come back now we made a mistake'. So, we briefed John Basten and went to the Full Court of the Federal Court and they found the release extinguished the warrant and there was no power to arrest him so he was out. There was an amendment to the *Crimes Act* to deal with that situation after that. John Basten was absolutely ruthless in his efficiency. You briefed him and within 24 hours you would not only have an advice but you would have pleadings and documents and you were ready to go. It was pretty exciting, all that crime work.[601]

Ben Slade, a Centre solicitor in the mid-1980s, had come straight from law school to work at RLC and was participating in the PLS with Bill Dickens. They would visit two gaols in a day. You would 'see a queue of 30 people in one gaol and another 30 in the afternoon.'[602] There was no other free legal advice at the gaols.

The Centre's activities clearly antagonised the Department of Corrective Services. John Fahey, Minister in the NSW government publicly criticised the PLS, claiming it was being abused by prisoners who appealed to the District Court when Visiting Justices punished them for misbehaviour. Fahey claimed these appeals 'clogged up the District Court and cost the State tens of thousands of dollars in transport and legal expenses'.[603]

In 1985 it was agreed that the government legal aid office, the Legal Aid Commission of NSW, would set up a separate section to deal with prisoners' matters to start around July that year.[604] The Centre handed over the PLS organisation to government though they retained casework in Visiting Justice matters, occasional test cases[605] and representation on the PLS Advisory Committee. The Centre's mission in this area was accomplished. The project to provide legal services and a voice for prisoners in New South Wales had been established by the Centre and was now to develop into State-wide government funded service to prisoners in NSW gaols.[606]

In the transfer to the Legal Aid Commission, though possibly something was lost. The new PLS did not operate as an activist organisation. Brett Collins, now coordinator of prison activist group Justice Action, notes:

> Over the years legal aid became more and more reluctant to be activist and less prepared to expose what was actually happening in the prisons ... after a while they didn't want to put all that time into the meetings ... they tried to step away. Then they said they don't want a committee anymore [Advisory Committee] ... it was reinstituted after protests but then disbanded ... The Prisoner movement lost the network and being part of the processes with lawyers.[607]

Zdenkowski agrees:

> When the PLS went to legal aid there was a gap in advocating for prison rights. There are now very few people involved. Brett Collins and Justice Action have continued to hold the torch. However, there is no sustained public discourse about prison conditions.[608]

Basten has another view:

> There was a solicitor Jack Grahame who used to do a lot of the prisoners work and Richard Button... they did very well—they expanded the service to the whole state...there were a lot of test cases being run...one of the things that happened was that

> heroin got into the gaols and the sort of political motivation to improve conditions just collapsed.[609]

Despite these concerns, the innovation of the PLS has proved to be a sustainable service that today assists prisoners everywhere in NSW.[610] The staff and volunteers at the Centre identified a need, then designed and implemented a novel service to meet the need. The NSW government was persuaded to take on and run a service for prisoners in all gaols. In doing so, they made a significant contribution to delivering access to legal services to a previously excluded group of people—prisoners.

## INTELLECTUAL DISABILITY RIGHTS SERVICE

The history of people with intellectual disability is a history of marginalisation, oppression and abuse.[611] Around 1981, the Centre identified a gap in legal services for people with intellectual disability[612] and this focus culminated in the creation of a new organisation—the Intellectual Disability Rights Service (IDRS). The role of IDRS was to advocate for people with intellectual disability by undertaking strategic casework and education and to aim for the reform of law and policy to promote the rights of people with intellectual disability.[613] This innovative organisation was to make its mark on the legal services of NSW and Australia through its casework and reform agenda as well as innovations in the mode of delivery of its services.

In the 1970s, the topic of intellectual disability and the law was in its infancy in Australia but was starting to be discussed in progressive legal circles. In July 1978, a conference was held at the University of New South Wales by the NSW Council for the Mentally Handicapped entitled The Intellectually Handicapped: Citizens or Non Citizens. Lawyer Jim Simpson was struck by the contents of a speech by Edward St John QC in which he talked about people with intellectual disability as outlaws—'people truly outside the due process and equal protection of the laws.'[614]

Jim Simpson, who came to the service from a private firm, was a volunteer at RLC and describes the development of work relating to intellectual disability at the Centre:

> By 1980 there was a social worker on every evening roster and there was a woman called Anne Louise Carlton who was the Friday night social worker and worked in intellectual disability in Parramatta and she introduced us to problems faced by people with intellectual disability ... She would get clients referred from the NSW Council for Intellectual Disability and a group of people from there came along wanting advice about wills to provide for their children.
>
> It was a time with very little community-based supported accommodation so they wanted advice about how parents could pool money to purchase housing. We did quite a lot of work around that issue and that was the main thing that was coming in. Anne Louise went off to Melbourne but arranged for Janene Cootes to replace her.[615] She was very influential in getting us to think about the problems that people with intellectual disability had but who were not coming in to see us. There was a lot of discussion about how rotten the institutions were and possibilities for people moving out into the community. It was obvious the vulnerability of people with intellectual disability and in about 1983 we decided to take a more CLE focus and the Friday night roster people started running forums about the rights of people with intellectual disability. This was extra work on top of the usual volunteer work. People included Tony Payne, Julia Hall and Jill Anderson. Then we started to get cases where people's rights were abused. We had a guy who was taken advantage of by a marriage agency—they took a lot of money to find him a wife. We got media about that on a current affairs show. There was a horrendous case where a guy was in respite care in an institution and his parents picked him up after a week's respite and all his fingernails were gone.

## 'THE BABIES': SPECIALIST SERVICES DEVELOPED AT RLC

No clear explanation and the Department of Health concluded that their son had a disease that affected his fingernails. The parents went to Ombudsman who exposed no proper investigation and found that the most likely thing was that a staff member had done this. He eventually got compensation but whoever did it was not discovered. In about 1984, there was a planning weekend at Bundanoon and a decision made that each evening would take on a particular specialty which cemented that we were doing intellectual disability and a particular staff member was associated with each night ... Then we started seeking funding to set up IDRS.[616]

The Centre had no specific funding for intellectual disability work and Bill Dickens was the first staff lawyer assigned to the night. Dickens recalls: 'my father who was a GP in Dubbo was involved in services for people with intellectual disability in western NSW so that struck a bit of a chord with me ... I used to go out and talk to groups of people with intellectual disability about what the law was.'[617]

Between 1980–85 seven major State Government Reports were published on services to intellectually disabled Australians. These presented pictures of service delivery, which was fragmented, uncoordinated, and poorly resourced.[618] In 1983, the then Federal Minister for Community Services, Senator Don Grimes satisfied a pre-election commitment by establishing the Disability Advisory Council of Australia, which provided a mechanism for disabled people to directly advise the government. This initiative was closely followed by the Handicapped Programs Review (HPR) (1983–85) and its legislative outcome, the *Disability Services Act 1986*. The HPR involved a comprehensive public examination of government social policy as it affected people with disability. The review was based 'on the principle that future government funds should be directed towards services and programs that provided the individual with the greatest amount of flexibility.'[619] The Centre staff wrote a publication on legal needs of institutionalised people in 1985.[620] In 1986, the Australian Parliament approved the *Disability Services Act*. This legislation set out a 'new direction'—and signalled a move away from segregation to the integration of people with disabilities in Australian society. The object of the legislation included:

1. to assist persons with disabilities to receive services necessary to enable them to work towards full participation as members of the community;
2. to promote services provided to persons with disabilities that:
   (i) assist persons with disabilities to integrate in the community, and complement services available generally to persons in the community;
   (ii) assist persons with disabilities to achieve positive outcomes, such as increased independence, employment opportunities and integration in the community.[621]

Roger West, co-ordinator of the Centre, worked with Jim Simpson on how to lobby government and get funding to set up IDRS. The proposal for the new service was successful at the end of 1985 and was the culmination of five years of involvement by Redfern Legal Centre in the problems of people with intellectual disability. The NSW Government gave the Centre $60,000 in 1985 and IDRS was established at the Centre in one of the rooms upstairs in Redfern Town Hall. Initially the staff consisted of a solicitor, a part-time community educator and the administrator. The Service provided initial advice to anyone either by telephone or in person and then generally provided an appropriate referral rather than conducting the case

## 'THE BABIES': SPECIALIST SERVICES DEVELOPED AT RLC

entirely. The aim of the Service was to build up the capacity of mainstream lawyers to act for people rather than seeking to provide a comprehensive casework service. (This was in accord with the principle of normalisation. This principle says that people with intellectual disability should be allowed to live as normal a life as possible in the general community and as far as possible obtain services from mainstream channels rather than specialist channels).[622]

Shortly afterwards in 1986, Senator Grimes funded several demonstration projects—innovative programs to improve the lives of people with disability. Simpson notes that 'we got $250,000 for 18 months which was really big money back then. We grew quickly and after Redfern Legal Centre Publishing moved out, we shared space on the top level of the Centre with another new service, The Accommodation Rights Service.'[623]

The work of IDRS was always collaborative. The Service's work in casework, education and policy and the way in which it offered its services was developed in conjunction with other community services. Simpson recalls:

> We had support from community groups—NSW Council for Intellectual Disability and Action for People with a Disability which was a parent group who had a rights-based focus and very progressive. Soon after we developed the interest at RLC a similar interest developed at Macquarie Legal Centre and they were doing similar stuff. I wasn't aware of anything similar overseas and the model we developed was very much based on our experience. We were very clear from the start we wouldn't just do advice and casework but we would do community education with people with intellectual disability themselves, their families and support workers. That was the way to go. In the early years, we did about one third advice and casework, one third systemic advocacy and one third education. We would do test cases where there were glaring outrages

and there was no other source of assistance. Part of this was about building up a network of private lawyers and building up expertise in Legal Aid for people with intellectual disability.[624]

The new service worked on a wide variety of human rights issues such as the use of physically restrictive and intrusive methods of managing challenging behaviour, employment issues such as wages, conditions of work, self-determination, use of psychotropic medication, discrimination, guardianship and the establishment of a Guardianship Board, criminal law, education of lawyers, victims of crime including sexual assault, housing, wills, sterilisation, work on *Disability Services Act* standards and issues to do with boarding houses/hostels. Litigation was generally restricted to test cases. The Service provided education to help people with intellectual disability to recognise violations of their rights and what they could do about such violations. Similar training was conducted through workshops and publications for relatives, friends and advocates, and disability service providers.[625] Simpson recalls:

> In 1986, I became the first Principal Solicitor and Coordinator. I was a pig in mud! For a long time, I was just a square peg in a round hole in the private firm. I got good experience there but it was for pretty well-off people and I gradually developed clarity that where I was comfortable was working where people were doing it tough and especially the systemic change advocacy I particularly enjoyed. The world was ripe for that. I had done a fair bit of litigation so had the confidence to take on issues.[626]

The Service took on test case litigation.[627] In the 1980s, there was a great deal of debate about who should have responsibility for decisions of sterilisation of minors with intellectual disabilities.[628] In 1988, IDRS was involved with a case before the Family Court in relation to a proposed hysterectomy on a 14-year-old girl with intellectual disability.[629] The girl's parents organised the

## 'THE BABIES': SPECIALIST SERVICES DEVELOPED AT RLC

operation as they were concerned about how she would react to menstruation. IDRS became aware of the proposed operation and obtained an interim injunction on behalf of a parent active in an organisation of parents of people with intellectual disability the night before the planned operation to prevent the operation occurring until there had been a full hearing in the Court.[630] The Human Rights and Equal Opportunity Commission sought and was granted leave to intervene in the proceedings. This was the first case of its type in Australia. In *Re a Teenager*, Cook J held the operation could go ahead. In his remarks on the case, the judge said that the decision was one for the parents stating:

> The Court was concerned as to how the proceedings came before the Court and as to how a complete stranger to the child and the family, could prosecute an action which, seemingly, involved most intimate and sensitive awareness and appraisal of that particular child's interests. It does not seem appropriate to the Court that representatives of interest groups, no matter how well-intentioned or motivated, can bring to all essential judgments, arising both before and during such litigation as the present, the cool and pragmatic approach required.[631]

The Service was involved in two of these sterilisation cases which were controversial and attracted significant publicity. Simpson notes:

> Sterilisation was one of the biggest issues we took on. I remember Justice Powell was getting cases where he was authorising hysterectomies on women without any representation for the woman. I wrote to him and said how about having separate representatives in those cases. He was unwilling to talk to me about this. So I wrote to Chief Justice Street and got a very urbane response which said that he looked forward to the assistance of legal representation in this sensitive area of the law… We were in the thick of

the development of the guardianship legislation which was going to have in it that sterilisation of women who lacked capacity could only occur with permission of the Tribunal. But then we were really concerned about anecdotes we were hearing where young girls were given hysterectomies even pre-menstruation. We got alerted by a local government disability service who rang us and told us they were worried about a particular case where a hysterectomy was to be done the day after tomorrow. The girl was prepubescent so we took the bit between our teeth and I rang up the doctor. At that point, a body of law had developed overseas that non-therapeutic sterilisation of people with intellectual disability was illegal, at least without court approval. The doctor told me that he had advice that the operation was both legal and ethical. It was going to happen the next morning.

I talked to a member of our management committee who was a parent and with her as plaintiff I rang up the duty judge of the Equity Division and gained an *ex parte* injunction that night. We then got John Basten involved as barrister. John said there were complex jurisdictional issues so it was moved to the Family Court ... It was very difficult. There was no doubt about the bona fides of the family. It was an issue about whether the operation was necessary and in the child's interests. There was another similar case which we pursued before the first case was heard. Parallel to this the Victorian Public Advocate brought a similar case before Nicholson CJ in the Family Court. He looked at overseas case law and concluded that non-therapeutic sterilisation did require Family Court approval.[632] His decision was followed by a decision of the Full Court of the Family Court that said it didn't require approval. So, the issue went to the High Court.

The High Court in *Re Marion*[633] said Family Court approval was required for sterilisation. We saw this as a big step forward in the rights of people with intellectual disability. We didn't know what to expect. It was such a roller coaster with the different decisions in the Family Court. It was so difficult. We were barging in on these families who were loving caring families. We were worried about what our standing would be. The first judgment had a lot of publicity and the parents did an interview in the *Women's Weekly* and on TV. We were worried about our reputation and our relationships with others in the disability community. But in fact, there didn't seem to be any negative effect whatsoever and in fact in the month after the first Family Court decision we had a real spike in our advice work.[634]

Funding bodies and organisations supported a community development ideal in this period, but a question arises as to whether those involved at the time addressed the equity issues surrounding participation in such models of community functioning. Marginalised groups remained on the periphery, excluded from the mainstream ideals, so missing out on the opportunities offered by 'community development'.[635] IDRS had its own management committee which included parents, a representative from the Centre staff and people with intellectual disability [636]and the Rights Forum which was a group of people with intellectual disability who met regularly to provide advice to IDRS on issues. 'At the time this was ground-breaking and very valuable.'[637] In the case of IDRS significant efforts were made to ensure marginalised people had a real voice in the service's activities and policies. The Service recognised the 'value of the unique insight on intellectual disability issues possessed by people who themselves have an intellectual disability'.[638] A publication addressed at people with intellectual disability participating in management of advocacy services was produced by the Service.[639] Another publication was a guide to the law and rights in group homes, hostels, institutions and other supported accommodation and was entitled Rights in Residence.[640] IDRS worked to highlight the vulnerability of people with intellectual disabilities as victims of crime as well as working on systemic change in the criminal justice system's approach to offenders with intellectual disability. IDRS engaged criminal barrister Mark Ierace to write 'Intellectual Disability: A Manual for Criminal Lawyers' which filled in the gaps in lawyers' training about law which applied to people with intellectual disability.[641] A number of other publications have been produced by the service.[642]

By 1991, IDRS had moved their education focus to a train the trainer model—training workers in the intellectual disability field to ensure widest impact.[643] The main focus of the service was now primarily on preventative law by means of education rather than casework. Since that time IDRS has continued providing essential legal advice, education and reform work for people with intellectual disability and their families. The service operates the Criminal Justice Support Network (CJSN) which provides assistance to people with intellectual and other cognitive disability at police stations and at court.[644] The value of the service has been nationally recognised with calls for similar organisations to be established in all states.[645]

The IDRS provided the first legal service dealing with the topic of intellectual disability in Australia, a legal service that employed people with intellectual disability on staff to deliver services and a service that had people with intellectual disability as an integral part of the management of the service and in the Rights Forum. It fulfilled the role of a non-profit being an active agent in shaping solutions to social problems, as opposed to being merely a service provider or advocate for policy related reform.[646] IDRS, as part of and Redfern Legal Centre and now an independent organisation, is an organisation that enables action and change and was innovative in its manner of providing services being primarily by education and retaining people with disabilities to do education and training work.

The Service continues to work alongside people with cognitive impairment who need help with legal problems or support dealing with the legal system. The introduction of the National Disability Insurance Scheme opened up a new field of work. IDRS provides support, to people with cognitive impairment, to appeal decisions made by the National Disability Insurance Agency (NDIA) to be externally reviewed by the Administrative Appeals Tribunal (AAT). Following a grant of funding IDRS is to provide the Justice Advocacy Service (JAS) to people with cognitive impairment across NSW. In 2019, plans to separate the Community Legal Centre (CLC) functions of IDRS from the Justice Support functions were put in place.

## REDFERN LEGAL CENTRE PUBLISHING
### (INCLUDING LAWYERS PRACTICE MANUAL AND STREETWIZE COMICS)

During the twentieth century, in western industrialised countries, economic, social and political changes led to increased legislation, administrative regulation and litigation. 'The number of courts and judges, and their caseloads, increased, and the quantity and length of judicial decisions multiplied. More laws were enacted and more administrative regulations were promulgated. The result was more paper, more books, higher library and research costs, and the need for new approaches to both research and publishing.'[647] Encel points out that the strength of the legal profession is heightened by a written constitution and the intricacies of the Federal system but also by the 'complex web of judicial, quasi-judicial and administrative tribunals which constitute one of the pillars of the bureaucratic ascendancy—an ascendancy which gives an enormous social role to the judge, the lawyer.'[648]

From 1984–85, the RLC publishing section evolved into Redfern Legal Centre Publishing—first just as an imprint of the legal centre, then a formal name and later in 1987, a separate business.⁶⁴⁹ RLCP was an innovation in the form of a self-funding community legal service that published plain English guides to the law with a focus on areas of poverty law.⁶⁵⁰ It was created as part of Redfern Legal Centre and came into being at a time of movements having an impact on the reform of legal services in the 1970s and 1980s, the Plain English movement, preventative law, a focus on consumer rights and notions of deprofessionalisation.

Legal language and written materials that lawyers produce about the law had been criticised for centuries on the basis of their inaccessibility to general readers.⁶⁵¹ Despite this, most publishing houses were unenthusiastic about legal projects directed at the layman.⁶⁵² The Australian Law Reform Commission described the problem:

> Many legal documents are unnecessarily lengthy, overwritten, self-conscious and repetitious. They consist of lengthy sentences and involved sentence construction. They are poorly structured and poorly designed. They suffer from elaborate and often unnecessary cross-referencing. They use confusing tautologies such as 'ordered, adjudged and decided' and 'let, allow and permit'. They retain archaic phrases such as 'know all men by these presents' and 'this indenture witnesseth'. They use supposedly technical terms and foreign words and phrases, such as *inter alia* and *res ipsa loquitur*, even when English equivalents are readily available. They are unintelligible to the ordinary reader, and barely intelligible to many lawyers. Language which suffers from some or all of these defects is called 'legalese'. Linguists regard it as an identifiably different dialect or class of language.⁶⁵³

Critics argued that the language of the professions was a symbol and a tool of power creating dependence and ignorance on the part of the public.⁶⁵⁴ The Plain English movement was the name given to the first effective effort to change this. The movement aimed to write legal documents, importantly those used by consumers, in a manner that could be understood—not just by the legal technicians who draft them, but by the consumers who are bound by their terms.[655] The Plain English movement for legal writing is widely claimed to have started in the USA with Executive Order 12044 signed 23 March 1978 by President Jimmy Carter, requiring US government regulations to be written 'as simple and as clear as possible'.[656] The 'plain language movement' sought to demystify the law to make it comprehensible to all[657] and as Felsenfeld notes 'The Plain English movement of 1975–80 may be usefully thought of as part of a longer evolution in consumer protection.'[658]

In a parallel development originating in the 1960s and 1970s, researchers were beginning to note a move towards a challenge to the autonomy, monopoly and social privilege of established professions. By 1969, Haug and Sussmann were identifying a 'new stage in the interaction between professionals and the society, a stage we have called the revolt of the client.'[659] Theories advanced as to the cause of this included a higher level of knowledge in the community, doubt as to claims of altruism by the profession and concerns that 'the organisational delivery system supporting their authority is defective and insufficient.'[660] Also relevant was standardisation and routinisation of activities and an increasing demand by clients to play a part in decisions affecting their needs.[661] Queries were raised as to whether the aims of professionals were in society's best interests.[662] This anti-professional stance or 'Deprofessionalisation' was being discussed with reference to psychiatry,[663] social work,[664] accountants,[665] teachers[666] as well as medicine and law. As Haug stated 'medicine and law, two of the classic learned professions, are suffering the pangs of splits and cleavages in which part of their former work domain is being claimed by new workers, with new titles, training and responsibilities.'[667]

Concerns were being raised that professionals, 'even if they are not venal, are cold, elitist, and divorced from human concerns.'[668] Writers were discussing the dominance, the authority and the autocracy of the professions. [669] Deprofessionalisation was an approach often adopted by early CLC workers and others[670] as illustrated in a discussion on the need for lawyers at the NSW conference on legal services held in St. Luke's Community Centre, Redfern on 7 June 1975. Discussion at the conference focused on the desirability of community control over lawyers, and of encouraging individuals to conduct their own cases or control their lawyer's conduct of them more closely than was usual. The group decided that it would be desirable to continue the discussion at a separate meeting with the idea of forming a group, perhaps called 'Up Against the Law' or 'People Against the Law'. This suggestion was adopted by the conference as a whole. The feeling was that such a group could have three main aims:

a) Help people who are up against the law to defend themselves;
b) Explain to school and community groups about how the law operates;
c) Provide a pressure group for people who have come into conflict with their lawyers, courts, the police or prison officials.[671]

Another parallel movement was the recognition of the notion of preventative law (or preventive law as it is often termed in the United States). The concepts that '(1) mistakes, controversies, and lawsuits are not likely to arise between persons who want and know how to prevent them; and that (2) one who is informed is prepared to protect himself against persons who deal unfairly' had no doubt always been recognised.[672] It was Louis M Brown[673] who brought the notion into prominence in the legal profession and defined preventive law as 'that part of the practice of law which concerns itself with helping a client to minimize risks and maximize rights, not over the entire arena of lawyer-client affairs, but in that part of a lawyer's activity which is commonly called planning.'[674]

Early legal centres including Fitzroy Legal Service had adopted an ethos of demystification of the law[675] and Attorney–General Lionel Murphy adopted this approach in the establishment of the ALAO declaring 'The law must be brought out into the light of day.'[676] It was in the midst of this move for a Plain English approach to the law and an increasing appreciation of the importance of preventative law that Redfern Legal Centre Publishing (RLCP) was born.

At the time there was little, if any, available information in plain English about the law. Responses to a NSW Law Foundation survey of 1976 recorded 'a damning indictment of the mystification and obscurantism that is perceived to be the law. The fact that over 70 per cent of the sample questioned complained of the complexity of the law is a clear case for urgent action to both simplify the law and at the same time educate the public as to their legal rights and obligations.'[677] The legal profession however did not see it as their role to educate the public. Keon-Cohen commented in 1978 that community legal education 'was a relatively new concept to Australian lawyers, its existence, let alone the nature of this responsibility, has yet to be recognized.'[678] In respect of legal publishing in Australia at this time it was noted that 'outmoded policies and monopoly practices have led to an almost total disregard of the laymen's need for legal literature.'[679]

The first product of RLC's publishing efforts came from a Victorian CLC publishing innovation. In May 1977, Fitzroy Legal Service produced the *Legal Resources Book*—a loose-leaf plain English guide to the law written and updated by volunteer lawyers and designed for use by the public, as well as community and social workers and teachers who often approached the FLS for advice. The book was a huge success selling out its first edition of 4,000 copies in eight days receiving considerable favourable publicity, selling well and raising funds for the Centre.[680]

The expansion of community legal education was seen to be a 'wider critical response to the monopolies enjoyed by the professions who it is argued exploited the inaccessibility of their domain expertise to maintain their power, financial privilege and their elite status'.[681] The Centre's philosophy relating to CLE was set out in an article presented at a Commonwealth Legal Aid Commission seminar in 1979 and included the statement that 'A community based legal centre maximises the impact of its scarce resources by reaching more people through its CLE activities than by just taking on individual cases'.[682]

The way that Redfern Legal Centre responded to the need for CLE and preventative law was by developing an entirely new style of legal publisher. RLC developed a specialist legal and educational publishing service. Through assessing legal casework demand from clients at the Centre, RLC (and later RLCP) staff identified the need in the community for accessible legal information. They designed and developed an organisation devoted wholly to the production of Plain English resources on the law aimed at informing and empowering young people (*Streetwize Comics*) and the general public, community (*Law Handbook*) and social workers and lawyers (*Lawyers Practice Manual*). Operating from December 1978,[683] these publications were designed as educational and preventative resources. Many were able to be

## 'THE BABIES': SPECIALIST SERVICES DEVELOPED AT RLC

distributed free or at minimal cost through the assistance of profits from sales and government grants. Surplus funds were used to develop new resources.[684] This was a first in the fields of both community legal education and publishing.

A crucial factor in RLCP's success was the availability of funding for projects developed by the Centre. One source of this funding was the NSW Law Foundation. In 1967, a Bill was put forward to the NSW Parliament to require solicitors to deposit a proportion of funds placed in their trust accounts with the Law Society to create the Statutory Interest Fund. This fund was to be used to expand legal aid services and encourage law reform research amongst other things[685] and was administered by the Law Foundation. The amount to be deposited was increased over the years.[686] The Law Foundation made a major financial contribution to ensure the successful publication of Redfern Legal Centre's legal resources book.[687]

The Centre started work on a NSW version of the Legal Resources Book. Michael Mobbs was a lawyer who had spent time in the USA with Ralph Nader's organisations and consumer advocacy groups.[688] (Ralph Nader is an auto-safety reformer and consumer advocate and had a big influence on the developing consumer movement.) Mobbs describes the development in NSW:

> Nader was a big influence on many people and was known to us all… I came back to Australia in the middle of 1976 and felt like a shag on a rock. I was mixed up with the campaign to stop the Ranger Uranium mine [[689]] and was casting around to see what I could do in law… I got mixed up with the Legal Resources Book and became the founding editor. I worked out at the University of New South Wales. I worked 9–12 months on that. It was excruciating. Just like herding cats. It really was appalling. Many of the contributors came from the Law Faculty and they all wanted to control the job. Egos were offended. Often people

couldn't write clearly. There were about 24 chapters. It was a real learning experience. I had no authority. It was the worst job but years and years later people would say to me how useful it was—doctors, social workers etc. John Kirkwood, a UNSW academic very involved with RLC also worked on the book ... I would say the book was 90 per cent John's Kirkwood's creation. The book really had a substantial impact—it made the law accessible to a whole lot of people who needed to understand it. ... The book was printed in Melbourne and there was a pilots' strike the day of the launch. I persuaded everybody to go ahead with the launch and managed to get the books brought down in a small plane. The LRB was part of John's vision in providing access to the law. The idea of having the law plainly available to everyone—social workers, teachers etc was a great idea.[690]

Centre workers understood the comment that the fact the law is not accessible 'condemns the citizen to alienation from the experience of justice that law promises him.'[691] The book was published by Redfern Legal Centre and its black hard cardboard cover had an illustration of a seated blindfolded female justice figure. Little figures including a judge were sitting on her knee. The cover stated: 'Adapted from the Victorian Edition by Gardner, Neal, Cashman.'[692] The book was a looseleaf production and Virginia Bell jokes; 'I think we had this idea that families would sit around the hearth updating their Legal Resources book. There was a certain level of naivety that was breath-taking.'[693] As Sean Kidney notes the book 'was certainly influenced by the plain English movement, in that accessible legal information required it to be written in a more accessible style than was the norm. Individual Centre lawyers pushed very hard for easy to understand material—that was a key part of the push to set up RLCP.'[694]

Anne Healey was working at IBM in 1980 when she saw an ad for a publication manager for the Centre to work with Bob

## 'THE BABIES': SPECIALIST SERVICES DEVELOPED AT RLC

Fox, the editor who took over from Michael Mobbs. Healey's job was to take care of the financial side of the *Legal Resources Book* and she was partly motivated by a belief that she had to make enough money to go towards the cost of a solicitor's salary as Virginia Bell's solicitor's position at the Centre was unfunded. The publishing involved…

> contacting all these fantastic people to write the chapters. None of them were paid for their work … I worked upstairs in the back room surrounded by boxes … I used to have stalls at various places, went to book launches, I knew everyone in the legal publishing world. We wanted to sell to social workers, workers in other agencies, law students, volunteer lawyers at the Centre.[695]

The book was also used as a basis for the Centre's community legal education. It could be used for the types of activities outlined in a 1979 article on the Centre and community legal education including radio programs, pamphlets, videos, newspaper articles, talks at community groups and schools, training social workers, do it yourself kits and community 'teach ins'.[696] The Centre's first solicitor (later barrister), John Terry, thought it was important to get Aboriginal Liaison officers education in the law so they would have more power and confidence in their work. He set up a course for Aboriginal field officers through UNSW in 1981/82.[697] Healey developed a series of talks based on the Legal Resources Book and used to go out and talk to the field officers on a regular basis.[698]

The Centre built on this first publishing initiative with the publication of the *Lawyers Practice Manual* (commonly known as 'the Red Book') in 1983. Neil Rees, John Basten and Chris Ronalds had come up with the idea of a practice manual for lawyers. 'Nothing of the sort existed at the time. All the existing legal information services were just black letter law and there was nothing for junior lawyers.'[699] The Manual was innovatory in two ways. It had chapters on numerous areas of law especially relevant to a poverty law practice such as criminal law, discrimination, tenancy, motor vehicle law. This publication also did something that no previous law book in Australia had done, which was to describe in detail the practical steps to be taken in each type of matter from examples of completed court forms to instructions on where to sit at the Bar table and what documents to file. Law School education did not include this type of material and this manual allowed junior lawyers to more effectively assist clients as well as conduct community legal education sessions in areas of law they were not specialised in. Chapters were written by solicitors and barristers—usually staff or volunteers of the Centre. Ronalds notes that 'this was an incredibly useful resource for new practitioners. People would send in very boring treatises on law and we would send it back and say "No! It has to be practical". We had to choose the right people to write it.'[700] This initiative was subsequently replicated in most other states.[701] Chris Ronalds chaired the LPM committee for over ten years with regular meetings held at her house in Rozelle. This was voluntary work and the main difficulty was getting copy on deadlines. Finances, etc, were handled by RLC. Originally it was not looseleaf.'[702] After the split, half the profits would go to RLCP and half to Redfern Legal Centre. In Victoria the CLCs produced version of the LPM known as 'the Green Book' (now online).[703]

In the mid-1980s, the Centre decided to look at possibilities for an expanded role for the publishing work. The staff were wedded to the preventative approach to the law and took the view that it was possible to prevent citizens acting to their detriment in legal problems, overcome dependence on lawyers, reduce feelings of powerlessness and promote community interest and involvement in law reform through publications work.[704] Publishing worker,

## 'THE BABIES': SPECIALIST SERVICES DEVELOPED AT RLC

Sean Kidney, describes his arrival at the Centre and his adoption of the preventive approach to legal problems:

> I was a publisher and I'd dropped out of the commercial sector and worked in community publishing. I had a friend, Debbie Whitmont, who was working at RLC. She used to tell me stories about RLC. My friend, Ian Close and I applied to RLC in 1983 for a job share position. The job was called something like Coordinator of Publishing ...We had a job share at first then both went to full-time. We shared a cubicle upstairs in the Town Hall.
>
> After a few years, in 1985, we set up RLCP as a separate organisation. The year after that I pushed to turn the Legal Resources Book into the paperback which significantly improved sales. This later turned into the *Law Handbook*. We launched a whole catalogue of books and publications. RLCP had become bigger, had more staff and the Redfern Legal Centre Management Committee thought it needed its own management committee ...RLCP gave RLC a different profile. These were smart professional publications for people to buy. All of these activities helped burnish the credentials of RLC and crystallised one method of dealing with the ongoing tensions between casework and non-casework. RLCP was another version of specialisation of work to head off the endless repeat stuff from clients coming through the door. I would regularly go downstairs and see what was happening at the front desk or be at CLC conferences and think this should be put into a publication... I saw myself as part of the Redfern Legal Centre team—I worked on campaigns on interest rates and other areas of law. I used to go to community education meetings of CLCs which led to a sense of community ... I had the privilege of not doing casework but I could see what was happening to people and see that something should be done. And what I could do was to get the publications out. I wanted to be engaged in the overall work of the Centre.
>
> I saw the publication side as a means to solve social problems and stop unnecessary repeating casework. We got a fair bit of

attention at RLCP so RLC had a much bigger reputation than other legal centres ... You get trapped by constraints such as government money. There were always arguments about that at the Centre. We constantly had to document the success of our lobbying and the publishing work was useful. It was high profile.[705]

## Ian Close remembers:

Sean and I were employed by RLC in October 1983 to finalise the production of the first *Law Handbook* which at that stage was being typeset. We took over managing the roll-out of the new book from Sarah White who was also the centre's administrator and was about to leave to get married. There were two other part-time employees for that first *Law Handbook* edition: Margaret White as editor and Anne Healey as marketing manager. The book was launched late in December 1983 by Michael Kirby. At that stage the publishing operation was very much part of RLC. The process of separation was gradual.

The publishing arm of RLC slowly expanded between 1984 and 1986. As well as supplements to the Law Handbook and new editions every two years (1986 and 1988) we started to publish other plain English guides to other areas of the law. 'Legal Rights & Intellectual Disability: a short guide' in 1986 was the first of these. We also took over management (for RLC) of the *Lawyer's Practice Manual*. The manual didn't require a lot of work from us as the production and distribution was handled by the Law Book Company, but the royalties of the manual were an important source of income for the publishing operation.

By 1986, *The Law Handbook* was accepted as an essential source of Plain English information about the law. The Clerk of the Local Court, Bankstown, Bill Wheeler wrote 'My union, the Petty Sessions Officers Association of NSW, whose members work in Local Courts, has decided that there will be a copy of The Law Handbook in every court office. I suspect barristers will have it under the bar table, and that solicitors will put it in the drawer of their desks!'[706] Decisions about the work of RLCP had to be signed off by the Centre Management Committee but Kidney notes: 'I don't think the Management Committee had any idea much about publishing. But if I could get a grant for a publication, people just said yes. They wanted to be sure the publications would be useful in terms of the Centre's practice. Often I would make the decision and then put the decision to the Committee for ratification.'[707]

The lack of accessible information about the law for young people[708] led to the genesis of *Streetwize Comics*—an RLCP innovation to create comics for young people with legal education themes. Streetwize was mainly aimed at young people outside educational institutions, where there is no teacher to act as intermediary.[709] *Streetwize* was also eventually to become its own separate organisation and the comic concept was so successful that it was emulated in other states of Australia, the United Kingdom, Canada and New Zealand.[710]

The *Streetwize* idea was that:

> conventional methods of providing information to young people, such as government pamphlets and formal education, were often judgemental, inaccessible and full of jargon, and failed to relate to the everyday lives of young people. It was hoped that by using comics, the information would be more accessible to young people, particularly young people with low levels of literacy.[711]

Features of the comics were that they involved young people in the production, included female characters, young people from Aboriginal, disabled, gay and lesbian, and a range of ethnic backgrounds, a character facing a problem, and their peers helping them to overcome the problem by utilising existing sources of information and support.[712] The Streetwize comics focused on groups who were thought of as alienated from society, and whose actions were often attributed to subjective, psychological aberration.[713] A number of government departments recognised the importance of delivering information to young people in comic form but *Streetwize* did cause some controversy and encountered opposition from some politicians and bureaucrats, making distribution in schools in some states a problem.[714] Kidney recalls:

> I had this idea about comics which led to *Streetwize Comics*. We put this together with Julie Melbourne from Marrickville Legal Centre, brought in Dominic Gibson to RLCP then got government funding. I had to do Canberra visits all the time. When it came to *Streetwize*, I had to continually explain to politicians the research evidence about how we were doing the comics. I pushed reality stories. We told funders that workers had to go out and research real stories. Some were amazing. For example, the guy who missed out on a welfare payment and went out and shot his dog. I got respected social and academic researchers to write academic reports in order to persuade the funders this was the way to go. They were approving each issue.
>
> We had some good times and we got really good feedback. We produced thousands of copies of the comics. Distribution was always a problem. Towards the end, we got asked by DSS to do a social security comic which turned into a consultancy on welfare payments for homeless kids ... I'm very proud of the *Streetwize Comics*. They would pop up everywhere. It was read by kids and were also useful as a way to explain to politicians what was going on.[715]

In August 1986, RLCP moved out of the Redfern Town Hall to 18 George Street, Redfern. *RLC News* reported that: 'the apron strings are not severed yet ...the enthusiasm, craziness and non-legal approach of the Press is sorely missed at Pitt Street... The

## 'THE BABIES': SPECIALIST SERVICES DEVELOPED AT RLC

move has enabled us to spread out a little providing the closest yet to barely reasonable working conditions for the staff.'[716] In 1987, RLCP split from Redfern Legal Centre and became an entirely separate organisation. Ian close comments:

> As we expanded and took on more professional publishing staff, the arrangement became more problematic for RLC. There was a worry that the grants-based funding model of the centre would be jeopardised by a growing publishing operation that was signing large printing contracts. Publishing by its nature is a high-turnover operation: a lot of money out to produce and print books before (hopefully) a lot of money in from their sale. It just disrupted the financial stability of the centre. RLCP still relied on grant money (eg for *Streetwize*) but it was at least a semi-commercial business.[717]

The process was not easy. Andrew Haesler, Principal Solicitor at the Centre at the time reflects:

> RLCP wanted to be an independent organisation. The finances were merged with RLC. They wanted to run as a collective and be a publishing agency with everyone getting the same pay. RLC realised RLCP would never make RLC a lot of money. We had to get the Community Justice Centre in to help facilitate the split up of assets etc. It was a bit like a divorce.[718]

RLCP operated as an independent organisation for almost 30 years and produced a significant collection of publications. The organisation ran the *Law for Non Lawyers* course which allowed people including social workers, counsellors, health professionals, public servants and other a guided accessible introduction to many areas of the law. Eventually the organisation was dissolved and the rights to the publications sold to University of New South Wales Press Ltd, a publishing organisation at the University of New South Wales. Initially, UNSW Press was asked to take over only the *Environmental Law Handbook* because RLCP faced a downward cash flow, but agreement was made to acquire the whole list and maintain the publishing program. RLCP was dissolved and several of its staff joined UNSW Press. The print versions of the main books continued to be successful (with new editions of *The Law Handbook* in 2004 and 2007 and the *Environmental Law Handbook* in 2006) but 'it proved more difficult to commission and develop books on specific topics.'[719] Demands for online publications and issues relating to subscription models were outside the framework of UNSW Press publishing and an approach from Thomson Reuters who had specialist expertise in this type of law publishing seemed the best arrangement for the future of the main RLCP reference works. On 20 July 2009 they were acquired by Thomson Reuters. Redfern Legal Centre Publishing Ltd was deregistered as a company on the 17 April 2004.[720]

The acquisition by Thomson Reuters did not please everybody. Kidney recalls:

> Eventually, the Committee sold the *Law Handbook* off to the fuckers in suits essentially. I was really annoyed. It shows you, you need people who have a vision of what can be, and enthusiasm. The RLCP Management Committee was made up of lawyers who were doing other stuff. They just looked for an easy path to jettison it. It needed work. They gave it to Law Book Company. And the Law Book Company put up rates. But what did they expect?[721]

Chris Ronalds, who had chaired the Lawyers Practice Manual Committee for ten years, says: 'I was never happy over selling the manual to the Law Book Company [Thomson Reuters]. I thought it was a really short-term decision. It was a good seller.'[722]

Despite these concerns however, RLCP left its mark on the history of Australian community legal education as well as Australian legal publishing. As Kidney reflects: 'It was a very innovative time. The innovations were modest but the breeding ground for later in life cannot be underestimated. All those people were informed for their future careers and that's incredibly important.'[723] The Law Handbook is still sold in every state and in NSW under the imprint of Redfern Legal Centre Publishing and the name is well known in legal circles. Little public attention has been paid to the importance and innovation of RLCP as an organisation despite their publications receiving considerable praise.

As a result of the proliferation of law in the late twentieth century, discovering what the law was had never been more difficult. Fitzroy Legal Service's Legal Resource book was a catalyst that led to RLCP changing the face of legal publishing in Australia. No longer were law books designed to be read only by lawyers. RLCP developed publications that were accessible to the public as well as welfare and other professionals. These people needed a gateway to understanding complex laws to assist disadvantaged clients, develop policy proposals and the publications made the law understandable to many in the general public. As Kidney notes RLCP certainly had an influence on the craft of legal writing and efforts to make legal language simple.[724] There is a limited amount of literature relating to the effectiveness of CLE measures in Australia and internationally[725] and there was little formal evaluation of the products produced by RLC and Streetwize, though demand from public and targeted audiences indicate that they were seen to be useful. Neil Rees, noted legal academic, has observed that the work of RLCP has been of extraordinary significance in the field of public access to the law.[726]

The innovations of RLCP and *Streetwize* were new solutions to the problem of a lack of accessible practical information for many in the community. This practical legal information was not provided by the government and the publishing market had yet to recognise the possibility of sales of this type of product. Works by RLCP were used by unrepresented people in courts and tribunals,[727] were quoted by judges in court proceedings,[728] informed members of the public and were the basis of the NSW Legal Information Access Centre providing self-help services to the public.[729] The publishing outputs provided practical information on court processes and the legal system to junior lawyers or those working in a new area of law in the *Lawyers Practice Manual*, put complex legal information in comic format to increase accessibility to young people and involved the recipients of the legal information in a role in designing the material (*Streetwize*). The RLCP model embedded a legal publisher in a shop-front legal office to ensure publications directly addressed client needs and developed an entrepreneurial self-funded community legal centre focused on publishing a catalogue of books, films etc on specialist areas of the law in plain English and available to the public, community/welfare workers, law students and lawyers thereby increasing accessibility of the legal information. Innovation is a multidisciplinary activity and researchers have shown the positive impact of a good working climate on knowledge flows and innovation performance.[730] Collaboration, open forms of communication and relationships between publishers, lawyers at the Centre and with other community legal workers in external organisations were well developed and communication systems were effective—factors conducive to innovation.[731] Both RLCP and *Streetwize Comics* were organisations and innovations that had a major impact on community legal education and legal publishing in Australia.

## WOMEN'S DOMESTIC VIOLENCE COURT ASSISTANCE SCHEME (WDVCAS)

> The history of law is full of sorrows greater than many of us will ever know[732]

From the 1960s, activists such as the Battered Women's movement in the UK and USA had brought the issue of domestic violence to public attention and highlighted the grievous problems with the traditional approach of the law and prosecuting authorities that domestic violence was a private matter to be sorted out inside the family.[733] Feminist theorists in the 1980s were particularly concerned with exploring the ways that dominant ideologies such as heterosexuality, motherhood, monogamy and the public/private dichotomy contribute to male dominance and patriarchy[734] but this was still an era when there was little focus by government on domestic violence. As Graycar *et al* point out there was a belief that it is for family members to sort out their personal relationships and this was not an area where the law should venture although of course as they discuss this ignores the power inequalities inside the family affected by the structures external to it.[735] As the Australian Law Reform Commission noted in 1986:

> In the long term, the public and private attitudes which have allowed the phenomenon of domestic violence to flourish need to change. These are based on the view that an assault in the home is not a private matter. The resources of the community are called on to deal with the consequences of violence in the home, be they the damaged children, the victim's injuries, the disruption to the neighbourhood, the wrecked lives. It is the business of the whole community to reduce domestic violence as much as possible.[736]

Government inquiries in Australia included an Australian Law Reform Commission Inquiry into Domestic Violence in 1986[737] which found that the most frequent complaint about the law's response to domestic violence (DV) is that it offered inadequate protection to victims. This report highlighted police reluctance to take complaints seriously and noted criticism that courts fail to provide adequate measures (such as enforceable injunctions or restraining orders) to prevent further violence, and that injunctions against violence can be ignored with impunity or, at least, with little fear of serious consequences. The Inquiry found: 'in short, the substance of the most common criticism made of the legal system in this area is that spouse beating is not regarded as really criminal. This perception encourages offenders to think that they can "get away with it" and helps to perpetuate violence.'[738]

In the 1980s, legislation providing for specific domestic violence orders led to a significant increase in the number of women applying for protective orders.[739] In NSW in 1982 amendments to domestic violence orders (S547AA *Crimes Act NSW*) empowered courts of summary jurisdiction to make orders imposing restrictions or prohibitions on the behaviour of those from whom violence is apprehended.[740] Where a lawyer was representing the complainant, the complainant was much more likely not to withdraw the application for protection and the application was more likely to be successful. Research demonstrated that a shift to an increase in legal representation for women seeking orders was associated with a marked reduction in the number of applications for Apprehended Violence Orders (AVOs) being withdrawn or dismissed.[741] Family violence legislation was enacted in most states and territories in the 1980s and 1990s as a response to growing recognition that existing legal mechanisms failed to protect victims—predominantly

## 'THE BABIES': SPECIALIST SERVICES DEVELOPED AT RLC

women—from family violence[742] and by the 1990s, domestic violence was recognised internationally as a significant social and legal problem.[743] Violence against women was recognised as a fundamental infringement of human rights in the 1993 United Nations Declaration on the Elimination of Violence against Women and was a major topic at the 1995 Beijing Fourth World Conference on Women (UN Women, 1995).[744]

Redfern Legal Centre had been acting for victims of domestic violence since it opened. Virginia Bell[745] was rostered on at the Centre as a solicitor in the evenings and then at the beginning of 1978 started working at the Centre full-time.

> There was a fair bit of appearance work in the Local Court—mainly Redfern Court doing domestic violence cases in the days when police tended not to prosecute those. There was a decent chamber magistrate at Newtown Court who would refer matters to us. The woman had to bring the proceedings themselves.[746]

The Centre also assisted women who had separated from their partners with related matters. Bell continues:

> For a period of six months, they needed evidence that in the view of a solicitor there was no practical means of getting assistance from the partner before they could get Commonwealth [social security] benefits. This was the kind of thing the Australian Legal Aid Office wouldn't help with.[747]

The Centre continued assisting victims of domestic violence and working on policy and law reform issues in this area as an integral part of its work over the next ten years.[748] In 1988, Jane Goddard started working as a solicitor at the Centre after studying in Canberra and working at the student legal centre run at ANU. 'I was very much in awe of the Centre—it was the first legal centre in NSW and had quite a reputation.'[749] Her job involved assisting women victims of violence. She often found the job confronting:

> I had to prepare victims compensation claims for women who had been assaulted. The other component was working with women who had survived domestic violence. This involved a lot of collaboration with support services in the area. Women could drop in or make evening appointments. On the duty days at Redfern Local Court, community agencies would refer cases. We worked closely with sexual assault centres at local hospitals and the South Sydney Women's Centre (the Shop), government and community services ... I was thrown into the job and expected to do it with very little supervision. I had never worked as a lawyer before ... The volunteers on the evening advice sessions were often experienced practitioners though. My job included casework and education.[750]

Goddard's job was to represent victims of DV in the magistrates' court. These matters were initiated through the chamber magistrate.[751] Goddard describes the situation that led to the development of the Domestic Violence Court Assistance Scheme proposal.

> Every Wednesday was DV list day. There would be five to seven women who were appearing that morning at Redfern Court. There was nowhere really for claimants to sit that was safe. The perpetrator would turn up and it was very hard to talk to one client and at the same time be able to manage all the other clients who were upset and I didn't think I was providing a very good service. People would be standing on the lobby or the steps of the court.[752]

Ben Slade remembers Goddard considering the concept of a domestic violence court assistance scheme at a legal centre conference in Maroochydore around 1990. 'Jane went hell for leather about how dreadful the domestic violence situation was. The idea came from Jane saying how horrible the situation is and

## 'THE BABIES': SPECIALIST SERVICES DEVELOPED AT RLC

we decided we should do something more about it and decided why don't we set up a service. Jane then took it on.'[753] Goddard devised a scheme:

> We talked to the chamber magistrate and magistrate to see if there was a room we could use. Then we started a roster of support workers. Workers from local agencies would come to court to assist the women and would be able to do associated work on housing, medical issues, etc. All these workers had to get permission from their employers to work at court as an ongoing obligation and a commitment of time and resources. We then got other lawyers doing list days at the court too, so lawyers from the Domestic Violence Advocacy Service would come out. We saw it a new way of delivering a legal service but also a way of looking at all of the non-legal issues that were important to the women involved. We all saw it as a new way of doing things.[754]

The WDVCAS scheme commenced in March 1990. Goddard lists the benefits of the scheme.

> It empowered women to go through the legal process and reduced the possibility of being harassed at court. This was the very early days of awareness of DV—the fact there was a dedicated service took away the stigma to some degree. There was close collaboration with community agencies.[755]

Mary Perkins was the coordinator of the Centre at the time.

> I remember Jane was really keen and Ben [Slade] was really pushing it. We were trying to sort out what sort of support women needed in DV cases. There was a series of interviews with women to sort out their needs. The Centre put a lot of resources into this project. We got the support of the local magistrate at Redfern Court. There was a committee set up by lawyers and non-lawyers and a report issued.[756]

Once the scheme was operating as a pilot, funding from the Law Foundation was used to evaluate the scheme.[757] The Centre and community agencies were assisted by the positive attitude of Redfern Court. Mark Randall, the Clerk of the Court was supportive—sending people down to the Centre for advice and really helped the DVCAS.[758]

An evaluation of the scheme in 1991 showed that 74 per cent of women represented by the scheme were granted protective orders compared with 50 per cent represented by other practitioners and 40 per cent represented by the police.[759] The scheme was recognised as a markedly effective method of providing court assistance to women. This was instrumental in getting other legal centres to develop similar services. The model was discussed at Community Legal Centre conferences and criminology conferences.[760]

Louise Blazejowska started work at the Centre in 1991 and recalls her time at the Centre working on the DV scheme. 'I remember at a staff meeting when we were talking about the DVCAS. It was fantastic. Ben [Slade] said "take it to the world". At that time, there were DVCAS schemes at Marrickville, Newtown, Parramatta ... none in rural areas.'[761]

Blazejowska developed the Domestic Violence Court Assistance Kit which was funded by the Federal Government's Office of Status of Women in 1995.[762] This kit provided a model for the setting up of schemes statewide. Blazejowska describes her work:

> I was looking after the DVCAS. I can remember the DVCAS was in a pilot stage and the Law Foundation was doing a review of it. This produced a report which was very positive about the model. It showed two things—when you have lawyers and social workers working together you get a better legal outcome and clients are more willing to participate in the system and you get

## 'THE BABIES': SPECIALIST SERVICES DEVELOPED AT RLC

> a better outcome for other issues like housing, income support etc. Also, if you have legal representation you are far more likely to get a final order … As I was at RLC I got more and more calls about DVCAS and realised it was bigger than just RLC as there were schemes being established all over the State and calls were coming from all over NSW. It was about 1992. I felt quite overwhelmed as I'd had no experience with DV.
>
> Jane Goddard and Jane Mulroney had done all the work on the training manual so I added to it and then we got some money from the State Government's Department for Women and we decided to do a manual for all the WDVCAS so we could establish it as a State-wide model. So, my job was to turn that work into a model that could be used anywhere. I developed a relationship with RLCP. They got the funding to produce the kit.[763]

In 1994, the Australian Law Reform Commission produced a report entitled *Women's Equality Before the Law*.[764] In it, the Commission noted the introduction of court support services operating in parts of urban and rural Australia and that 'all the schemes have been based on the Women's Domestic Violence Court Assistance Scheme which has been operating at Redfern Local Court and coordinated by Redfern Legal Centre since March 1990.'[765]

The Report confirmed the overwhelming success of the court support scheme. Practical results of the scheme as evaluated at Redfern Court were that the percentage of withdrawals (both with and without undertakings) for proceedings was significantly less for complainants represented by the scheme than either those unrepresented or those complainants making applications prior to the scheme's inception. Also, the number of successful orders obtained markedly increased under the operation of the scheme. Recognition by government of the value of the schemes led to support for the scaling up of the project. By 1999 there were 33 funded schemes located at 47 Local Courts across NSW[766] with the specific objectives being:

a) improve the accessibility of the local court system for women seeking AVOs;

b) familiarise women with the court process, layout and personnel, in order to increase their knowledge of the criminal justice system and its operations;

c) arrange legal representation from appropriately trained, sympathetic legal practitioners/police prosecutors for women seeking AVOs;

d) advocate on behalf of women during local court proceedings. To be able to follow up on the order and make appropriate referrals to other legal matters;

e) assist women to identify their needs and then advocate on their behalf in relation to those needs;

f) provide referral to other appropriate services in the area of income support, housing, order enforcement, counselling and other needs as required;

g) provide court assistance services in a manner that ensures access and equity principles are applied which meet the particular needs of special need groups within local communities;

h) assist in ensuring the personal safety of women and children is of the highest priority at all times whilst in the precinct of the court and its surroundings.[767]

Establishing the services under the project across the State however was not without its problems. Blazejowska, working for the Attorney–General's Department at the time, recalls:

> The Department for Women decided to set up 21 schemes. I got kicked off the committee as I was arguing for lawyers to be part of the scheme. When it came to Attorney–Generals signing off

## 'THE BABIES': SPECIALIST SERVICES DEVELOPED AT RLC

on the model, I refused to sign off on it. But when the money came in for a State-wide network, the Department for Women refused to let the money be used for legal representation and that's how it stayed for about 20 years until I could persuade Legal Aid you had to build lawyers into the schemes. So, for the schemes in the next 20 years people just had to try and get any legal assistance they could beg or borrow or people would be unrepresented. When I got to the [Legal Aid] Commission, I argued for the need for legal representation. I did an audit of what representation was out there and there was very little assistance, so I did a report on legal aid responses and one recommendation was to establish legal representation.

Bill Grant [CEO Legal Aid Commission] agreed to fund it and over half the courts the DVCAS were in got lawyers and I developed a training package. I did talk to different states about the scheme. WA wasn't interested. Queensland had something similar but only in the main court in Brisbane and not a network. "DV" schemes are now a flagship at Legal Aid. They are very proud of the systems. They are formally part of the justice system and integrated.[768]

Helen Campbell, now Executive Officer, Womens Legal Service notes:

This model of court assistance is one of many mighty achievements Redfern Legal Centre has. The model has been widely replicated. It is now in practically every court in NSW, there are still rosters of private practitioners ... There is something similar in the Northern Territory. The DVCAS also meant the Centre was assisting more Aboriginal women.[769]

The scheme incorporated many of the underlying philosophies of the Centre—the partnership and collaboration with other organisations, support for innovation from other staff at the Centre and the outlook of the Centre that law was not to be kept distinct from other aspects of individual welfare. The Centre received the 2007 Human Rights Law Award from the Australian Human Rights and Equal Opportunity Commission.[770] The award especially recognised the establishment of the Women's Domestic Violence Court Assistance Scheme which aims to provide women seeking restraining orders as a result of domestic violence with legal advice as well as any other support required (including housing, income support and counselling).

The DVCAS system has expanded since the early days. The DV team went offsite about 2010 when the whole DV scheme expanded. They were part of the Centre but from about 2010 were based at the Downing Centre Court complex in Sydney city—there were 8–10 of them and a coordinator, assistant coordinators, and an Aboriginal and CALD specialist worker. The service is funded by Legal Aid NSW and as Administrator Hilary Chesworth mentions:

> We have to keep reminding them they are part of an independent organisation... There are information barriers between RLC and the DVCAS and though discussions have been had about setting up the WDVCAS as a separate service there are no plans on foot for this to happen... The service is growing, becoming a launch site for a project called the Waverley Local Coordination point and women are referred in and our employees contact them and if we assess they are at serious risk they get referred to a meeting of various service providers—housing/social security etc.[771]

The scheme has developed including processes whereby workers get the details of every woman who has reported DV to the police in the Centre's area. The Centre then calls them as an early intervention system, explaining the process to the women. There is also a pilot scheme of safety action meetings where police ask victims a series of questions and then decide if there was a threat or serious threat. For everyone classified as a serious threat the woman's position would be discussed every week with lawyers, social service and housing.[772]

In 2021, there is significantly increased focus by governments on family violence.[773] The WDVCAS scheme was clearly one of the Centre's great achievements. It is firmly entrenched in the legal system of NSW,[774] has a website, facebook page[775] and is still expanding to new courts.[776] The scheme has received public recognition on many occasions. The NSW Ombudsman endorsed the scheme stating in 2006:

> Finally, we note that many locations do not have a women's domestic violence court assistance scheme or have access to a scheme but its coverage is limited. Given the prevalence of domestic violence, the needs of victims and the very valuable service that court assistance schemes provide, we recommend that the Attorney–General consider extending its Women's Domestic Violence Court Assistance Program.[777]

The Australian Law Reform Commission has stated 'Victim support is also crucial at court… The NSW Domestic Violence Court Assistance Schemes are useful precedents.'[778] The scheme has provided information and resources for research on domestic violence.[779] There is no doubt that the Centre's innovation not only changed legal practice in supporting domestic violence victims through court processes but provided invaluable help to thousands of women. Unlike most of the CLC innovations in the form of new services at RLC, the DVCAS remained a service still firmly ensconced at RLC until 2018 (though geographically based at the Downing Centre Court, the workers at the RLC scheme were all employed by RLC until 2018). In September 2018 the NSW State government decided to put the WDVCAS services out to tender and Redfern Legal Centre announced that after 30 years of providing a court service for women in Sydney it would not be tendering. In a statement explaining its decision, the Centre cited "significant changes made to the new service model and the significant increase in demand for the service." [780]

The WDVCAS service was innovative in several ways being the first holistic legal service offered in courtrooms in Australia for women in family violence offering support in areas of housing, income security and avenues of assistance for other legal problems such as family law. WDVCAS also offered the first multidisciplinary legal service at local courts in NSW.[781] The support, enthusiasm for a new idea and the Centre's willingness to develop the WDVCAS proposal were crucial to its success. The argument[782] that for innovation, the spaces between separate unconnected networks—'structural holes'—are especially useful since they allow actors to connect different knowledge networks is relevant here in development of a service that involved workers from differing professional backgrounds—unusual in the legal industry. The 'local embeddedness' of the Centre and the connections and ties with other local organisations leading to collaborative practices[783] were clearly a factor in the development of the scheme and its effectiveness.

## WELFARE RIGHTS CENTRE

A constitutional amendment in 1947 empowered Federal Parliament to make laws with respect to providing certain pensions, allowances and benefits and meant that the Federal government took over responsibility for income maintenance schemes.[784] Section 51(xxiiiA) was inserted into the Constitution granting the Australian Government power to make laws with respect to:

> (xxiiiA) The provision of maternity allowances, widows' pensions, child endowment, unemployment, pharmaceutical, sickness and hospital benefits, medical and dental services (but not so as to

authorise any form of civil conscription), benefits to students and family allowances.[785]

This income maintenance came to be seen as a matter of right for people who fell within the relevant categories rather than a privilege. This was exemplified by the repeal in 1974 of sections in the *Social Services Act 1947–1975* that provided a claimant was not to receive a pension unless he was of good character and deserving of a pension.[786]

Recognition of a right to income security brought as a consequence, an acceptance that lawyers had a role in the social security sphere by providing advice as well as representation in challenging determinations.[787] Sackville noted that until the 1970s, lawyers had rarely represented people applying for pensions or benefits.[788] The Department of Social Security discouraged the involvement of lawyers and there was no formal system of review until 1975. The Australian Assistance Plan had provided for some welfare rights officers to assist people[789] but generally there was little assistance for clients.

The Centre had long assisted clients with social security problems and been involved in policy work in that area of law. John Kirkwood who was very involved with the Centre's development was at UNSW teaching welfare law, a subject which had not been taught before in Australian Law Schools.[790] Toward the end of 1976, the Sydney office of the Department of Social Security (DSS) learned of an alleged arrangement under which medical practitioners would assist members of the Greek community to obtain invalid pensions fraudulently, in return for payment. The matter was called to the attention of the Health Department and then to the Commonwealth Police. 181 people, virtually all of Greek ethnic background, were arrested and charged with conspiracy to defraud the Commonwealth. There was huge publicity about the case.[791] Although legal aid was provided for many defendants by the federal government legal aid office the advice from that office to clients was to plead guilty.⁷⁹² Redfern Legal Centre provided initial legal representation to those charged in the committal proceedings and in the efforts to get the pensions restored.⁷⁹³

As Tomsen notes, from the late 1970s, the politicisation of legal aid issues after the controversial introduction of the Whitlam's Australian Legal Aid Office meant the active involvement in legal aid issues by previously excluded lay groups, including such welfare organisations as ACOSS and its various State affiliates.⁷⁹⁴ In the late 1970s—early 1980s, a proposal arose to set up a specialist Centre focusing on social security issues as a result of discussions between the New South Wales Council of Social Services, Australian Council of Social Services and the Centre. At the time Joan McClintock and Phillipa Smith from ACOSS were developing policies around social security benefits and working on social security eligibility issues and drew on the expertise of the Centre.⁷⁹⁵ Clare Petre and Roger West from RLC were very involved with ACOSS at a policy level. ACOSS's efforts were supported by the Combined Pensioners Association, NSW Council of Social Service, Social Workers Action Group, and the Disabled Persons Resource Centre. Joan McClintock led ACOSS in developing the proposal for a Welfare Rights Centre and she then tried for quite a long time to get funding for it. The NSW Treasurer at the time, George Booth had a chief of staff, Percy Allan who was Phillipa Smith's partner. Coming up to the NSW Budget in 1982, Booth said there is some spare money around and Allan drew his attention to the ACOSS submission advocating setting up a welfare rights Centre.⁷⁹⁶ ACOSS were able to convince the NSW Treasurer (as Smith recalls) 'that it was smart strategically to set up a specialist welfare rights group because we thought a lot of people were being taken off their

## 'THE BABIES': SPECIALIST SERVICES DEVELOPED AT RLC

entitlements and the consequence for the State Government was that emergency relief was going through the roof.'[797]

This collaboration in an area of law ignored by the private legal profession, led to the establishment of an entirely new service.

West notes:

> All of these organisations were encountering problems with the Department of Social Security and clients who had difficulty negotiating the system. We worked closely with both ACOSS and NCOSS. They had been trying to get funding for a specialist advice service from the Commonwealth, but with no success... We [RLC] tweaked the ACOSS/NCOSS model to make it a legal Centre, not just a general welfare advice service. When WRC got funded, we persuaded the South Sydney Council to let us take over the caretaker's quarters at the back of RLC.[798]

On 2 October 1982, the *Sydney Morning Herald* announced that 'An $80,000 social welfare rights Centre is to be established at the Redfern Legal Centre with State funds.'[799] Sydney City Council contributed $10,000 to help RLC.[800] The Centre was opened on 5 May 1983 by the Lord Mayor Doug Sutherland and the NSW Treasurer, Ken Booth.[801] A plaque was put up on the Redfern Town Hall to recognise their contribution. The State Government funding was a real victory for the coalition, being state funding for what was usually seen as a Commonwealth responsibility. As Smith notes 'it was an unusual funding thing for the State Government to do at that time.'[802] At the opening Booth stated:

> The Welfare Rights Centre is the first of its kind in Australia. It is hoped that it will act as a prototype for other similar Centres in high unemployment areas such as Newcastle and Wollongong. The Welfare Rights Centre will be working closely with other established Community Legal Centres, which can provide

assistance on a range of legal matters, including some Social Security matters.[803]

The Welfare Rights Centre was a new type of legal centre dealing primarily with one specific area of law—almost one statute—rather than say, a defined clientele or type of issue.[804] As Smith notes 'for us [ACOSS] it was a really useful collaboration working with the Welfare Rights Centre as it provided real life examples of what was happening on the ground.'[805] The collaboration continued with work on invalid pensions test and unemployment benefits work tests. As we have seen an effective network structure with a range of different sources of knowledge types and ensuring access to knowledge both within the network and outside helps knowledge and information flow between different actors and encourages innovation.[806] The Welfare Rights Centre was an example of this process and as the first legal centre focusing on social security entitlements in Australia led the way to a network of centres around Australia which have made a significant impact in this important area of administrative law.[807]

## THE ACCOMMODATION RIGHTS SERVICE (SENIORS RIGHTS)

RLC had been involved with issues facing people in nursing homes from the early 1980s. As discussed above a phone in was held in 1982 in a Senior Citizen's Week project in a collaboration with the Combined Pensioners and the Australian Consumers Association.[808] A report of the phone-in was launched in a blaze of media attention and the abuse of older people in nursing homes was squarely on the agenda for the first time.[809]

Over the following three years campaigning continued and The Aged Care Coalition was formed to identify a means of improving the quality of life for older people living in supported accommodation. The coalition was comprised of seven organisations: Redfern Legal Centre, Social Welfare Action Group, Disabled Persons International, NSW Council of Social Service, NSW Combined Pensioners Association, the Ethnic Communities Council and the Australian Consumers Association. Members of the Coalition started visiting aged care organisations to follow up on complaints that kept coming in after the phone-in. Evidence of the abuse noted in the phone-in was provided to the Senate Enquiry on Nursing Homes and Private Hospitals and taken up in national policy debates, over time leading to a range of user rights measures being incorporated into state and later national laws.[810]

A proposal was developed to establish an advocacy service in the aged care field. Dominic Gibson, lawyer/policy worker at RLC recalls:

> We formed an extremely tight working relationship with the Combined Pensioners ... A big driver was John Barber as the policy officer and Noreen Hewitt. In one of my first jobs in 1983, the Commonwealth flew us down to Canberra to Department of Social Security as they were the people who managed nursing homes to give evidence about management of those facilities. ... RLC put a proposal up for an advocacy service in this area of law. We applied to lots of funders—the Legal Aid Commission, the Department of Housing, Law Foundation and they all provided some funding. In 1983, the Commonwealth flew us down to Canberra to give evidence about the TARS service.[811]

The Aged Care Coalition which included RLC studied the experience of residents of supported accommodation which resulted in a report entitled *If Only I'd Known* published in March 1986.[812] This report along with other research in aged care was highly influential in demonstrating the serious need for a new advocacy service.[813] As a result of RLC's work with the Combined Pensioners and the Aged Care Coalition, The Accommodation Rights Service was established in 1986 under the auspices of Redfern Legal Centre, and with the support of the then Housing Commission and NSW Department of Community Services. In 1986 a national conference was held to focus on user rights with the Combined Pensioners Association and TARS advocating for a greater role for consumers in the planning monitoring and delivery of community services.[814] TARS began operating as advocacy service for elderly residents. The service later changed its name to Seniors Rights. These services now operate in most states in Australia. Again the success of the service was due to the high level of collaboration between agencies external to the Centre and the links formed in pursuit of the end result of service provision to a disadvantaged community.

1. Natalie Ross.
2. Andy Haesler.
3. Clare Farnan.
4. Paul Farrugia, Tamara Sims, Nick Patrick, Kristin van Barneveld and Faye Williams, Peter Stapleton. Helen Campbell in front.
5. Workers at the front desk of Redfern Legal Centre.
6. Heather McGilvray.

## CHAPTER 8
# CONFERENCES AND SOCIAL LIFE

RLC has of course been a leading member of the State and National Community Legal Centre movement over the years. Much of the Centre's activist, policy and law reform work was developed and carried out in conjunction with other Centres and this was facilitated by State and National CLC conferences. These were also a chance for people to let their hair down.

Penny Quarry went to the Jindabyne CLC conference when she moved to Sydney and was a law student at the University of Sydney.

> At Jindabyne, it was really cold, she didn't know anyone, there weren't enough blankets. There were 40 or 50 people there. I was on the outskirts of the group when they would sit outside round a fire. It was freezing. John Basten would sit in the middle of the group and was a prime mover in the group. I think there was a fair bit of dope smoking. They had a dance in a large hall—hardly anyone there. There was me and another student who was an a excellent dancer and we were dancing. Anne Summers was there.

Ben Slade recalls:

> In 1982 a student legal referral service was set up at ANU. Nick Seddon was the staff member who assisted. After a year or so we found about legal centres' conferences and went to our first legal centre conference at Lane Cove. It was a lot of fun. It was like being at an endless slumber party with all your chums.

Collective decision making: effective but takes work!

> I realised that people were multi skilled and multi-talented. People could do handstands. It was near the Lane Cove National Park. The conference dinner that year was a harbour cruise. It was all going well until we swung past Milsons Point. I happened to know that [fellow ANU law student] Will Stubbs was staying with a friend at a flat in North Sydney. On the ferry, I was aware that the flat was close to the harbour and Will pointed it out. He then decided he was going to head over to the place. He left his shoes and jumped off the back of the boat to head over there. We watched him swim away. There was concern but it was judged to be too dangerous to turn the boat around. This gave us crowd from ANU a certain notoriety.[815]

Later the number of people from ANU Law School in the early 1980s to end up working or volunteering at RLC during this period led to the term "the Canberra Mafia." Members included Ben Slade, Jane Goddard, Frances Gibson, Christian Mikula, Will Stubbs, Cathy Kerr, Helen Campbell, Phillip Kellow and others. At Ben Slade's job interview at the Centre in 1984, John Basten said that if Ben was the person who jumped off the Sydney ferry at the NSW Legal Centres Conference that the interview would stop right there.[816] 'There were big parties associated with National Legal Centres conferences.'[817]

Lansdowne remembers: 'The Centre life was very social… a lot of informal parties, at the Town Hall… John Basten, Peter Cashman and Julian Disney and Stan Ross had a house at Bundanoon and so in the late 1970s we used to spend a lot of weekends there working on the house and a lot of legal centre functions were there.'[818]

In the early Management Committee meetings there were often entries under the headings 'Parties' often held at Phil Burgess' place. Petre says 'We would regularly go to Virginia Bell's in Redfern and my house. 'Just about everyone was under 35—most under 30 at the start. People lived in the moment as people of that age tend to do.'[819] 'We slept and ate cheek by jowl. We ate together, went to parties and saw bands together. Some people from UNSW and RLC became shareholders in the newly established Regular Records.[820] Most people didn't have kids, some partners were involved—others were not. It was a very cohesive group. People were as dedicated to partying as they were dedicated to the work during the day.'[821] 'There was a bit of drinking, going to the pub, bottles of cheap wine, a bit of marijuana… there were romances.'[822]

Dominic Gibson remembers a party at the Redfern Town Hall when the party was raging. 'I found myself dancing to the Rolling Stones and I remember lifting John Basten high into the air on to the meaty beats of 'Get Your Ya-Ya's Out!'… I used to bring my big speakers in and we would dance. I remember Anne Healey at one party dancing around 2am and running up and down the corridor of the Town Hall and sliding down the bannisters. Mark Austin was a party regular and used to always finish the evening singing Irish ballads in honour of his Irish ancestry.'[823]

In the 1980s and 1990s, the Canberra mafia and colleagues continued the tradition of an active social life revolving around the Centre. Shivaun Inglis lived in a house with Jane Goddard in Abercrombie Street in 1987. She remembers; 'A lot of volunteers ended up at our house. We had parties. Ben Slade, Jane Goddard and Gordon Renouf, Fran Gibson all worked at Redfern. We went to the Cricketers Arms Hotel [now Tudor Hall] every Friday after work. There were parties at the Town Hall. They spent a lot of time hanging round the Centre. Andy Haesler would tell us stories like about Sallie-Anne Huckstepp and the pond at Centennial Park… fascinating Sydney history.'[824]

Biber remembers the 1990s. 'As soon as the Friday afternoon shift finished, all the volunteers and all the staff went across the road to the pub. I do remember we would sit towards the back and the cops would be in the front bar and the clients would be around-it was kind of an equalising place. There was a lot of lunches at the Pron Prohm—that was the first time I ever ate Thai food. I remember it being so exotic and spicy.'[825]

## MUTANT DEATH—RLC GETS ITS OWN SONG

Bands listed as playing at the RLC parties in early years include bush bands "Blue tongue" with Tempe Tipsters (Colonial Dress preferred) (1981), Franz Lizt and the Labels (1981), Ice Nine (1981) but it was a punk band called Mutant Death that will always be associated with the Centre.

Andy Nehl from the band Mutant Death:

> People in the band did some work on Radio Skid Row and 2SER on the Prisoners Programs on those stations. We did a lot of interviews with the lawyers from Redfern Legal Centre on Radio Skid Row in the basement of the Wentworth building at Sydney uni. We covered issues for disadvantaged people on tenancy, prison issues etc.' The song Mutant Death recorded was called 'Police Verbals (Redfern Legal Centre Blues)'. It was written and sung by Mutant Death's bass player, Tony Collins.
>
> The song was actually recorded at Radio Skid Row...Skid Row played that song a lot at the time. It was our hit!...This was at the time when police corruption was really bad and verballing people was at its height. When the band played the song live, one line was sung as "I went with Roger Rogerson to another room". The line in the recording was "I went with the detective into another room" cause of defamation and not wanting to be killed. [826]

## LYRICS—POLICE VERBALS (REDFERN LEGAL CENTRE BLUES)'

*I was sitting home watching my TV*
*When three fat pigs came bustin' in on me*
*'We got you red handed, with three grams and a gun'*
*'Come on down the station, we're gonna have some fun'.*
*I was being verballed, I was being framed*
*The cops had set me up, I was going down the drain.*
*I didn't know what was going on, I was in a state of fright*
*Alone with three pigs, in the middle of the night*
*They said 'go with the detective, he'll treat you real nice'*
*I'm not saying anything, till I get legal advice.*
*I was being verballed, I was being framed*
*Had to get in touch with Redfern Legal Centre straight away.*
*I went with the detective, into another room*
*There was no chairs or tables, I knew it was coming soon*
*Then he took off his jacket, and he punched me in the face*
*Said 'plead guilty to the charges or you'll never leave this place'.*
*I was being verballed, I was being bashed*
*And the law couldn't help me 'cause I didn't have the cash.*
*I woke up next morning, still bleeding in my cell*
*Got on to Redfern Legal Centre, spoke to Virginia Bell*
*When she got on to the cops they said 'you haven't got a chance'*
*'Your client signed a record of interview before we broke his hands'.*
*I was being verballed, I was being framed*
*The cops had set me up, and I was going down the drain.*
*Next thing I knew, I was standing up in court*
*The evidence was bullshit, and the witnesses were bought*
*I told the judge and jury but the bullshit didn't stop*
*They were gonna take the word of a lousy drug dealin' cop.*
*I was being verballed, I was being framed*
*The cops had loaded me up, I was going down the drain.*
*The cops had done their homework, they knew they couldn't fail*
*The jury found me guilty, I got 16 years in jail*
*And now I know what justice is, but what a price I paid*

*I should have read the law book from Redfern Legal Aid.*
*I was being verballed, I was being framed*
*The cops had loaded me up, and I was going down the drain.*

© Mutant Death 1984

Bill Dickens, solicitor at the Centre, was a friend of the band when they played at a Christmas RLC event in the Town Hall upstairs. It did not go down too well with everyone. 'John Basten turned the power off at the powerboard because he didn't like the music they were playing at the time. There was some pretty hot debate about it between everyone and him but he was the boss! It was very embarrassing 'cause they were my friends.'[827]

Nehl remembers: 'The acoustics in Redfern Town Hall are 'appalling—it's just a square box and sound bounces back to you on stage and it makes it hard to play. But Mutant Death could sometimes sound great and sometimes dreadful... There was no sound mixer that night, just a DIY mixing desk. That night it did not go down well.' Halfway through the set John Basten got up on stage and said to Andy 'If there was a vote of people in this room right now you would be offstage and out the door'. 'This probably reflected the views of most of the people in the room. After Mutant Death, Coupe De Ville played. They weren't a punk band and were well rehearsed and everyone liked them a lot better. Later that night Mutant Death went on to play another show between 3 am and 5 am at another Christmas party and we played really well and it sounded great.'[828]

Simon Rice recalls[829] 'Redfern Legal Centre's 1984 Christmas party, was 'at home', in the Redfern Town Hall. The night was hot, the hall packed, the music loud. Mutant Death was undeterred by a threat from one of Redfern's lawyers to pull the plug on them and, in a tribute to their hosts, the band performed — a more apt word than 'sang' — 'Police Verbals', *aka* 'Redfern Legal Centre Blues'...Police Verbals' describes bluntly and

## CONFERENCES AND SOCIAL LIFE

vividly the notorious nature of NSW policing at the time, later the subject of the Wood Royal Commission. Virginia Bell—formerly Justice Bell of the High Court—was counsel assisting that Commission, thirteen years after Mutant Death had put on record her reputation for taking on the NSW police.

On 10 March 1992, RLC celebrated its fifteenth anniversary with speakers Gough Whitlam, Mayor of South Sydney, Vic Smith, Law Society President John Marsden, Mark Richardson from Legal Aid and Robyn Lansdowne—There was a ceremonial cutting of the fifteenth anniversary cake with Gough Whitlam, Clare Petre and client, Mr Santalab.

Stephen O'Neil recalls the band The Cannanes (featuring RLC solicitor Frances Gibson and writer of this tale) playing at Redfern Legal Centre's twentieth birthday party in 1997 at South Sydney Leagues Club.

> Despite some initial angst, the twentieth birthday party saw the largest group of dancers ever for the band. Unfortunately the Redfern evening was marred by a complete arsehole whom no doubt was paid handsomely for spending the evening bossing us around. We thought at first he was OK, just someone a bit officious doing a difficult job despite his stupid phone calls asking us "Where does each muso stand on stage etc" but when bands ran seven minutes overtime as of course they are wont to do he ordered us off the stage despite the aforementioned exceptionally large group of enthusiastic and by now very vocal dancers. He completely harassed our mixer, the delightful John Rafferty all evening and deserves a nasty punishment though I am at the moment at a loss to think of a suitable one. Tony Pooley suggested that we should drag him into the toilets and put thongs on him so we could have the satisfaction of seeing him thrown out by the also rather officious Souths Leagues club bouncers but we failed to seize the moment.[830]

Wilson's restaurant at 91 Pitt Street Redfern, the first Lebanese restaurant in Sydney was a favourite with the RLC workers, as was the Cricketer's Rest Hotel—later renamed the Tudor Hall Hotel—across the road from the Centre.[831] 'Wilson's is a Lebanese restaurant which is about 50 metres from the Centre in Pitt Street and was the unofficial Redfern Legal Centre restaurant and many shifts, many Centre meetings and many management committee meetings adjourned from the Town Hall to Wilsons. We spent a lot of time there.'[832] Later the Centre staff and volunteers spent many happy hours at a Thai restaurant on Redfern Street named the Pron Prohm (Tup Tim).

Redfern Legal Centre volunteers and staff continue to enjoy social occasions, celebrations, trivia nights, RLC birthdays etc though perhaps more focused on fund raising and possibly in a more mature fashion than the early years.

# INDEX OF PEOPLE

## A
Rick Abel  33
Serena Afa  119
Yasmin Alali  11, 274–275, 281
Percy Allan  236
Jill Anderson  28, 196
Kevin Anderson  74, 187
Pam Anderson  11
Zelie Appel  158, 281
Mick Appleby  27
Mark Austin  245

## B
Irene Baghoomians  105, 275
Clinton Bamberger  33, 45, 266
Sharmilla Bargon  158
John Basten  32–34, 37–38, 45, 48, 60, 63, 77, 106, 118, 170, 183, 186, 193, 202, 213, 242, 244–245, 248, 264, 266–269, 271–273, 281–282, 285–287, 290, 296
Trevor Bates  131
Sir Phillip Baxter  30
Kevin Bell  71, 265, 271–272

Virginia Bell  53, 56, 59, 72, 79, 87, 183, 186, 212–213, 225, 244, 247, 249, 266, 269, 271, 285, 291, 294
Bob Bellear  34, 39
Michael Berg (photograph)  92
Laura Bianchi  120, 159, 162–164, 277, 281
Katherine Biber  86, 102, 106, 126, 273–275, 278–279, 298
Julie Bishop  124
Tony Blackshield  64
Erhard Blankenberg  17, 263
Louise Blazejowska  11, 169, 228, 294, 295
Annabel Bleach  95
Steve Bolt  85, 104, 136, 273, 275, 279
George Booth  236
Ken Booth  237
Daniel Brezniak  53, 269
Dave Brown  34, 55, 266
Louis M Brown  209, 290–291
David Buchanan  45, 50, 54, 56–57, 268–269, 274
Terry Buddin  30, 32, 38, 40, 42, 48, 62, 77, 92, 183, 266–272, 297
Phil Burgess  38, 42, 244, 268
Meredith Burgman  164
Richard Button  194

## C

Alan Cameron  183
Helen Campbell  86, 101, 104, 140, 142–143, 145, 151, 231, 241, 244, 273–276, 280, 295
Anne Louise Carlton  196
Bob Carr  136, 284
President Jimmy Carter  207
Peter Cashman  49, 244, 269

## INDEX OF PEOPLE

Steven Catt  43
Michael Chesterman  61
Hilary Chesworth  140, 141, 153, 232, 275, 277–278, 280–281, 295
Richard Chisholm  35, 37–38
Selena Choo  183
Simon Cleary  116, 118, 277
Ian Close  215, 216, 289, 293
Paul Coe  40
Brett Collins  190, 194, 286–287
Janene Cootes  196, 287–288
Russell Cox  52
Gerard Craddock  10, 59, 66–67, 87, 96, 102, 262, 270–271, 273–274, 297–298
Sarah Crawford  85, 105, 273–275
Reverend Bill Crews  134
Deneale Crozier  140

## D

Sue Davitt  45, 183
Bill Dickens  58, 87, 101, 192–193, 197, 248, 270, 275, 287, 298
Romano Di Donato  92
Julian Disney  32, 37–39, 48, 244, 266, 267–269, 282, 283, 297
David Donnison  170, 282
Bronwyn Dyer  11, 277, 281

## E

Natalie Egan  295
Bob Ellicott  45

## F

John Fahey  193
Felicity Faris  21, 265
Clare Farnan  28, 169, 241
Sophie Farrell  148, 280
Paul Farrugia  60, 72, 110, 183, 270, 271, 275
Tom Fawthrop  33, 266
Regina Featherstone  158
Bill Ferguson  41
Nick Franklin  188

## G

Marc Galanter  33
Julian Gardner  170
Mary Gaudron  179, 288, 294
Ann Genovese  12, 187, 262, 285, 286
Dominic Gibson  42, 87, 101, 218, 239, 245, 268, 273, 275, 297–298
Frances Gibson  88, 94, 138, 167, 183, 244, 249
Robin Gibson  11
Jeff Giddings  38, 112, 151, 174, 267, 275, 280–283
Hal Ginges  53
Greg Glass  76
Jane Goddard  11, 27, 28, 75–76, 167, 169, 225–227, 229, 244–245, 272, 294
Helen Golding  34, 49, 50, 53, 55, 63, 188
Joanne Golding  55
Emma Golledge  133, 150, 279, 280
Alexis Goodstone  96, 156, 274
Lyndal Gowland  180
Harriet Grahame  11, 183, 276
Jack Grahame  194, 287

## INDEX OF PEOPLE

Alex Greenwich  163, 281
Senator Don Grimes  197
Bradley Gundy  114
David Gundy  95, 114

## H
Andy Haesler  11, 27–28, 32, 42–43, 74–75, 83–84, 86, 88, 90–91, 105, 113, 131, 149, 192, 219, 241, 245, 266–268, 272–274, 276, 280, 286–287, 293, 298
Julia Hall  95, 196, 287, 289
Denis Harley  48
Don Harley  69, 271
Penny Harrington  28
Danae Harvey  11
Bruce Hawker  179, 284
Matthew Hazard  183
Anne Healey  53, 191, 212, 216, 245, 269, 286, 291–292, 296
Mr Henderson SM  58
Cherilyn Herbert  11, 275, 281
Mick Hillman  11, 28, 88, 274
Eric J. Hobsbawm  12, 262
Russell Hogg  43
Sekai Holland  64
Ray Hood  74
Brian Huckstepp  75, 114
Sallie-Anne Huckstepp  114, 245, 276

## I
Mark Ierace  118, 204, 289
Shivaun Inglis  245, 298
Joyce Ingram  180

## J
Owen Jessup 61–62
Beth Jewell 11, 116, 132, 140, 183, 278–280
Lindy Jones 77

## K
Phillip Kellow 104, 244
Brian Kelsey 35–36, 38
Cathy Kerr 11, 79, 104, 244, 272, 275
Sean Kidney 212, 215, 217–218, 220–221, 291–293
Kylie Kilgour 132, 183
Michael Kirby 216
Jeremy Kirk 107
Chris Kirkbright 40
John Kirkwood 27, 33, 43, 48, 55, 59, 64, 71, 212, 235, 270–271, 273

## L
Warren Lanfranchi 114, 276
Robyn Lansdowne 11, 33, 38, 63, 69, 189, 249, 266–275, 282, 286, 297
Samantha Lee 138, 161, 279
Craig Lenehan 183
Dixie Link-Gordan 180
Peter Livesey 36, 42, 49, 54, 268–270
Janet Loughman 11

## M
Chips Mackinolty 42
Marianne Maguire 145
Dylan Maher 115, 276
Nick Manning 141

## INDEX OF PEOPLE

George Allen Mansfield  40
Janet Manuel  118
John Marsden  249
Bernie Matthews  51–52, 264, 269, 286
Joan McClintock  236, 269
Pat McDonough  11, 102, 104, 275
Rod McGeoch  72
Heather McGilvray  27–28, 241
Don McKay  71
Nora McManus  46
Julie Melbourne  218
Carrie Menkel-Meadow  98, 100, 274, 275
Christian Mikula  244, 276
Andrew Miles  103, 105, 132
Bruce Miles  64
Julian Millar  66
Michael Mobbs  44, 55, 165, 211, 213, 268–269, 291
Phil Molan  38
Clover Moore  88, 134
Tim Moore  137, 279
Elizabeth Morley  108, 142, 151, 275, 280
Jane Mulroney  229, 295
Amy Munro  107, 154, 162, 275, 281
Lionel Murphy  71, 209, 283, 291
Greg Murray  67

## N

Ralph Nader  211, 291
John Nagle  186
Andy Nehl  246, 286, 298
Garth Nettheim  68, 263
Eddie Neumann  32, 67

Max Neutze  14, 262
David Nichols  11, 267
Mary Anne Noone  11, 82, 100, 112, 148, 150–151, 172, 271,
　　273–275, 278, 280–284, 290, 295

## O

Michael O'Donnell (photograph)  27
Frank O'Grady  40
Finn O'Keefe  159, 281
Stephen O'Neil  3, 249

## P

Christine Parker  22, 265, 282
Sophie Parker  138
Nick Patrick  147
Catherine Payne  114, 196, 287
Tony Payne  196
Mary Perkins  11, 89, 143, 169, 227, 274, 294, 298
Clare Petre  16, 27, 44, 77, 87–88, 95, 183, 236, 249, 263,
　　267–269, 271, 283
Kathy Pierce  76
Tony Pooley  180, 249
Polly Porteous  132, 137, 153, 279, 281
David Porter  138
Andrea Powell  95
Terry Purcell  16, 263, 267, 285, 291

## Q

Penny Quarry  47, 115, 242, 269, 276

INDEX OF PEOPLE

## R

Rick Raftos  43, 92
Mark Randall  228
William Redfern  14
Neil Rees  213, 221, 293
Gordon Renouf  28, 76, 85, 102, 127, 142–143, 169, 245, 273, 276, 283
Simon Rice  28, 34, 61, 66, 83, 88, 183, 248, 266, 270–273, 281, 298
Mark Richardson  249
Bruce Roberts  189, 286
Violet Roberts  189, 286
Francine Rochford  11
Nanette Rogers  59, 87, 191, 273
Chris Ronalds  57, 213–214, 220, 270, 292–293
Natalie Ross  241
Stan Ross  244

## S

Mehera San Roque  106
Mr Santalab  27, 96–98, 102, 171, 249
Sue Schreiner  74–76, 95, 272
Nick Seddon  242
Steven Sellars  54
Vicki Sentas  138
Jeff Shaw  135
Nicholas Shehadie  41
Sargent Shriver  33
Jo Shulman  135, 140–141, 145–147, 153, 160, 276, 280–281
Carolyn Simpson  58
Jim Simpson  195–196, 198, 287, 288
Tamara Sims  97, 106, 160, 274–275, 281

Ben Slade  11, 28, 87, 101, 102, 105, 117–118, 132, 169, 183, 193, 226, 242, 244–245, 272–274, 277, 287, 294, 297
Edward 'Jockey' Smith  54
Phillipa Smith  236
Roger Smith  41, 267
Susan Smith  180
Peter Stapleton  59, 164, 183, 270, 275, 281
Sean Stimson  128–129
Edward St John  195, 287
Julius Stone  36
Judith Stubbs  144
Will Stubbs  102, 244, 274
Doug Sutherland  237
Kim Swan  38
Jacqui Swinburne  121, 134, 141, 152, 161, 183, 279, 281
Garth Symonds  50, 53, 57, 62–63, 269–270, 275, 282, 286, 291–292
Anik Shapiro  95–96

# T
John Terry  27, 45–47, 51, 56–57, 63, 71, 213, 272, 292
Lloyd Tidmarsh  54
Pam Todd  95
Mark Twain  42

# V
David Vaile  119, 125, 127, 169, 277–278

## W

Johnnie Wade  41
Janet Wahlquist  53
Frank Walker  23, 27, 179, 190, 284–285
Wendy Wang  141
Angus Webb  76, 272
Roger West  28, 38, 61, 77–78, 86–87, 90, 110, 176, 183, 198, 236, 267, 270–273, 282–283, 288, 297
Bill Wheeler  216, 292
Margaret White  216
Sarah White  216
Gough Whitlam  27, 171, 249
Debbie Whitmont  46, 60, 63, 67, 73, 96, 215, 269–271, 274, 283
Harry Whitmore  30, 35, 266
Alex Wodak  137
Justice Hal Wootten  15, 30, 37, 51, 263, 266

## Y

Justice Yeldham  70–71
Sir John Young  22

## Z

George Zdenkowski  34, 37–38, 72, 175, 186–187, 194, 266–267, 269, 271, 283, 285–287

# ENDNOTES

1. Eric Hobsawm in David Snowman, 'Eric Hobsawm' (1999) 49 (1) *History Today* 17,18.
2. Interview with Gerard Craddock (Frances Gibson, Sydney, 1 May 2013).
3. Ann Genovese, 'A Radical Prequel: Historicising the Concept of Gendered Law in Australia' in Margaret Thornton (ed), *Sex Discrimination in Uncertain Times* (ANU Press, 2010) 56.
4. Eric J. Hobsbawm, *The Age Of Empire 1875–1914*.
5. Andrew Jakubowicz, *Changing Patterns of Community Organization* (Government IV Honours Thesis, Sydney University, 1969); David Neal, 'Law and Power: Livin' in the 70s' (2013) 29(2) *Law in Context* 99.
6. Paul Convy, *The Lebanese Quarter: Mapping the Syrian Lebanese Quarters at Redfern. Time, Place and Extent* (Australian Lebanese Historical Society, 2006) 14.
7. See 'Remembering the Strike that Stopped the Nation', *City of Sydney* (Web Page, 8 June 2017) <https://news.cityofsydney.nsw.gov.au/media-releases/remembering-the-strike-that-stopped-the-nation >.
8. Max Neutze, *People and Property in Redfern: Post War Changes in the Population and the Properties in an Inner Suburb of Sydney* (Urban Research Unit, Research School of Social Sciences, Australian National University, 1972) 19.
9. 'Redfern Estate Heritage Conservation Area', *Office of Environment and Heritage NSW* (Web Page, 28 July 2006) <http://www.environment.nsw.gov.au/heritageapp/ViewHeritageItemDetails.aspx?ID=2421496 >.
10. Paul Convy and Anne Mansour, 'Lebanese Settlement in NSW: A Thematic History' *NSW Office of Migration and Heritage* (Web Document, July 2008) <http://www.migrationheritage.nsw.gov.au/mhc-reports/ThematicHistoryOfLebaneseNSW.pdf>.
11. Max Neutze, *People and Property in Redfern: Post War Changes in the Population and the Properties in an Inner Suburb of Sydney* (Urban Research Unit, Research School of Social Sciences, Australian National University, 1972) 120.
12. For a short history of Reserves in NSW see 'Living on Aboriginal Reserves and Stations' *NSW Office of Environment and Heritage* (Web Page) <http://www.environment.nsw.gov.au/chresearch/ReserveStation.htm>.
13. WD Scott and Company, 'Problems and Needs of the Aboriginals of Sydney: A Report to the Minister of Youth and Community Services, New South Wales, Sydney and Foundation for Aboriginal Affairs, Aborigines in Sydney' (unpublished document in Murphy papers, 1971) cited in KJ Anderson, 'Place Narratives and the Origins of Inner Sydney's Aboriginal Settlement, 1972–73' (1993) 19(3) *Journal of Historical Geography* 314.

# ENDNOTES

14. The Block is an area of houses which were acquired by the Aboriginal Housing Company in the 1970s and 1980s. See 'Aboriginal Housing Company and the Block', *Redfern Oral History* (Web Page, 9 September 2019) <http://redfernoralhistory.org/Organisations/AboriginalHousingCompany/tabid/209/Default.aspx>.
15. See Chris Cuneen, 'Aboriginal-Police Relations in Redfern', *Human Rights and Equal Opportunity Commission* (Web Document, 1990). <https://www.humanrights.gov.au/sites/default/files/content/pdf/race_discrim/redfern_1990.pdf>.
16. Hal Wootten, 'Aboriginal Legal Services' in Garth Nettheim (ed), *Aborigines Human Rights and the Law* (Australian and New Zealand Book Company, 1974) 60.
17. 'History', *Aboriginal Legal Service* (Web Page) <https://www.alsnswact.org.au/about>.
18. See recognition by Sackville of the importance of the chamber magistrate role in NSW in the legal aid system. Ronald Sackville, Commission of Inquiry into Poverty (1975) *Law and Poverty in Australia* (Australian Government Publishing Service, Canberra) 42.
19. Clare Petre, 'Specialisation: The Sydney Push Legal Centres in New South Wales' in David Neal (ed) *On Tap not on Top: Legal Centres in Australia 1972-1982* (Legal Services Bulletin, 1984) 12.
20. Paul Mortimer, *Unfinished Business: The Story of the Tenants Union of NSW 1976-1996* (Tenants Union of NSW, 1996) 14. Note that it is arguable that the Tenants Union was the first community legal centre in NSW. The fact that it did not call itself a community legal centre and did not receive any funding for paid workers until 1979, however, have led to it being regarded as another activist group rather than a CLC as such, though it was later to join the national CLC movement.
21. Interview with Terry Purcell (Frances Gibson, Sydney, 6 September 2016).
22. Erhard Blankenberg, *Innovations in the Legal Services* (Oelgeschlager, Gunn & Hain, 1980) 1.
23. Erhard Blankenberg, *Innovations in the Legal Services* (Oelgeschlager, Gunn & Hain, 1980) 1.
24. See discussion in Jude McCulloch, Megan Blair and Bridget Harris (Web Page, 2011) *Justice for all: A history of the Victorian Community Legal Centre movement*. Federation of Community Legal Centres Victoria, Australia < https://eprints.qut.edu.au/104428/>. Also Adam Jamrozik, Cathy Boland and Robert Urquhart, Social Change and Cultural Transformation in Australia (Cambridge University Press, 1995).
25. Robert D Benford, 'Review of Sixties Radicalism and Social Movement Activism: Retreat or Resurgence?' (2015) 44(1) *Contemporary Sociology* 71.
26. @Michelle Arrow, *The Seventies: The Personal, the Political, and the Making of Modern Australia* (NewSouth Publishing, 2019) 6.
27. Michelle Arrow, *The Seventies: The Personal, the Political, and the Making of Modern Australia* (NewSouth Publishing, 2019) 8.
28. Angela Melville, 'Barriers to Entry into Law School: An Examination of Socio-Economic and Indigenous Disadvantage'(2014) 24 *Legal Education Review* 45, 48.
29. Bob Bessant, 'Robert Gordon Menzies and Education in Australia' (1977) *Melbourne Studies in Education* 163.
30. Angela Melville, 'Barriers to Entry into Law School: An Examination of Socio-Economic and Indigenous Disadvantage' (2014) 24 *Legal Education Review* 45, 48.
31. Alan Barcan, 'The Arrival of the New Left at Sydney University, 1967-1972' (2011) 40(2) *History of Education Review* 156.
32. J Handler, E Hollingsworth and H

Erlanger, *Lawyers and the Pursuit of Legal Rights* (Academic Press, 1978) 135–153.

33  Alan Barcan, 'The Arrival of the New Left at Sydney University, 1967–1972' (2011) 40(2) *History of Education Review* 156, 159.

34  Richard Gordon (ed), *The Australian New Left* (Heinemann Australia, 1970) 24.

35  Stephen Foster and Margaret Varghese, 'The Making of The Australian National University 1946–1996 Chapter 8: Who were the Students?', *ANU Press* (Web Document, 2009) < https://press.anu.edu.au/publications/making-australian-national-university >.

36  In a review of research concerning participation in education generally, Julie Smith concluded that 'certain groups of students sharing particular attributes (rural, female or low family socioeconomic background) are particularly susceptible … (to) these financial or economic factors and are likely to be the students 'tipped out' by an unfavourable balance of financial and economic incentives. These students can be characterised as the 'marginal' groups', Julie P Smith, *Education Participation and Financial Incentives*, Office of Youth Affairs Working Paper, undated) quoted in Don Anderson, 'Tertiary Fees and the Social Mix' (1985) 28(1) *Vestes* 20, 21.

37  Bruce Chapman, 'Positive and Negative Aspects of Australian Higher Education Financing' (Background paper at Towards Opportunity and Prosperity, *Melbourne Institute* and *The Australian Economic and Social Outlook Conference*, April 4 and 5, 2002) 2; Neville Wran, Committee on Higher Education Funding, Department of Employment, Education and Training, *Report of the Committee on Higher Education Funding* (Australian Government Publishing Service, 1988); David Weisbrot, *Australian Lawyers* (Longman Professional, 1989) 94. See also 'What is Whitlam's Higher Education Legacy?' *Andrew Norton* (Web Page, 2014) <https://andrewnorton.net.au/2014/10/21/what-is-whitlams-higher-education-legacy/>.

38  Frank Crowley, *Tough Times: Australia In the Seventies* (William Heinemann Australia, 1986) 35.

39  Frank Crowley, *Tough Times Australia In the Seventies* (William Heinemann Australia, 1986) 229.

40  John Emerson, 'Women in the Legal Profession: A Historical Review' (2004) 26(19) *Bulletin (Law Society of S.A.)* 22.

41  The biggest change in the legal profession in the twentieth century was the entry of women, and from the late 1970s on, 'a critical mass seemed to have been reached … Women began studying law in greater and greater numbers.' See John Emerson, 'Women in the Legal Profession: A Historical Review' (2004) 26(19) *Bulletin (Law Society of S.A.)* 23.

42  Bryn Jones and Mike O'Donnell, *Sixties Radicalism and Social Movement Activism: Retreat or Resurgence?* (Anthem Press, 2012) 227, 228.

43  John Basten, Regina Graycar and David Neal, 'Legal Centres in Australia' (1983) 6 *UNSW Law Journal* 113, 135. See also Megan Blair and Jude McCulloch, 'From Maverick to Mainstream: Forty Years of Community Legal Centres' (2012) 37(1) *Alternative Law Journal* 12.

44  Bernie Matthews, *Intractable: Hell has a Name. Katingal* (Pan Macmillan, 2006) 89.

45  Brian Martin, 'The Anti Uranium Movement' (1982) 10(4) *Alternatives: Perspectives on Society and Environment* 56.

46  Geoffrey Holloway, 'The Wilderness Society: The Transformation of a Social Movement' (Occasional Paper No.4, Department of Sociology, University of Tasmania 1986).

47  Gwendolyn Jamieson, *Reaching for Health: The Australian Women's Health Movement and Public Policy* (ANU E Press, 2012) 3 < https://www.jstor.org/stable/j.

ctt24h7z0>.
48. Jack Doig, 'New Nationalism in Australia and New Zealand: The Construction of National Identities by Two Labo(u)r Governments in the Early 1970s' (2013) 59(4) *Australian Journal of Politics and History* 560.
49. John Chesterman, *Law and the New Left: A History of Fitzroy Legal Service, 1972–1994* (University of Melbourne, 1995) iii.
50. Rowan Cahill, *Notes on the New Left in Australia*, (Australian Marxist Research Foundation,1969) 2.
51. Richard Neville and Dean Letcher, *OZ 40* (September 1968) https://issuu.com/libuow/docs/ozsydney40, 9.
52. Alan Barcan, *The Socialist Left in Australia 1949–1959* (Australian Political Studies Association Occasional Monograph no 2, 1960).
53. Felicity Faris in David Neal (ed) *On Tap, Not on Top. Legal Centres in Australia 1972–1982*, (Legal Service Bulletin Co-operative Ltd, 1984) 57.
54. John Chesterman, *Law and the New Left: A History of Fitzroy Legal Service, 1972–1994* (University of Melbourne, 1995) 84.
55. David Weisbrot, *Australian Lawyers* (Longman Professional,1989) 94. See also Margaret Hetherton, *Victoria's Lawyers : the First Report of a Research Project on Lawyers in the Community* (Victoria Law Foundation, 1978)12 and John Goldring, *Admission Policy in Legal Education in Australia* (Discussion Papers, Law Foundation of New South Wales, 1976) 34.
56. Angela Melville, 'Barriers to Entry into Law School: An Examination of Socio-Economic and Indigenous Disadvantage' (2014) 24 *Legal Education Review* 45.
57. The Bar is a legal profession of specialist advocates and advisers called barristers.
58. Sol Encel, *Equality and Authority* (Cheshire, 1970) 76.
59. Roman Tomasic and Cedric Bullard, *Lawyers and their Work in New South Wales* (Law Foundation of New South Wales,1978) 271.
60. Michael Sexton and Laurence W Maher, *The Legal Mystique: The Role of Lawyers in Australian Society* (Angus and Robertson, 1982) 7-9.
61. David Weisbrot, *Australian Lawyers* (Longman Professional, 1989) 95.
62. Christine Parker, 'Justifying the New South Wales Legal Profession: 1976 to 1997' (1997) 2(2) *Newcastle Law Review* 1, 5.
63. David Weisbrot, *Australian Lawyers* (Longman Professional, 1989) 184.
64. New South Wales Law Reform Commission Report, 'Chapter 7', *First Report on the Legal Profession: General Regulation and Structure* (1982) 31.
65. See Michael Sexton and Laurence W Maher, *The Legal Mystique: The Role of Lawyers in Australian Society* (Angus and Robertson, 1982) 35.
66. New South Wales Law Reform Commission, 'The Legal Profession' (Background Paper III, Sydney, 1980). See also Michael Sexton and Laurence W Maher, *The Legal Mystique: The Role of Lawyers in Australian Society* (Angus and Robertson, 1982) 30, 174.
67. David Weisbrot, *Australian Lawyers* (Longman Professional,1989) 184.
68. For an example see Kevin Bell, 'Politics of Reforming the Legal Profession in Australia: A Case Study of the Western Region Community Legal Centre' 7 *Law and Policy* 143.
69. See Michael Sexton and Laurence W Maher, *The Legal Mystique: The Role of Lawyers in Australian Society* (Angus and Robertson 1982) 35.
70. George Williams, 'Whitlam's Legacy of Law Reform' (2014) 88(12) *Law Institute Journal* 26.
71. *Family Law Act 1975* (Cth), *Trade Practices Act 1974* (Cth), *Administrative Appeals Tribunal Act 1975* (Cth), *Ombudsman Act 1975* (Cth).

72. Alan Barcan, 'The Arrival of the New Left at Sydney University, 1967–1972' (2011) 40(2) *History of Education Review* 156, 172.
73. Frank Crowley, *Tough Times: Australia In the Seventies* (William Heinemann, Australia, 1986) 6.
74. See Ronald Sackville, Commission of Inquiry into Poverty (1975) *Law and Poverty in Australia* (Australian Government Publishing Service, Canberra).
75. George R Palmer and Stephanie D Short, *Health Care & Public Policy: An Australian Analysis* (Springer Link, 1989) 235.
76. Chief Justice Robert French AC, 'University of New South Wales Law School 40th Anniversary', *High Court of Australia* (Web Document, 17 September 2011) 5 <http://www.hcourt.gov.au/assets/publications/speeches/current-justices/frenchcj/frenchcj17Sep11.pdf>.
77. See Hal Wootten, 'Living Greatly in the Law' (2008) 31(1) *The University of New South Wales Law Journal* 258.
78. John Basten, The 2017 Harry Whitmore Lecture 17 October 2017 Separation Of Powers – Dialogue And Deference,1.
79. Frank Carrigan, 'They Make a Desert and Call it Peace' (2013) 23(2) *Legal Education Review* 313.
80. Marion Dixon, *Thirty Up: The Story of the UNSW Law School* 1971–2001 (UNSW Law School, 2001) 32.
81. A law journal focusing on issues such as legal aid, alternative legal service delivery, crime, discrimination etc. later to be renamed the Alternative Law Journal.
82. Interview with Robyn Lansdowne (Frances Gibson, Melbourne, 6 July 2016).
83. Brien Kelsey, 'What's Wrong with the Law School?' *Tharunka* (UNSW Student Paper), 15 September 1976.
84. Interview with Andrew Haesler (Frances Gibson, Sydney, 7 July 2015).
85. Interview with 1?)
86. Interview with Terry Buddin (Frances Gibson, Sydney, 4 August 2015).
87. Doug Donovan and Jacques Kelly, E. Clinton Bamberger Jr., pioneer in legal aid for poor (Baltimore Sun 13 February 2017)
88. Christopher Brown, Interview with *E. Clinton Bamberger, Jr.* National Equal Justice Library Oral History Collection, (4 June 2002).
89. Interview with Terry Buddin (Frances Gibson, Sydney, 4 August 2015).
90. Interview with John Basten (Frances Gibson, Sydney, 27 July 201?). See Tom Fawthrop, Biography <https://tomfawthropmedia.com/biography/>. Fawthrop was the co-editor of *Up Against the Law*—a self-help manual on how a defendant can represent himself in a criminal case under UK law applying the precedent of McKenzie versus Mckenzie. Worm --- "Up Against the Law" [1977] AltCrimJl 4
91. Interview with Andrew Haesler (Frances Gibson, Sydney, 7 July 2015).
92. Interview with Robyn Lansdowne (Frances Gibson, Melbourne, 6 July 2016).
93. See George Zdenkowski and David Brown, *The Prison Struggle: Changing Australia's Penal System* (Penguin Books, 1982).
94. Marion Dixon, *Thirty Up: The Story of the UNSW Law School 1971–2001* (UNSW Law School, 2001) 29–34; Interview with Andrew Haesler (Frances Gibson, Sydney, 7 July 2015).
95. Simon Rice, 'A Reflection on Justice Virginia Bell' (2009) 1 *Peppercorn* 18.
96. Interview with Andrew Haesler (Frances Gibson, Sydney, 7 July 2015).
97. Interview with Julian Disney (Frances Gibson, Sydney, 25 July 2016).
98. This piece is republished in the booklet *Critique of Law: A Marxist Perspective* (1978) published by the Critique of Law editorial group edited by Dave Brown and Gill Boehringer at Macquarie University.
99. Email Dave Brown to Frances Gibson (4 November 2015).

# ENDNOTES

100 Interview with Robyn Lansdowne (Frances Gibson, Melbourne, 6 July 2016).

101 Mary Jane Mossman, 'Report to the Academic Policy Committee on Clinical Legal Education' (Undated, UNSW) See Marion Dixon, *Thirty Up: The Story of the UNSW Law School 1971–2001* (UNSW Law School, 2001) 29–34; Interview with Andrew Haesler (Frances Gibson, Sydney, 7 July 2015).

102 Clare Petre, 'Specialisation: The Sydney Push Legal Centres in New South Wales' in David Neal (ed) *On Tap not on Top: Legal Centres in Australia 1972–1982* (Legal Services Bulletin, 1984) 12.

103 Interview with George Zdenkowski (Frances Gibson, Sydney, 28 October 2017).

104 Legal Aid Clinic, *UNSW Memorandum* File MP/SC Secretariat 29 November 1976 (Copy held by Robyn Lansdowne).

105 UNSW Law, *Report of the General Meeting to discuss the setting up of a legal aid clinic held at UNSW Law School* (19–20 November 1976) (Copy in possession of Robyn Lansdowne) 1. Note that the first clinical legal education program in Australia began at Springvale Legal Service, Monash University. See Kerry Greenwood, *It seemed like a good idea at the time: a History of Springvale Legal Service 1973-1993* (1994. Springvale Legal Service).

106 Interview with Terry Buddin (Frances Gibson, Sydney, 4 August 2015).

107 Jeff Giddings et al, 'The First Wave of Modern Clinical Legal Education The United States, Britain, Canada, and Australia' in *The Global Clinical Movement: Educating Lawyers for Social Justice* (Oxford University Press, 2011) 4.

108 David Nichols, *From the Roundabout to the Roundhouse: 25 years of KLC* (Kingsford Legal Centre, 2006). Evans, Adrian, et al, *Australian Clinical Legal Education: Designing and operating a best practice clinical program in an Australian Law School* (ANU Press, 2017) 103.

109 Interview with Roger West (Frances Gibson,Sydney, 9 December 2016).

110 Interview with Julian Disney (Frances Gibson, Sydney, 25 July 2016).

111 Interview with Julian Disney (Frances Gibson, Sydney, 25 July 2016).

112 Interview with Terry Buddin (Frances Gibson, Sydney, 4 August 2015).

113 Interview with John Basten (Frances Gibson, Sydney, 27 July 2016).

114 Interview with Terry Purcell (Frances Gibson, Sydney, 6 September 2016).

115 Interview with Terry Buddin (Frances Gibson, Sydney, 4 August 2015).

116 George Mansfield built many notable buildings in Sydney including the original Royal Prince Alfred Hospital and History House and the Macquarie Street offices for the Royal Australian Historical Society.

117 For example, the Labor party launched their campaign there in 1904. Premier of NSW McCall, made his policy speech upstairs in 1944.

118 'Tradition', *Rabbitohs* (Web Page, 2015) <https://www.rabbitohs.com.au/news/2018/12/15/the-story-of-south-sydney/>.

119 J Hartley, 'Black, White... and Red? The Redfern All Blacks Rugby League Club in the Early 1960s' (2002) 83 *Labour History* 149,158.

120 Known as the Bing Crosby of Australia, Johnny Wade was one of the most popular performers to emerge from the local scene.

121 N Shehadie, 'City of Sydney Oral History Program Redfern, Waterloo and Alexandria' *Sydney Oral Histories* (Web Page, 2015) <https://www.sydneyoralhistories.com.au/sir-nicholas-shehadie/.

122 Roger Smith,' Redfern Legal Centre' 1992 *Legal Action* 9. Roger Smith is an expert in domestic and international aspects of legal aid, human rights and access to justice. He writes regularly in the specialist legal press in England

and Wales, with regular op-ed pieces in the Law Society Gazette and the New Law Journal. He edits the newsletter of the International Legal Aid Group (see http://www.ilagnet.org) on international developments in legal aid, and is a Visiting Professor of Law at London South Bank University and an honorary professor at the University of Kent. He is a solicitor and has been director of the Legal Action Group, JUSTICE and West Hampstead Community Law Centre as well as director of policy and legal education at the Law Society, London, and solicitor to the Child Poverty Action Group.

123 Interview with Andrew Haesler (Frances Gibson, Sydney, 7 July 2015).

124 Minutes of the First Meeting of the Redfern Legal Centre Management Committee Meeting 20 March 1977 (From the collection of Robyn Lansdowne).

125 Interview with Andrew Haesler (Frances Gibson, Sydney, 7 July 2015).

126 Interview with Dominic Gibson (Frances Gibson, Sydney, 4 July 2015).

127 Interview with Peter Livesey (Frances Gibson, New South Wales, 5 September 2016).

128 Phil Burgess, *Choices Open for Formation of Legal Aid Clinic*, (10 December 1976) (Copy in possession of Robyn Lansdowne).

129 UNSW Law, *Report of the General Meeting to discuss the setting up of a legal aid clinic held at UNSW Law School* (19–20 November 1976) (Copy in possession of Robyn Lansdowne) 3.

130 Undated Discussion paper (Copy in possession of Robyn Lansdowne).

131 See Australian Securities and Investment Commission, Companies Register, *Redfern Legal Centre Ltd CAN 001 442 039*.

132 Clare Petre, 'Specialisation: The Sydney Push Legal Centres in New South Wales' in David Neal (ed) On *Tap not on Top: Legal Centres in Australia 1972–1982* (Legal Services Bulletin, 1984) 12.

133 Interview with Terry Buddin (Frances Gibson, Sydney, 4 August 2015).

134 Interview with Andrew Haesler (Frances Gibson, Sydney, 7 July 2015).

135 Minutes of the Meeting of the Redfern Legal Centre Management Committee Meeting 10 November 1977, 4. (From the collection of Robyn Lansdowne).

136 Interview with Clare Petre (Frances Gibson, Sydney, 21 May 2013).

137 Interview with Michael Mobbs (Frances Gibson, Sydney, 29 April 2016).

138 Draft letter from Redfern Legal Centre to the Attorney–General, The Hon R.J. Ellicott QC undated (From collection of Robyn Lansdowne).

139 Minutes of the Meeting of the Redfern Legal Centre Management Committee Meeting 29 September 1977 (From the collection of Robyn Lansdowne).

140 Minutes of the First Meeting of the Redfern Legal Centre Management Committee Meeting, 20 March 1977 (Copy in possession of Robyn Lansdowne).

141 Interview with Robyn Lansdowne (Frances Gibson, Melbourne, 6 July 2016).

142 Interview with John Basten (Frances Gibson, Sydney, 27 July 2016).

143 Redfern Legal Centre, *Annual Report* 2016-2017.

144 RLC News RLC News Vol 1 No 1 (October 1977).

145 Interview with Andy Haesler (Frances Gibson, Sydney, 7 July 2015).

146 Interview with David Buchanan (Frances Gibson, Sydney, 20 October 2016).

147 Fr Peter G. Williams Homily for the Funeral Liturgy of Terry Gordon Terry Convocation Newsletter Burgmann College July 1994,5.

148 Rob Brennan, *A Sermon in the cemetery* (8 October 2016) Bobby Dazzler's Blog <https://dazzlerplus.wordpress.com/2012/07/13/a-sermon-in-the-cemetery/>

149 See John Basten and Julian Disney,

# ENDNOTES

'Representation by Special Advocates' (1975–1976) 1 *University of New South Wales Law Journal* 168, 174, advocating for use of trained non-lawyers in social security and criminal matters. Disney also notes '[w]e knew of a law firm in London which used a social worker.' Interview with Julian Disney (Frances Gibson, Sydney, 25 July 2016).
150 Interview with Robyn Lansdowne (Frances Gibson, Melbourne, 6 July 2016).
151 Interview with Debbie Whitmont (Frances Gibson, Sydney, 28 April 2016).
152 Interview with Debbie Whitmont (Frances Gibson, Sydney, 28 April 2016).
153 Interview with Penny Quarry (Frances Gibson, Sydney, September 2016).
154 Interview with Penny Quarry (Frances Gibson, Sydney, September 2016).
155 Interview with Clare Petre (Frances Gibson, Sydney, 21 May 2013).
156 Interview with John Basten (Frances Gibson, Sydney, 27 July 2016).
157 Interview with George Zdenkowski (Frances Gibson, Sydney, 28 October 2017).
158 Interview with Terry Buddin (Frances Gibson, Sydney, 4 August 2015).
159 Interview with Michael Mobbs (Frances Gibson, Sydney, 29 April 2016).
160 Interview with Peter Cashman (Frances Gibson, Sydney, 30 August 2016).
161 Interview with Peter Livesey (Frances Gibson, NSW, 6 May 2016).
162 Interview Garth Symonds (Frances Gibson, New York, 20 September 2016).
163 Email David Buchanan SC to Frances Gibson, 19 October 2016.
164 'The Law Business Under Inspection,' *Sydney Morning Herald*, (Sydney) 9 February 1977, 26.
165 Quotes from Bernie Matthews from *Intractable – Hell has a name Katingal* (Pan Macmillan, 2006) at 227-228.
166 Les Kennedy, 'Final release for Katingal, misguided experiment in extreme jails', *Sydney Morning Herald* (Sydney), 19 May 2004.
167 New South Wales, Royal Commission into NSW Prisons, *Report* (1978), Chapter 8, 153.
168 Letter Bernie Matthews to Frances Gibson 3 October 2016.
169 Bernie Matthews, *Intractable – Hell has a name Katingal* (Pan Macmillan, 2006) at 229.
170 Interview with Garth Symonds (Frances Gibson, New York, 20 September 2016).
171 Interview with Virginia Bell (Frances Gibson, Sydney, December 2016).
172 In late 1970s Janet Walquist and Monica McCrae and Ian McClintock and Daniel Brezniak were trying to set up a poverty practice in Marrickville.
173 Interview with Garth Symonds (Frances Gibson, New York, 20 September 2016).
174 Interview with Anne Healey (Frances Gibson, Sydney,24 July 2016).
175 Interview with Peter Livesey (Frances Gibson, New South Wales, 5 September 2016).
176 Interview with David Buchanan (Frances Gibson, Sydney, 20 October 2016).
177 Interview with Peter Livesey (Frances Gibson, New South Wales, 5 September 2016).
178 Redfern Legal Centre, Management Committee Meeting 23 June 1977. (Copy held in collection of Roby Lansdowne).
179 Redfern Legal Centre, Management Committee Meeting 21 July 1977. (Copy held in collection of Roby Lansdowne).
180 Drew Hutton and Libby Connors, *History of the Australian Environment Movement* (Cambridge University Press 1999) 141.
181 'History', *Sydney Gay and Lesbian Mardi Gras* (Web Page) http://www.mardigras.org.au/history/.
182 Interview with Virginia Bell (Frances Gibson, Sydney, 1 December 2016).
183 David Marr, 'A Night Out at the Cross', *National Times*, Sydney, 2 July 1978.
184 Interview with Peter Livesey (Frances

Gibson, New South Wales, 5 September 2016).
185 Interview with Chris Ronalds (Frances Gibson, Bawley Point, 24 January 2016).
186 Interview Chris Ronalds (Bawley Point, 24 January 2016).
187 *RLC News* (Redfern Legal Centre, 1980) 4.
188 Interview with Peter Livesey (Frances Gibson, New South Wales, 5 September 2016).
189 Interview with Bill Dickens (Frances Gibson, Dubbo, 8 February 2017). John Kerr, *The Hit Men* (Penguin 2010) at 63.
190 Redfone 8 September 1981,4.
191 MacPherson v R [1981] HCA 46
192 Interview with Peter Stapleton (Frances Gibson, Sydney, 20 July 2016).
193 Redfern Legal Centre, Minutes of Management Committee meeting 2 February 1978, 2 (Copy held in collection of Roby Lansdowne).
194 Interview with Gerard Craddock (Frances Gibson, 1 May 2013).
195 Interview with Peter Stapleton (Frances Gibson, Sydney, 20 July 2016).
196 Interview with Peter Stapleton (Frances Gibson, Sydney, 20 July 2016).
197 Interview with Paul Farrugia (Frances Gibson, Sydney, 27 April 2016).
198 Interview with Paul Farrugia (Frances Gibson, Sydney, 27 April 2016).
199 Interview with Paul Farrugia (Frances Gibson, Sydney, 27 April 2016).
200 Interview with Paul Farrugia (Frances Gibson, Sydney, 27 April 2016).
201 Interview with Roger West (Frances Gibson, Sydney, 9 December 2016).
202 Interview with Simon Rice (Frances Gibson, Canberra, 20 May 2013)
203 Garth was working as a more or less full=time volunteer at the Centre from 1978-1979– but was paid for a few months from April 1978. Redfern Legal Centre, Minutes of Management Committee meeting 13 April 1978, 3. (Copy held in collection of Robyn Lansdowne).
204 Interview with Garth Symonds (Frances Gibson, New York, 20 September 2016).
205 Interview with Garth Symonds (Frances Gibson, New York, 20 September 2016)
206 Interview with Garth Symonds (Frances Gibson, New York, 20 September 2016).
207 Interview with Peter Stapleton (Frances Gibson, Sydney, 20 July 2016).
208 Interview with Garth Symonds (Frances Gibson, New York, 20 September 2016).
209 Interview with Debbie Whitmont (Frances Gibson, Sydney, 28 April 2016).
210 Interview with Judith Kirkwood (Frances Gibson, Sydney, 5 December 2016).
211 Interview with Judith Kirkwood (Frances Gibson, Sydney, 5 December 2016).
212 Interview with Terry Buddin (Frances Gibson, Sydney, 4 August 2015).
213 Interview with Judith Kirkwood (Frances Gibson, Sydney, 5 December 2016).
214 Interview with Judith Kirkwood (Frances Gibson, Sydney, 5 December 2016).
215 John Kirkwood, *Social Security Law and Policy*, (Law Book Company, 1986). In a review of this book (Gillian Moon, 'Reviews', (1986) 11 (4) *Legal Service Bulletin*, 188-189) wrote "In 1985, the Welfare Rights Centre (Sydney) sought access under the *Freedom of Information Act* to copies of Social Security Appeals Tribunal recommendations which were, in practice, being used by the Department of Social Security as 'precedents'. When the huge file of FOI papers arrived, WRC was intrigued to realise that most of the 'precedents' were cases which had come before John Kirkwood in the SSAT. His recommendations had been referred to DSS in Canberra, where concerted efforts had been made by the Department to find fault with his reasoning and recommendations, but to no avail. His arguments were too compelling, and his cases became 'precedents'.
216 Redfern Legal Centre, *1977-1987 Redfern Legal Centre Tenth Year Report* (December 1987). For further information about

# ENDNOTES

John Kirkwood see Terry Buddin, 'In Memoriam' and John Basten, 'John Kirkwood and legal Centres', 1986 11(4) *Legal Service Bulletin*, August, 187-189.

217 Interview with Roger West (Frances Gibson, Sydney, 9 December 2016).
218 Redfern Legal Centre, Minutes of Management Committee meeting 13 April 1978. (Copy held in collection of Roby Lansdowne).
219 Interview with Clare Petre (Frances Gibson, Sydney, 21 May 2013).
220 Interview with Debbie Whitmont (Frances Gibson, Sydney, 28 April 2016).
221 Interview with Virginia Bell (Frances Gibson, Sydney, 1 December 2016).
222 Interview with Simon Rice (Frances Gibson, Canberra, 20 May 2013).
223 Interview with Gerard Craddock (Frances Gibson, 1 May 2013).
224 Interview with Gerard Craddock (Frances Gibson, 1 May 2013).
225 Interview with Debbie Whitmont (Frances Gibson, Sydney, 28 April 2016).
226 For more on Roger the Shoeman see 'Old Shops', *Sydney Morning Herald* (online, 2014) < https://www.smh.com.au/interactive/2014/OldShops/roger-shoe-repairs.html >.
227 See attacks on the Australian Legal Aid Office described in Mary Anne Noone and Stephen Tomsen, *Lawyers in Conflict* (Federation Press, 2006) 75–95; Don Fleming and Francis Regan, 'Re-visiting the Origins, Rise and Demise of the Australian Legal Aid Office' (2006) 13(1) *International Journal of the Legal Profession* 69, 87; Kevin Bell, 'Politics of Reforming the Legal Profession in Australia: A Case Study of the Western Region Community Legal Centre' (1985) 7 *Law and Policy* 143.
228 Interview with Robyn Lansdowne (Frances Gibson, Melbourne, 6 July 2016).
229 Memorandum Management Committee Redfern Legal Centre (2 April 1977) (Copy in possession of Robyn Lansdowne).
230 Various authors' Legal Centre Practice Problems – November 1983 (Confidential document held in collection Robyn Lansdowne).
231 *Dunlop v Lawton & Ors* 9 November 1977
232 Robyn Lansdowne, Note of telephone call to Don Harley 22 February 1976. (Copy held by Robyn Lansdowne) and Minutes of Meeting of the Management Committee of Redfern Legal Centre (24 March 1977) (Copy in possession of Robyn Lansdowne). Various authors' Legal Centre Practice Problems – November 1983 (Confidential document held in collection Robyn Lansdowne) 33.
233 RLC News (1977, Vol 1, 3 p. 4)
234 Minutes of the Meeting of the Redfern Legal Centre Management Committee Meeting 10 November 1977, 2.(From the collection of Robyn Lansdowne).
235 Kevin Bell and John Dixon 'Lawyers: Making the Industry More Flexible' (1981) 6 *Legal Services Bulletin* 241.
236 Kevin Bell and John Dixon 'Lawyers: Making the Industry More Flexible' (1981) 6 *Legal Services Bulletin* 241.
237 John Basten, *Community Control of Community Legal Centres*, undated (Copy in possession of State Library of New South Wales) 6.
238 Dilina's was a Italian restaurant upstairs above the shops in Redfern Street Redfern. (Clare Petre email to Frances Gibson 2 November 2015).
239 John Basten, Regina Graycar, David Neal 'Legal Centres in Australia' *UNSW Law Journal* 163, 172.
240 Interview with George Zdenkowski (Frances Gibson, Sydney, 28 October 2017).
241 Interview with Virginia Bell (Frances Gibson, Sydney, 1 December 2016).
242 Interview with Paul Farrugia (Frances Gibson, Sydney, 27 April 2016).
243 Interview with Debbie Whitmont (Frances Gibson, Sydney, 28 April 2016).

244 *RLC News* (Redfern Legal Centre, August 1984).
245 See for instance Kevin Bell, 'Politics of Reforming the Legal Profession in Australia: A Case Study of the Western Region Community Legal Centre' 7 *Law and Policy* 143.
246 SMH at page 6
247 *Daily Telegraph* 2 March 1898, 5.
248 Andy Haesler elaborates: 'Kevin Fitzpatrick SM – who could be a bit of a prick – I can't recall if he convicted John Terry or let him go but best avoided … John was out on the town near Taylor Square. He saw an Aboriginal woman being bundled into a police van – he intervened. He was thrown in too. When he asked why – he was told "farting in church. "He was charged with offensive language /behaviour. Etc. many of the details are lost in time.' Email to Frances Gibson (Sydney, 31 July 2021).
249 Email Andy Haesler to Frances Gibson ((9 March 2021).
250 See NSW Bar Association, Sue Schreiner < https://nswbar.asn.au/the-bar-association/bar-history/pioneering-women#/view/10_sue_schreiner>.
251 Interview with Sue Schreiner (Frances Gibson, Canberra,7 March 2017)
252 Email Andy Haesler to Frances Gibson 10 March 20201.
253 Email Jane Goddard to Frances Gibson 11 March 2021
254 Email from Angus Webb To Andy Haesler 9 March 2021.
255 Emails, Jane Goddard and Ben Slade to Frances Gibson (9 March 2021).
256 Gerard Noonan, (9 December 2004) *Sydney Morning Herald*, https://www.smh.com.au/politics/nsw/your-courthouse-will-just-have-to-go-minister-20041209-gdka4d.html..
257 Order under the *Local Courts Act* 1982 2005 No 368
258 Minutes of the First Meeting of the Redfern Legal Centre Management Committee Meeting 20 March 1977 (From the collection of Robyn Lansdowne).
259 Redfern Legal Centre, Minutes of Management Committee meeting 6 April 1977, 2 (Copy held in collection of Roby Lansdowne).
260 Interview with Terry Buddin (Frances Gibson, Sydney, 4 August 2015).
261 Interview with Terry Buddin (Frances Gibson, Sydney, 4 August 2015).
262 Interview with John Basten (Frances Gibson, Sydney, 27 July 2016).
263 Interview with Roger West (Frances Gibson, Sydney, 9 December 2016).
264 Interview with Roger West (Frances Gibson, Sydney, 9 December 2016).
265 Interview with Robyn Lansdowne (Frances Gibson, Melbourne, 6 July 2016).
266 Interview with Roger West (Frances Gibson, Sydney, 9 December 2016).
267 Interview with Simon Rice (Frances Gibson, Canberra, 20 May 2013)
268 Interview with Roger West S(Frances Gibson, ydney, 9 December 2016).
269 Cathy Kerr was a volunteer at RLC, later worked with Legal Aid in the NT, Principal Lawyers Northern Rivers CLC and Senior Project Officer at Office of Environment and Heritage (NSW).
270 Interview with Cathy Kerr (Frances Gibson, Bendigo, 2 September 2016).
271 See for instance Warren Feek, *Management Committees: Practising Community Control* (National Youth Bureau, 1982); Richard M Hessler and Carolyn Sue Beavert, 'Citizen Participation in Neighborhood Health Centers for the Poor: The Politics of Reform Organizational Change, 1965–77' (1982) 41(3) *Human Organization* 245.
272 Norman I Fainstein and Susan S Fainstein, 'The Future of Community Control' (1976) 70(3) *The American Political Science Review* 905.
273 Jerome Carlin, 'Store Front Lawyers in San Francisco' (1970) 7(6) *Trans-action* 66.
274 See John Chesterman, *Law and the New*

*Left: A History of The Fitzroy Legal Service 1972–1994*, (PhD Thesis, University of Melbourne, 1995) 115-121.
275 John Basten, *Community Control of Community Legal Centres*, undated (Copy in possession of State Library of New South Wales) 15.
276 Robyn Lansdowne, *Community Involvement in Redfern Legal Centre* (November 1977) (Copy in possession of Robyn Lansdowne) 7.
277 See Memo to Centre meeting 5 July 1979 from Roger West and John Kirkwood containing proposals for the establishment of a 3-tier structure for the Centre to include more involvement from the community (probably welfare workers, students and solicitors) and Centre restructure proposals in 1988 and 2000 and 2008 discussed later in this chapter.
278 Kirsty Macmillan, 'Community Legal Centres: Second National Conference' (1980) 5(2) *Legal Services Bulletin* 77.
279 John Basten and Robyn Lansdowne, 'Community Legal Centres: Who's in Charge? (1980) 5(2) *Legal Services Bulletin* 56.
280 Interview with Roger West (Frances Gibson, Sydney, 9 December 2016).
281 See discussion on community participation in Ronald Sackville, Commission of Inquiry into Poverty, *Law and Poverty in Australia* (Australian Government Publishing Service, 1975) 49, noting difficulties involved in the approach.
282 See John Basten and Robyn Lansdowne, 'Community Legal Centres: Who's in Charge? (1980) 5(2) *Legal Services Bulletin* 57.
283 John Basten, Regina Graycar and David Neal, 'Legal Centres in Australia' (1983) 6(2) *UNSW Law Journal* 163, 173.
284 Mary Anne Noone, 'Mid-Life Crisis: Australian Community Legal Centres' (1997) 22 *Alternative Law Journal* 25.
285 Interview with Andrew Haesler (Frances Gibson, Sydney, 7 July 2015).
286 Interview with Simon Rice (Frances Gibson, Canberra, 28 January 2016)
287 Interview with Gordon Renouf (Frances Gibson, Sydney, 28 January 2016).
288 *RLC News* (Redfern Legal Centre, January/February 1988) 2.
289 Interview with John Basten (Frances Gibson, Sydney, 27 July 2016).
290 Interview with Gordon Renouf (Frances Gibson, Sydney, 28 January 2016)
291 Interview with Sarah Crawford (Frances Gibson, Sydney 3 February 2017).
292 Interview with Steve Bolt (Frances Gibson, 21 February 2017).
293 Interview with Katherine Biber (Frances Gibson, Sydney, (7 September 2016).
294 Interview with Helen Campbell (Frances Gibson, Sydney, 23 November 2016).
295 Welfare Rights Centre see page
296 Interview with Dominic Gibson (Frances Gibson, Sydney, 4 July 2015).
297 Interview with Dominic Gibson (Frances Gibson, Sydney, 4 July 2015). Craddock adds: ' The bit about the interview for the consumer credit job leaves out the reason why I took the 6-pack – I told the panel they should hire Gig Moon. Alexis Hailstones and I had done a joint thesis on setting up a consumer credit legal centre and Gig had asked me to help with her application and we'd worked on her application. She was by far the better candidate and she got the job. From my perspective it wasn't a real interview and I knew the panellists, so why not take some beers?' Gerard Craddock Email to Frances Gibson, 18 July 2021.
298 Spelling luckily corrected by Frances Gibson prior to submission. Interview with Ben Slade (Frances Gibson, Sydney, 8 December 2015).
299 Nan Rogers, solicitor at the Centre was to become Crown Prosecutor in Alice Springs for over twelve years and is currently a Crown Prosecutor in Melbourne.

300 Interview with Ben Slade (Frances Gibson, Sydney, 8 December 2015). This of course was actually Will Stubbs on a mad romantic expedition to see a girlfriend. Will was later to become well known Aboriginal Arts curator.
301 Interview with Slade or D Gibson?
302 Interview with Andrew Haesler (Frances Gibson, Sydney, 7 July 2015).
303 Interview with Mick Hillman (Frances Gibson, Sydney, 16 February 2017).
304 Interview with Mick Hillman (Frances Gibson, Sydney, 16 February 2017).
305 Interview with Mick Hillman (Frances Gibson, Sydney, 16 February 2017).
306 Interview with Mick Hillman (Frances Gibson, Sydney, 16 February 2017).
307 Interview with Mick Hillman (Frances Gibson, Sydney, 16 February 2017).
308 Interview with Mick Hillman (Frances Gibson, Sydney, 16 February 2017).
309 Interview with Mick Hillman (Frances Gibson, Sydney, 16 February 2017).
310 Interview with Mary Perkins, (Frances Gibson, Sydney, 22 July 2016).
311
312 Frank Bongiorno, *The Eighties* (Black Inc, 2016) 202–203.
313 Julie Hamblin, Nick Crofts and Jamie Gardiner, 'Health Workers, AIDS and Patients' Rights' 17 *Alternative Law Journal* 15 (1992) 18.
314 One case included *Spooner, Richard (Tenant) v NSW Department of Housing (Landlord)* [1992] NSWRT 32 (11 March 1992), an application for compensation brought by the deceased tenant against the landlord based on the alleged failure by the landlord to provide adequate security for premises let to the tenant pursuant to a residential tenancy agreement, dated 14 June 1991.
315 David Buchanan and John Godwin, 'AIDS: The Legal Epidemic' (1988) 13(3) *Legal Service Bulletin* 111, 112.
316 Intellectual Disability Rights Service, *AIDS and Intellectual Disability* (IDRS, 1992).
317 Email from Alexis Goodstone, to Yasmin Alali 25 October 2021.
318 Interview with Robyn Lansdowne(Frances Gibson,
319 Interview with Debbie Whitmont (Frances Gibson, Sydney, 28 April 2016).
320 Interview with Gerard Craddock (Frances Gibson, Sydney, 1 May 2013).
321 Interview with Helen Campbell (Frances Gibson, Sydney, 23 November 2016).
322 Interview with Katherine Biber (Frances Gibson, Sydney, (7 September 2016).
323 Interview with Sarah Crawford (Frances Gibson, Sydney 3 February 2017).
324 Interview with Tamara Sims (Yasmin Alali, Sydney, 7 September 2021).
325 Carrie Menkel-Meadow, 'Nonprofessional Advocacy: The Paralegalization of Legal Services for the Poor' (1985) 19 *Clearinghouse Review* 403, 405.
326 Mark A Cohen, 'Clients Need Legal Services but Not Necessarily Lawyers' *Forbes* (Web Page, 19 February 2019) <https://www.forbes.com/sites/markcohen1/2019/02/19/clients-need-legal-services-but-not-necessarily-lawyers/#4589b58e702d>; Lisa Trabucco, 'Lawyers' Monopoly? Think Again: The Reality of Non-Lawyer Legal Service Provision in Canada' (2018) 96(3) *Canadian Bar Review* 460. Frank Regan and Julia Vernon, *Improving Access to Justice, the Future of Paralegal Professionals: Proceedings of a Conference Held 19–20 February 1990* (Australian Institute of Criminology Canberra, 1991); MA Noone, 'Paralegals and Legal Aid Organisations' (1988) 4 *Journal of Law and Social Policy* 146.
327 See for instance Law Council of Australia, 'Access to Justice: Let's Get Back to the Issues: Summary of Law Council of Australia's Response to Australia Access to Justice Advisory Committee' (1994) 29(8) *Australian Lawyer* 13, 15.
328 Carrie Menkel-Meadow, 'Nonprofes-

sional Advocacy: The Paralegalization of Legal Services for the Poor' (1985) 19 *Clearinghouse Review* 403, 404.

329 See John Hollister Stein, *Paralegals: A Resource for Public Defenders and Correctional Services* (U.S. Department of Justice, 1976); Michael Zander, 'Legal Aid Proposal' *The Guardian* (London, 1976); B Abel-Smith, M Zander and R Brooke, *Legal Problems and the Citizen* 80–82 (Heinemann, 1973).

330 Arthur Hayes, 'Activists Want to Pry Open Lawyers World' *Wall Street Journal* (New York, 1990); See *HALT* Facebook site (Web Page) <https://www.facebook.com/HALTdc/>.

331 Susan Armstrong, 'The Future of Legal Aid' in *Access to Law* quoted in Mary Anne Noone, 'Paralegals: A Growth Area in Times of Restraint?' (1988) 13(6) *Legal Service Bulletin* 253.

332 Nielsen, Marianne O, 'Indigenous-Run Legal Services in Australia and Canada: Comparative Developmental Issues' (2006) 16(3) *International Criminal Justice Review* 157,164.

333 Carrie Menkel-Meadow, 'Nonprofessional Advocacy: The Paralegalization of Legal Services for the Poor' (1985) 19 *Clearinghouse Review* 403, 405.

334 Mary Anne Noone, 'Paralegals: In the Community's Interest?' in Julia Vernon and Francis Regan *Improving Access to Justice* (Australian Institute of Criminology, 1991) 31.

335 See for instance discussion in Legal Aid and Family Services, *Paralegals and Legal Aid* (Attorney–General's Department, 1994).

336 Interview with Bill Dickens (Frances Gibson, Dubbo)

337 Interview with Dominic Gibson (Sydney, 4 July 2015).

338 Interview with Helen Campbell (Frances Gibson, Sydney, 23 November 2016).

339 Interview with Helen Campbell (Frances Gibson, Sydney, 23 November 2016).

340 Interview with Katherine Biber (Frances Gibson, Sydney, (7 September 2016).

341 Interview with Katherine Biber (Frances Gibson, Sydney, (7 September 2016).

342 Interview with Katherine Biber (Frances Gibson, Sydney, (7 September 2016).

343 Interview with Katherine Biber (Frances Gibson, Sydney, (7 September 2016).

344 Interview with Pat McDonough (Frances Gibson, 24 January 2016).

345 Interview with Pat McDonough (Frances Gibson, 24 January 2016).

346 Interview with Steve Bolt (Frances Gibson, 21 February 2017).

347 Interview with Cathy Kerr (Frances Gibson, Bendigo, 2 September 2016).

348 Interview with Sarah Crawford (Frances Gibson, Sydney 3 February 2017).

349 Interview with Sarah Crawford (Frances Gibson, Sydney 3 February 2017).

350 Interview with Sarah Crawford (Frances Gibson, Sydney 3 February 2017).

351 Interview with Irene Baghoomians, (Frances Gibson, Sydney 6 September 2016).

352 Interview with Tamara Sims, (Yasmin Alali.Sydney, 7 September 2021).

353 Interview with Amy Munro (Cherilyn Herbert, Sydney, October 2021).

354 Interview with Hilary Chesworth (Frances Gibson, Sydney, 9 July 2016).

355 Interview with Peter Stapleton (Frances Gibson, Sydney, 20 July 2016).

356 Interview with Elizabeth Morley (Frances Gibson, Sydney, 26 July 2016). Sydney, 21 July 2016).

357 Garth Symonds, Background paper to Policy Meeting, 3 February 1980. (Copy held in collection of Robyn Lansdowne).

358 Interview with Paul Farrugia (Frances Gibson, Sydney, 27 April 2016).

359 Redfern Legal Centre, *Annual Report* 1989–1990.

360 Jeff Giddings and Mary Anne Noone, 'Australian Community Legal Centres Move into the Twenty-First Century' (2010) 11(3) *International Journal of the*

*Legal Profession* 279.
361 Redfern Legal Centre *Annual Report 2014–2015*.
362 Interview with Jo Shulman (Frances Gibson, Sydney, 19 July 2016).
363 Michael Hogan, 'Towards A New South Wales Coronial System for the Nineties' (1991) 2(3) *Current Issues in Criminal Justice* 75-79.
364 Email from Andy Haesler to Frances Gibson (16 September 2019).
365 Email from Andy Haesler to Frances Gibson (16 September 2019).
366 See Vivian Altman, 'The Lanfranchi Affair: An Unsatisfactory Inquest' (1983) 8 Legal Service Bulletin 64.
367 Gregory Charles Glass, *Coroner's Inquest Finding into the Death of Sallie-Anne Huckstepp* [State Coroner NSW, 1991). See also J Dale, J *Huckstepp: A Dangerous Life*, (Allen & Unwin, Australia, 2004).
368 Parliamentary Joint Committee on the National Crime Authority, Parliament of Australia, *Witness Protection* (1988) 13.
369 Kevin Waller, State Coroner for NSW from 1988–1992 said of this matter, 'the media appeared to have gone berserk. I have never in my life seen a similar reaction to any such event' in Kevin Waller, *Suddenly Dead* (Pan McMillan, 1994) 18.
370 Geesche Jacobsen, 'Surry Hills Cell Death Triggers Inquiry', *Sydney Morning Herald* (online, 18 June 2011) <https://www.smh.com.au/national/nsw/surry-hills-cell-death-triggers-inquiry-20110617-1g7vu.html>.
371 Magistrate Harriet Grahame, 'Inquest into the Death of Dylan Maher', *Decision of Deputy State Coroner Grahame on 23 November 2015* (Web Page) <http://www.coroners.justice.nsw.gov.au/Pages/findings.aspx#2015findingsandrecommendations>.
372 Don Fleming, 'Australian Legal Aid under the First Howard Government' (2000) 33(2) *University of British Columbia Law Review* 343, 377.

373 'Tenth Year Report 1977–1987', *Redfern Legal Centre* (Web Document, December 1997) 17 <https://rlc.org.au/sites/default/files/attachments/1977-1987%20RLC%2010th%20year%20report.pdf>.
374 Betty Weule, 'The History Of Financial Counselling In Australia', *Financial Counselling Australia* (Web Page) <https://www.dropbox.com/s/h6cscq92bl5mhrp/Betty Weule The History of Financial Counselling in Australia.pdf?dl=0>
375 Interview with Helen Campbell (Frances Gibson, Sydney, 23 November 2016).
376 Interview with Penny Quarry (Frances Gibson, Sydney, September 2016).
377 'Tenth Year Report 1977–1987', *Redfern Legal Centre* (Web Document, December 1997) 17 <https://rlc.org.au/sites/default/files/attachments/1977-1987%20RLC%2010th%20year%20report.pdf>.
378 'Tenth Year Report 1977–1987', *Redfern Legal Centre* (Web Document, December 1997) 17 <https://rlc.org.au/sites/default/files/attachments/1977-1987%20RLC%2010th%20year%20report.pdf>.
379 Interview with Christian Mikula ((Frances Gibson, Canberra, 20 September 2018).
380 Australian Financial Counselling and Credit Reform Association, *Need or Greed? A Report on Consumer Credit Insurance* (Australian Financial Counselling and Credit Reform Association, 1987).
381 Karen Lavell, Redfern Legal Centre and Consumer Credit Legal Centre, *Debt Survival Guide* (Redfern Legal Centre Publishing, 1987).
382 Gordon Renouf, *Financial Over Commitment: The Consumer View* (Redfern Legal Centre, 1988).
383 Carolyn Huntsman and Redfern Legal Centre, *More More More: Lending Practices and Overcommitment* (Redfern Legal Centre, 1988).
384 New South Wales, *Parliamentary Debates*, Legislative Council, 23 November 1987,

816841 (The Hon.Virginia J Chadwick).
385 Margaret Roberts and Denis Nelthorpe, 'The Collective King Hit' (1985) 10 *Legal Service Bulletin* 26.
386 A bill of sale serves as legal evidence that full consideration has been provided in a transaction and that the seller has transferred the rights to the assets detailed in the bill of sale to the buyer.
387 'Congratulations Betty Weule, AM', *Financial Counselling Australia* (Web Page, 13 June 2016) <https://www.financial-counsellingaustralia.org.au/congratulations-betty-weule-am/>.
388 This followed the Walter Pugh case run by the Public Interest Advocacy Centre, in which a Sydney money lender charging 144.4 per cent interest on small loans averaging about $450 each, was ordered to forgo 80 per cent of interest on the debts owed to it. The NSW Commercial Tribunal reduced the combined interest bill owed to Walter Pugh Pty Ltd by $800,000 by ordering that the interest rate be reduced to 29 per cent: Interview with Ben Slade (Frances Gibson, Sydney, 8 December 2015).
389 *State Bank of New South Wales v Various Debtors* [1995] ASC 55–207 (Commercial Tribunal of NSW).
390 Interview with Ben Slade (Frances Gibson, Sydney, 8 December 2015).
391 Simon Cleary works as a barrister in Queensland and is also a novelist of some repute. See UQP, Simon Cleary,https://www.uqp.com.au/authors/simon-cleary.
392 Interview with Simon Cleary (Frances Gibson, Brisbane,9 March 2017).
393 Interview with Simon Cleary (Frances Gibson, Brisbane,9 March 2017).
394 Interview with Simon Cleary (Frances Gibson, Brisbane,9 March 2017).
395 Interview with David Vaile (Frances Gibson, Sydney, 18 July 2016).
396 Redfern Legal Centre *Annual Report* 1992/1993. Timeshares are a form of ownership or right to use a particular property or properties, such as a holiday villa, apartment or cabin for a set period of time. They are a long-term commitment and can be difficult to sell: Australian Securities Investments Commission, 'Timeshares', *Moneysmart* (Web Page) <https://www.moneysmart.gov.au/investing/property/timeshares>.
397 *Afa And Others* v *Garendon Investments Pty Ltd (Receiver and Manager Appointed) And Others* (1995) 37 NSWLR 221, *Afa v Garendon Investments Pty Ltd* (1994) ASC 56–280.
398 Application for leave to appeal to High Court refused: *Garendon Investments Pty Ltd & Annor v Serina Sainama Afa & Ors* [1995] HCA 297.
399 *Bass v Permanent Trustee Co Ltd* [1999] HCA 9 (*HomeFund* case)
400 Judith Yates, 'Ownership and Australia's Housing Finance System' (1994) 12(1) *Urban Policy and Research* 27, 33.
401 Judith Yates, 'Home Ownership and Australia's Housing Finance System' (1994) 12(1) *Urban Policy and Research* 27, 33.
402 See Greg Kirk, 'A History of Homefund' (2001) 13 *PIAC Bulletin* 1 (Web Document) https://www.piac.asn.au/wp-content/uploads/PIACBulletin13.pdf; *Bass v Permanent Trustee Co Ltd* [1999] HCA 9.
403 The Centre's archives still hold a photocopy of the cheque for $100,000 from the State Bank as part payment of costs to the Centre. *State Bank of New South Wales v Various Debtors* [1995] ASC 55–207 (Commercial Tribunal of NSW).
404 Interview with Hilary Chesworth.
405 Redfern Legal Centre Annual Report 2019/2020.
406 Interview with Laura Bianchi (Bronwyn Dyer, Sydney, 21 October 2021).
407 Frances Gibson, *When the Battles Lost and Won: Legal Aid in Civil Matters in New South Wales 1992–1994 Outline of a Community Legal Centre Campaign* (Kingsford Legal

Centre, 1997).
408 Jacquelyn Hole, 'Legal Aid Cuts Attacked as Blow to Civil Rights', *Sydney Morning Herald* (Sydney, 21 December 1992) 3; Editorial, 'A Phony Crisis in Legal Aid', *Sydney Morning Herald* (Sydney, 4 January 1993) 8.
409 See Combined Community Legal Centres Group (NSW) *NSW Community Legal Centres Directory* (NSW CLC State Office).
410 Just for the sake of clarity the solicitor selected was the author of this work.
411 For full details of the campaign and the way it was run see Frances Gibson, *When the Battles Lost and Won: Legal Aid in Civil Matters in New South Wales 1992–1994 Outline of a community legal Centre campaign* (Kingsford Legal Centre, 1997).
412 Sigrid Kirk, 'Legal Aid Restored for Most Cases', *Sydney Morning Herald* (Sydney, 14 October 1993) 5.
413 New South Wales, *Parliamentary Debates*, Legislative Council, 12 April 1994, (The Hon. Ron Dyer).
414 Mary Anne Noone, 'Mid-Life Crisis: Australian Community Legal Centres' (1997) 22 *Alternative Law Journal* 25, 28. See *Legal Aid Commission Act 1979* (NSW) s 14 which requires that the Board of the Commission include 'one is to be a person who, in the opinion of the Minister, represents such bodies, whether incorporated or unincorporated, as provide community legal services.'
415 Interview with David Vaile (Frances Gibson, Sydney, 18 July 2016).
416 Interview with David Vaile (Frances Gibson, Sydney, 18 July 2016).
417 'Origins and Nature of the Internet in Australia' *Roger Clarke* (Web Page, 29 January 2004) <http://www.rogerclarke.com/II/OzI04.html>.
418 Interview with David Vaile (Frances Gibson, Sydney, 18 July 2016).
419 Interview with Katherine Biber (Frances Gibson, Sydney, (7 September 2016).
420 Interview with David Vaile (Frances Gibson, Sydney, 26 July 2016).Sydney, November 2016).
421 Letter from Vanessa Chan SRC to Management Committee RLC, 6 August 1990 (Letter held at Redfern Legal Centre archives).
422 Interview with Hilary Chesworth (Frances Gibson, Sydney, 9 July 2016).
423 Email Sean Simson to Frances Gibson 21 July 2021
424 Email Sean Simson to Frances Gibson 21 July 2021
425 Email Sean Simson to Frances Gibson 21 July 2021
426 MLM was able to be realised thanks to the financial support of Study NSW, City of Sydney and the Fair Work Ombudsman, and the technical skills of ISLS's app development partner, Practera. Macquarie was the first education provider in NSW to subscribe to MLM, enabling its international students to have free access to the app.
427 Email Sean Simson to Frances Gibson 21 July 2021
428 *Tharunka* (Kensington, NSW: 1953–2010) Mon 9 Oct 1978 page 3 'Our Home'
429 *Nicholson v New South Wales Land and Housing Corporation* (unreported, NSW Supreme Court, Badgery-Parker J, 24 December 1991, No 30027 of 1991). Oter cases included *Swain v Residential Tenancies Tribunal of New South Wales* (unreported, NSW Sup Ct, Rolfe J, 22 March 1995, 30034 of 1994)
R v Spooner
430 Interview with Katherine Biber (Frances Gibson, Sydney, (7 September 2016).
431 Interview with Katherine Biber (Frances Gibson, Sydney, (7 September 2016).
432 Interview with Beth Jewell (Frances

# ENDNOTES

Gibson, Sydney, 26 July 2016).Sydney, 26 July 2016).

433 Interview with Beth Jewell (Frances Gibson, Sydney, 26 July 2016). Sydney, 26 July 2016).

434 Interview with Emma Golledge (Frances Gibson, Sydney, 13 February 2017). Emma is now Director of Kingsford legal Centre.

435 See Rentwatchers website archived by the National Library: 'Olympic Games 2000, Sydney: Anti-Olympics Campaigns and Activities' (Web Page, 12 September 2000) <http://pandora.nla.gov.au/nph-wb/20000911130000/http://www.rw.apana.org.au/about.html>. See also http://classic.austlii.edu.au/au/journals/UNSWLawJl/1999/30.pdf and For further information on the Centre's activity in this sphere see Beth Jewell, 'Sydney Housing: One Year After the Olympic Games' (2001) 26(6) *Alternative Law Journal* 299; Hazel Blunden, *The Impacts of the Sydney Olympic Games on Housing Rights*, Centre on Housing Rights and Evictions, Geneva, Switzerland (Web Document, 2007) <www.ruig-gian.org/ressources/Sydney_background_paper.pdf>.

436 Interview with Polly Porteous (Frances Gibson, Sydney, 16 February 2017).

437 Interview with Beth Jewell (Frances Gibson, Sydney, 26 July 2016).Sydney, 26 July 2016).

438 Interview with Beth Jewell (Frances Gibson, Sydney, 26 July 2016).Sydney, 26 July 2016).

439 Interview with Beth Jewell (Frances Gibson, Sydney, 26 July 2016).Sydney, 26 July 2016).

440 Interview with Jacqui Swinburne (Frances Gibson, Sydney, 5 July 2016).

441 Interview with Jacqui Swinburne (Frances Gibson, Sydney, 5 July 2016).

442 New South Wales, *Parliamentary Debates*, Legislative Council, 22 October 1998, 8840 (The Hon. JW Shaw).

443 Redfern Legal Centre < https://sharehousing.org/>.

444 Redfern Legal Centre, *Drug Law Reform Project Harm Reduction Model of Controlled Availability*, (Redfern Legal Centre, 1995).

445 Redfern Legal Centre, *Beyond Prohibition* (Redfern Legal Centre, 1996).

446 Interview with Katherine Biber

447 Email Steve Bolt to Frances Gibson, 12 May 2017.

448 Steve Bolt, *Rough Deal: Your Guide to Drug Laws*, (Redfern Legal Centre Publishing, 1998).

449 See New South Wales, *Parliamentary Debates*, Legislative Council, 19 November 1997, 2067 (The Hon. RS Jones).

450 Wodak, Alex and Baume, Peter, 'The New South Wales Drug Summit' (1999) 171(1) *Medical journal of Australia* 12.

451 Melanie Walker and Scott Davis, ' A tribute to Tim Moore, and his wide-ranging contributions to community health, Crikey 6 February 2015 https://blogs.crikey.com.au/croakey/2015/02/06/a-tribute-to-tim-moore-and-his-wide-ranging-contributions-to-community-health/.

452 Interview with Polly Porteous (Frances Gibson, Sydney, 16 February 2017).

453 Gary Christian, 'Blinded by the Dominant Ideology', *Quadrant Online* (Web Document, 1 November 2010) <https://quadrant.org.au/magazine/2010/11/blinded-by-the-dominant-ideology/>.

454 See urgent motion proposed by Alison Megarrity, ALP member for Menai in 2001, 'That this House expresses its opposition to calls by the Redfern Legal Centre to abandon the use of sniffer dogs for drug detection and other police activities in New South Wales.' The motion was successful, see New South Wales, *Parliamentary Debates*, Legislative Assembly, 23 October 2001,17744 (The Hon. A Megarrity).

455 Samantha Lee, Rise in strip searches in NSW damaging the credibility of police,

*Sydney Morning Herald*, https://www.smh.com.au/national/nsw/rise-in-strip-searches-in-nsw-damaging-the-credibility-of-police-20190213-p50xew.html.

456 Michael McGowan, NSW police watchdog finds common strip-search practices may not be legal, *The Guardian*, https://www.theguardian.com/australia-news/2020/feb/13/nsw-police-watchdog-finds-common-strip-search-practices-may-not-be-legal

457 Kate Allman, 'Report Shows 20-Fold Increase in NSW Police Strip Searches', *LSJ Online* (Web Page, 2019) <https://lsj.com.au/articles/damning-report-shows-20-fold-increase-in-nsw-police-strip-searches/>.

458 RLC Annual Report, 2019-2020 33.

459 Criminal Defence Lawyers Australia, 'Law on Police Using Body Worn Cameras in NSW' 24 January 2021 < https://www.lexology.com/library/detail.aspx?g=faefcc23-9b2b-4e34-bcf1-f05393e86b17>.

460 Hayley Gleeson, ABC News 'No One Will Believe You' 25 October 2020 < https://www.abc.net.au/news/2020-10-25/kate-was-charged-with-assaulting-her-police-officer-partner/12758060?nw=0>

461 Interview with Helen Campbell

462 Interview with Beth Jewell (Frances Gibson, Sydney, 26 July 2016).

463 Interview with Hilary Chesworth (Frances Gibson, Sydney, 9 July 2016).

464 Interview with Hilary Chesworth (Frances Gibson, Sydney, 9 July 2016).

465 Interview with Helen Campbell (Frances Gibson, Sydney, 23 November 2016).

466 Interview with Elizabeth Morley (Frances Gibson, Sydney, 21 July 2016).

467 Interview with Beth Jewell (Frances Gibson, Sydney, 26 July 2016).

468 Interview with Elizabeth Morley (Frances Gibson, Sydney, 26 July 2016).Sydney, 21 July 2016).

469 Interview with Elizabeth Morley (Frances Gibson, Sydney, 26 July 2016).Sydney, 21 July 2016).

470 Interview with Elizabeth Morley (Sydney, 21 July 2016).

471 Interview with Helen Campbell (Sydney, 23 November 2016).

472 Interview with Jo Shulman ( Frances Gibson, Sydney, September2016)

473 Interview with Jo Shulman (Frances Gibson, Sydney, 19 July 2016).

474 Interview with Jo Shulman (Frances Gibson, Sydney, 19 July 2016).

475 Mary Anne Noone, 'Imperatives for Community Legal Centres' (1992) 17 *Alternative Law Journal* 120, 123.

476 Interview with Sophie Farrell (Frances Gibson, Sydney 27 September 2016).

477 Interview with Sophie Farrell (Frances Gibson, Sydney 27 September 2016).

478 Interview with Sophie Farrell (Frances Gibson, Sydney 27 September 2016).

479 Interview with Sophie Farrell (Frances Gibson, Sydney 27 September 2016).

480 Interview with Sophie Farrell (Frances Gibson, Sydney 27 September 2016).

481 Interview with Andrew Haesler (Frances Gibson, Sydney, 7 July 2015).

482 Interview with Emma Golledge (Frances Gibson, Sydney, 13 February 2017).

483 Interview with Hilary Chesworth (Frances Gibson, Sydney, 9 July 2016).

484 Mary Anne Noone, 'Mid-Life Crisis: Australian Community Legal Centres' (1997) 22 *Alternative Law Journal* 25, 28.

485 Jeff Giddings and Mary Anne Noone, Australian Community Legal Centres Move into the Twenty-First Century' (2010) 11(3) *International Journal of the Legal Profession* 257, 276.

486 Jeff Giddings and Mary Anne Noone, Australian Community Legal Centres Move into the Twenty-First Century' (2010) 11(3) *International Journal of the Legal Profession* 257, 276.

487 Interview with Elizabeth Morley (Sydney, 21 July 2016).

488 Interview with Helen Campbell (Frances

# ENDNOTES

Gibson, Sydney, 23 November 2016).

489 Sarah Maddison, Richard Denniss and Clive Hamilton, *Silencing Dissent: Non-government Organisations and Australian Democracy* (Australia Institute, 2004).

490 Sandra Grey and Charles Sedgwick, 'The Contract State and Constrained Democracy the Community and Voluntary Sector under Threat '(2013) 9(3) *Policy Quarterly* 3, 8.

491 Interview with Jacqui Swinburne (Frances Gibson, Sydney, 5 July 2016). See also on restrictions to EDO's advocacy work detailed in Jeff Giddings and Mary Anne Noone, 'Australian Community Legal Centres Move into the Twenty-First Century' (2010) 11(3) *International Journal of the Legal Profession* 257, 269.

492 Interview with Jacqui Swinburne (Frances Gibson, Sydney, 5 July 2016).

493 Interview with Polly Porteous (Frances Gibson, Sydney, 16 February 2017).

494 Interview with Monique Hitter (Frances Gibson, Sydney, 7 February 2017).

495 Interview with Joanna Shulman (Frances Gibson, Sydney, 9 September 2021).

496 Note that local community legal education programs for community are still free.

497 Email from Hilary Chesworth to Frances Gibson, 22 September 2021.

498 Interview with Amy Munro (Cherilyn Herbert, Sydney October 2010).

499 Interview with Joanna Shulman (Frances Gibson, Sydney, 9 September 2021).

500 Interview with Joanna Shulman (Frances Gibson, Sydney, 9 September 2021). A commentator from a previous era at the Centre who shall remain nameless was somewhat aghast at this news. 'Such a load of total shit. Just sue the fuckers and get costs and stop pandering to the top end of town' were the exact words.

501 Simon Rice, 'Are CLCs Finished' (2012) 37 *Alternative Law Journal* 17.

502 Interview with Jacqui Swinburne (Frances Gibson, Sydney, 5 July 2016).

503 Interview with Joanna Shulman (Frances Gibson, 9 September 2021).

504 Interview with Zelie Appel (Bronwyn Dyer, 21 September 2021).

505 No relation to Guthrie.

506 RLC's volunteer coordinator. Interview with Finn O'Keefe, (Yasmin Alali, 29 October 2021).

507 Interview with Joanna Shulman (Frances Gibson, 9 September 2021).

508 Interview with Tamara Sims, (Yasmin Alali.Sydney, 7 September 2021).

509 Natassia Chrysanthos, 'Head of Sydney Law School condemns 'hard' policing of student protests' Sydney Morning Herald, 15 October 2020, <https://www.smh.com.au/national/nsw/head-of-sydney-law-school-condemns-hard-policing-of-student-protests-20201015-p565jc.html>

510 Sarah Keoghan, *Sydney Morning Herald*, 'COVID-19 fines in NSW alone totalled more than $1 million, 15 June 2020 < https://www.smh.com.au/national/nsw/covid-19-fines-in-nsw-alone-totalled-more-than-1-million-20200614-p552hf.html>.

511 Interview with Jacqui Swinburne (Frances Gibson, Sydney, 5 July 2016).

512 Interview with Amy Munro (Cherilyn Herbert, Sydney, October 2021).

513 Interview with Laura Bianchi (Bronwyn Dyer, Sydney, 28 October 2021).

514 Exact figures are difficult to obtain due to changes in statistical record keeping over the years. See Annual Reports, Redfern Legal Centre

515 New South Wales, *Parliamentary Debates*, Legislative Assembly, 30 March 2017, 51 (Alex Greenwich).

516 Interview with Peter Stapleton (Frances Gibson, Sydney, 20 July 2016).

517 Interview with Laura Bianchi (Bronwyn Dyer,Sydney, 20 July 2016).

518 John Basten, 'Neighbourhood Legal Centres in Australia: A Legacy of the Vietnam War?' (Paper presented at the

519 Interview with John Basten (Frances Gibson, Sydney, 27 July 2016).
520 David Donnison (Paper presented at Conference of International Schools of Social Work, Jerusalem, 1978) quoted in David Neal, *On Tap Not on Top: Legal Centres in Australia 1972–1982* (Legal Service Bulletin Cooperative Ltd, 1984) 32.
521 Garth Symonds, Background paper to Policy Meeting, 3 February 1980, 7. (Copy held in collection of Robyn Lansdowne).
522 Mary Anne Noone and Stephen Tomsen, *Lawyers in Conflict* (Federation Press, 2006) 200. See also generally Jeff Giddings, 'Legal Aid Franchising: Food for Thought or Production Line Legal Services?' (1996) 22(2) *Monash University Law Review* 344 ; Jeff Giddings, 'Legal Aid Services, Quality and Competence: Is Near Enough Good Enough and How Can We Tell What's What?' (1996) 1(3) *Newcastle Law Review* 67.
523 Interview with Roger West (Frances Gibson, Sydney, 9 December 2015).
524 Interview with John Basten (Frances Gibson, Sydney, 27 July 2016).
525 Christine Parker, 'Justifying the New South Wales Legal Profession 1976 to 1997' (1997) 2(2) *The Newcastle Law Review* 1, 8.
526 United Kingdom, *The Royal Commission on Legal Services*, Final Report Volume 1 (1979) 42.
527 Marshall J Breger, 'Legal Aid for the Poor: A Conceptual Analysis', (1981) 60 *North Carolina Law Review* 281, 298.
528 Hazel G Genn and Sarah Beinart, *Paths to Justice : What People Do and Think About Going to Law* (Hart, 1999). See OECD/Open Society Foundations (2019), *Legal Needs Surveys and Access to Justice*, OECD Publishing <https://doi.org/10.1787/g2g9a36c-en>, C Coumarelos et al, *Legal Australia-Wide Survey: Legal Need in Australia*, (2012, Law and Justice Foundation of NSW).
529 See for instance work on legal need in 70s and 80s, e.g. M Cass and Ronald Sackville, Commission of Inquiry into Poverty, *Legal Needs of the Poor*, AGPS, Canberra (1975); M Cass and John S Western, *Legal Aid and Legal Need*. Canberra: Commonwealth Legal Aid Commission (1980). Small research project at West Heidelberg described in Liz Curran and Mary Anne Noone, 'The Challenge of Defining Unmet Legal Need' (2007) 21 *Journal of Law and Social Policy* 63–89;C Coumarelos, Z Wei and A Zhou, *Justice Made to Measure: NSW Legal Needs Survey in Disadvantaged Areas* (Law and Justice Foundation of NSW, 2006); A Buck, P Pleasence and N Balmer 'Do citizens know how to deal with legal issues? Some empirical insights' (2008) *37 (4) Journal of Social Policy* 661,Liz Curran and MA Noone 'The Challenge of Defining Unmet Legal Need' (2007) *Journal of Law and Social Policy* 21(1), 63–89; Pascoe Pleasence et al, *Courses of Action: Civil Law and Social Justice* (UK Legal Services Research Commission, 2004); P Pleasance et al, 'The Legal Problems of Everyday Life', *Department of Justice Canada* (Web Document) <http://www.justice.gc.ca/eng/rp-pr/csj-sjc/jsp-sjp/rr07_la1-rr07_aj1/rr07_la1.pdf>; A Currie, 'Civil Justice Problems and the Disability and Health Status of Canadians' (2007) 21 *Journal of Law and Social Policy*, 71.
530 Julian Disney at al, *Lawyers* (Law Book Company, 1986) 355.
531 Except for specific circumstances such as notification of change of address. Julian Disney at al *Lawyers* (Law Book Company, 1986) 356.
532 NSW Law Reform Commission, *Third Report on the Legal Profession* (1982) 11.2.

533 See for instance 'The Restrictions on Advertising Personal Injury Services' *Legal Services Commissioner Queensland* (Web Document, 2008) <https://www.lsc.qld.gov.au/__data/assets/pdf_file/0015/106215/restrictions-on-advertising-personal-injury-services.pdf>.

534 Jeff Giddings, 'Lay People, for God's Sake!: Surely I Should Be Dealing with Lawyers? Towards an Assessment of Self Help Legal Services in Australia.' (2002) 11(2) *Griffith Law Review* 436, 438.

535 Interview with Clare Petre (Frances Gibson, Sydney, 21 May 2013).

536 Interview with George Zdenkowski (Frances Gibson, Sydney, 28 October 2016).

537 See L Rubinsten, *But I Wouldn't Want My Wife to Work Here: A Study of Migrant Women in Melbourne Industry* (Centre for Urban Research and Action, 1976); *Women and Shiftwork: A Study of Women Working at Night in Melbourne's Western Suburbs* (Western Region Council for Social Development, 1977); R Taft and D Cahill, *Initial Adjustment to Schooling of Immigrant Families* (Australian Government Printing Service, 1978).

538 Mark Wilson, *The British Environmental Movement: The Development of an Environmental Consciousness and Environmental Activism 1945–1975* (PhD thesis, University of Northumbria, 2014) 295, Ron Chapman, *Fighting for the Forests: A History of the West Australian Forest Protest Movement 1895–2001* (PhD Thesis, Murdoch University, 2008).

539 Interview with Roger West (Frances Gibson, Sydney, 9 December 2016).

540 Debbie Whitmont and Mark Austin, 'Rights of the Elderly' (1983) 8(4) *Legal Service Bulletin* 167.

541 Diane Gibson, *Aged Care: Old Policies, New Problems* (Cambridge University Press,1998) 114.

542 Email Gordon Renouf to Frances Gibson (6 August 2018).

543 See for instance 'Commission News' (2009) 94 *Australian Law Reform Commission Reform Journal* 45, detailing community consultation on domestic violence including phone ins; Dale Bagshaw and Thea Brown, *Family Violence and Family Law in Australia: The Experiences and Views of Children and Adults from Families Who Separated Post 1995 And Post 2006* (Monash University, University of South Australia, James Cook University for the Attorney–General's Department, 2010).

544 Disney et al included Aboriginal Legal Services and community legal Centres in this term 'legal aid' as well as the government legal aid services.

545 Julian Disney et al, *Lawyers* (Law Book Company, 1986) 507.

546 Julian Disney et al, *Lawyers* (Law Book Company, 1986) 63.

547 Julian Disney et al, *Lawyers* (Law Book Company, 1986) 63.

548 David Weisbrot, *Australian Lawyers* (Longman Cheshire, 1990) 232.

549 Julian Disney et al, *Lawyers* (Law Book Company, 1986) 511.

550 Though note Lionel Murphy's commitment to 'shopfront' legal aid offices in suburbs and regional cities by way of the Australian Legal Aid Office, possibly based on a visit to Fitzroy Legal Service in 1972. Jenny Hocking, *Lionel Murphy a Biography* (Cambridge University Press, 2000) 274.

551 Jeff Giddings and Mary Anne Noone, 'Australian Community Legal Centres Move into The Twenty-First Century' (2004) 11(3) *International Journal of the Legal Profession* 257, 259. See also David Neal (ed), *On Tap, Not on Top: Legal Centres in Australia 1972-1982* (Legal Service Bulletin Co–operative Ltd, 1984) 58 for a discussion of difficulties in client involvement; Ronald Sackville, Commission of Inquiry into Poverty, *Law and Poverty in Australia* (Australian Government Publishing Service, 1975) 22; Roy

Turner, Legal Aid Review Committee, Parliament of Australia, 'Legal Aid Review Committee Report' (Australian Government Publishing Service, 1974).

552 See Mary Anne Noone and Stephen Tomsen, *Lawyers in Conflict* (Federation Press 2006) 140–144.

553 See Ronald Sackville and Susan Armstrong, *Commission of Inquiry into Poverty Legal Aid in Australia* (Report by the Commissioner for Law and Poverty, 1975).

554 David Humphries, 'Activist Politician Delivered a Better Future for Others', *Sydney Morning Herald* (Sydney, 20 June 2012).

555 Bruce Hawker is a former Chief of Staff to Bob Carr, Labor Party campaign strategist, chairman and founder of the government relations and communications firm Hawker Britton.

556 Bruce Hawker, *The Lucky General* (Lecture Transcript, Web Page, 15 May 2018) <https://theluckygeneral.biz/2018/05/15/the-2018-frank-walker-lecture-populists-demagogues-and-celebrities-challenges-for-progressive-campaigning-in-the-age-of-trump/>.

557 Michaela Whitbourn 'A Labor Immortal' *Financial Review* (Sydney, 20 June 2012). Frank Walker was appointed NSW youngest Attorney–General at the age of 34 and later entered Federal politics. He was a determined and fearless campaigner with strong convictions whose reputation as a reformer and a passionate advocate for the underdog was well known. His record of support and funding for new innovative community services is widely acknowledged, including: Funding for the first government funded service specifically for transgender people in Australia, opening Tiresias House on 14 December 1983. Redfern Legal Centre worked closely with Tiresias House in later years ('Our history', *The Gender Centre* (Web Page) <https://genderCentre.org.au/about-us/our-history>); He is credited with a major role in saving the rainforest at Terania Creek after protests this was the 'first time citizens physically defended a rainforest by placing themselves in front of police and loggers', and he persuaded Neville Warn to act: Laurie Patton, 'Barbarians at the Gate: Don't let them Destroy Murray Valley National Park', *Independent Australia* (Web Page) <https://independentaustralia.net/australia/australia-display/barbarians-at-the-gate-dont-let-them-destroy-murray-valley-national-park,12915>); a program of law reform, including decriminalised public drunkenness, begging, vagrancy and most prostitution offences, raised the legal threshold for common public order offences such as offensive language and behaviour; establishing the Housing Information and Tenancy Services (HITS) Program in 1985, a network of twenty-one independent tenants' advice services throughout NSW, to be set up in 1986 and 1987, and the Tenants' Union would be funded to resource them. Shelter NSW and the inner-city based Housing Information and Referral Service (HIRS) also got funded under the program: Paul Mortimer, *Unfinished business: The story of the Tenants' Union of NSW 1976–1996* (Tenants Union, 1996) 27. One of these programs was at Redfern Legal Centre; In August 1979, the New South Wales Government announced that it would establish "Community Justice Centres" and three were in operation by January, 1981. These were the first such Centres in Australia: University of Sydney, Proceedings of the institute of Criminology No 51 Community Justice Centres 10 March 1982; Community Justice Centres (1979) 4(4) *Legal Service Bulletin* 152–154; Reformist policies in the juvenile justice area such as de-institutionalisation and the juvenile

cautioning scheme introduced by the ALP when Frank Walker was Minister for Youth and Community Services (YACS) came under strong attack from the Coalition in the lead-up to the election; Until 1979 the Law Foundation's funding was largely at the discretion of the Law Society but this changed in 1979 when during Frank Walker's tenure the Foundation was incorporated by its own Act which also provided for it to receive a 10% share of the income – this put the Foundation on a firm footing funding wise. Later during Terry Sheahan's tenure the Foundation received larger allocations from the mid-1980s until the mid-1990s. (Email Terry Purcell to Frances Gibson, 1 October 2019.)

558 NSW, *Parliamentary Debates*, Legislative Assembly, 1 April 1982, 3239 (Frank Walker).

559 'RLC Work Comes in Strange Ways', *RLC News* (February, 1984) 1.

560 For a history of prisoners' rights in Australia, see Mark Finnane and Tony Woodyatt, '"Not the King's Enemies": Prisoners and Their Rights in Australian History' in David Brown and Meredith Wilkie (eds), *Prisoners as Citizens: Human Rights in Australian Prisons* (Federation Press, 2002) 81. See also 'Chronology of the Prisoner Movement in Australia', *Justice Action* (Web Page) <http://www.justiceaction.org.au/index.php?option=com_content&view=article&id=111&Itemid=991>.

561 David Brown, 'The Nagle Royal Commission 25 Years on: Gaining Perspective on Two and a Half Decades of NSW Prison Reform' (2004) 29 *Alternative Law Journal* 135, 136.

562 Interview with Virginia Bell (Frances Gibson, Sydney, 1 December 2016).

563 Interview with George Zdenkowski (Frances Gibson, Sydney, 28 October 2016).

564 Interview with John Basten (Frances Gibson, Sydney, 27 July 2016).

565 John Basten, 'Neighbourhood Legal Centres in Australia: A Legacy of the Vietnam War?' (Paper presented at the Annual Meeting of the Law and Society Association and the ISA Research Committee on Sociology of Law, Madison Wisconsin, 5–8 June 1980).

566 Remission entitlements are entitlements to a reduction of the term of a prison sentence, usually due to good behaviour or conduct: *Attorney-General (Commonwealth) v Burcher* (1986) 86 ALR 457. In this case, the High Court accepted that Mr Burcher, a Commonwealth prisoner, was entitled to remission of his sentence in accordance with the law in the State in question.

567 Interview with John Basten (Frances Gibson, Sydney, 27 July 2016).

568 Interview with John Basten (Frances Gibson, Sydney, 27 July 2016).

569 George Zdenkowski and David Brown, *The Prison Struggle: Changing Australia's Penal System* (Penguin Books, 1982) 83.

570 George Zdenkowski and David Brown, *The Prison Struggle: Changing Australia's Penal System* (Penguin Books, 1982) 99.

571 Ann Genovese, 'A Radical Prequel: Historicising the Concept of Gendered Law in Australia' in Margaret Thornton (ed), *Sex Discrimination in Uncertain Times* (ANU Press, 2010) 56.

572 Les Kennedy, 'Final Release for Katingal, Misguided Experiment in Extreme Jails', *Sydney Morning Herald* (online, 19 May 2004) <https://www.smh.com.au/articles/2004/05/18/1084783517225.html>.

573 Les Kennedy, 'Final Release for Katingal, Misguided Experiment in Extreme Jails', *Sydney Morning Herald* (online, 19 May 2004) <https://www.smh.com.au/articles/2004/05/18/1084783517225.html>.

574 New South Wales, *Royal Commission into NSW Prisons*, Report (1978) 153.

575 George Zdenkowski and David Brown, *The Prison Struggle: Changing Australia's Penal System* (Penguin Books, 1982) 86–90.
576 George Zdenkowski and David Brown, *The Prison Struggle: Changing Australia's Penal System* (Penguin Books, 1982) 89.
577 George Zdenkowski and David Brown, *The Prison Struggle: Changing Australia's Penal System* (Penguin Books, 1982) 86–90. Although note that the gaol was reopened for several months in 1979.
578 Interview with Andy Nehl (Frances Gibson, Sydney, 9 February 2017).
579 Bernie Matthews, *Intractable: Hell Has a Name, Katingal. Life Inside Australia's First Super-Max Prison* (Pan Macmillan, 2006) 203. (The first time the program is listed in the *Sydney Morning Herald* is for a broadcast on 4 February 1979 'SMH 7-Day Guide', *Sydney Morning Herald* 29 January 1979, 14)
580 Women Behind Bars were a 'small … effective group of activists in NSW in the 1970s and early 80s, who changed public awareness about women, crime, punishment and imprisonment': see 'Women Behind Bars' *ABC Radio National* (15 April 2012). <http://www.abc.net.au/radionational/programs/archived/hindsight/hindsight-15-04-12/3941858>.
581 *Women Behind Bars* (Presented by Lorena Allam, ABC National Radio, 2012) 37:15:00.
582 2XX, 'Report on the Violet and Bruce Roberts Story in the 2XX collection', *2XX Collection*, 1979. For more on Violet Roberts, see Ann L Genovese, *The Battered Body: A Feminist Legal History* (PhD Thesis, University of Technology Sydney, 1998) (Web Document) <https://opus.lib.uts.edu.au/handle/10453/20131>.
583 Interview with Robyn Lansdowne (Frances Gibson, Melbourne, 6 July 2016).
584 Interview with Robyn Lansdowne (Frances Gibson, Melbourne, 6 July 2016).
585 Interview with Robyn Lansdowne (Frances Gibson, Melbourne, 6 July 2016).
586 'Violet and Bruce Roberts Released' (1980) *5 Legal Service Bulletin* 297.
587 'Sit-In by Prisoners', *Sydney Morning Herald* (Sydney, 14 January 1979) 3.
588 Garth Symonds, 'RLC Policy Meeting' (Non-casework Paper, Redfern Legal Centre, 3 February 1980) 2; See RW Henry, 'Report of Inquiry into Allegations of Misconduct by Prison Officers at Goulburn Gaol' (Report, NSW Government Printer, 1979).
589 Garth Symonds, 'RLC Policy Meeting' (Non-casework Paper, Redfern Legal Centre, 3 February 1980) 2.
590 Interview with Brett Collins (Frances Gibson, Sydney, 18 July 2016).
591 Interview with Brett Collins (Frances Gibson, Sydney, 18 July 2016).
592 Interview with Brett Collins (Frances Gibson, Sydney, 18 July 2016).
593 Interview with Anne Healey (Frances Gibson, Sydney, 24 July 2016).
594 Interview with John Basten (Frances Gibson, Sydney, 27 July 2016).
595 'Prisoners Legal Service Advisory Committee Report' (Committee Report, Legal Services Commission, 1981).
596 John Hunt, 'Free Legal Advice All Year', *Sydney Morning Herald* (Sydney, 13 May 1984) 116.
597 'Notes' (1986) 11(6) *Legal Service Bulletin* 282, 291.
598 J Basten, S Winters and G Zdenkowski, 'Prisons' in *Halsbury's Laws of Australia*, (Butterworths, 1996).
599 *Riley v Parole Board of New South Wales* (1985) 3 NSWLR 606.
600 Interview with Andrew Haesler (Frances Gibson, Sydney, 7 July 2015).
601 *Vella v Commissioner of Australian Federal Police* (1985) 9 FCR 81. Mr Vella was a Commonwealth prisoner who was re-

leased and subsequently rearrested. Proceedings were taken to obtain his release on the basis that there was no power to return him to custody even if the original release had been mistaken. Mr Vella was successful in the Full Federal Court Interview with Bill Dickens (Dubbo, 8 February 2017).
602 Interview with Ben Slade (Frances Gibson, Sydney, 8 December 2015).
603 Luis Garcia, 'Prison Drug Smugglers Face Jail', *Sydney Morning Herald* (Sydney, 1 June 1988) 3.
604 Letter from Andrew Haesler to Tony Woodyatt, 11 March 1985.
605 For example, 'in December 1988 … Redfern Legal Centre, acting on behalf of all prisoners sentenced to life imprisonment, commenced a representative action in the Supreme Court of New South Wales to have the policy declared null and void' New South Wales, *Parliamentary Debates*, Legislative Council, 1 March 1989, 5396 (Elisabeth Kirkby). This policy declared a mandatory higher security classification for any prisoner who had escaped: at 5391.
606 The contribution made by Legal Aid's PLS solicitor Jack Grahame, who had a longstanding commitment to civil liberties and prisoners' rights, should be noted.
607 Interview with Brett Collins (Frances Gibson, Sydney, 18 July 2016).
608 Interview with George Zdenkowski (Frances Gibson, Sydney, 28 October 2017).
609 Interview with John Basten (Frances Gibson, Sydney, 27 July 2016).
610 See Anne Grunseit, Suzie Forell and Emily McCarron, *Taking Justice into Custody: The Legal Needs of Prisoners* (Paper, Law and Justice Foundation of New South Wales, 2 June 2008) for research on issues relating to prisoners' access to legal assistance in NSW.
611 Hilary Little, 'Non-Consensual Sterilisation of the Intellectually Disabled in the Australian Context: Potential for Human Rights Abuse and the Need for Reform' (1992) 14 Australian Year Book of International Law 203, 204.
612 Redfern Legal Centre, IDRS Five Years of Rights 1986–1991 (Redfern Legal Centre, 1991).
613 Intellectual Disability Rights Service, Annual Report 2008–2009.
614 Edward St John QC, 'The Intellectually Handicapped and the Law' (Paper presented at The Intellectually Handicapped: Citizens or Non-citizens, UNSW Sydney, 15–16 July 1978) 11.
615 Fortuitously for Jim Simpson, who was later to marry Janene Cootes.
616 Interview with Jim Simpson (Frances Gibson, Sydney, 16 September 2016).
617 Interview with Bill Dickens (Frances Gibson, Dubbo, 8 February 2017).
618 Michael Steer, 'Review of Legal Rights and Intellectual Disability: A Short Guide Edited by Julia Hall, Tony Payne and Jim Simpson' (1986) 11(5) Legal Service Bulletin 227.
619 Rodney Sullivan, 'Donald James Grimes', The Biographical Dictionary of the Australian Senate (Web Page) <https://biography.senate.gov.au/grimes-donald-james/>.
620 Shane Rendalls et al, The Legal Needs of Institutionalised People (Australian Government Publishing Service, 1985).
621 National Council on Intellectual Disability, Submission to the Long-Term Disability Support Productivity Commission Inquiry 2010 (16 August 2010) 6.
622 Wolf Wolfensberger, The Principle of Normalization in Human Services (National Institute on Mental Retardation, 1972).
623 Interview with Jim Simpson (Frances Gibson, Sydney, 16 September 2016).
624 Interview with Jim Simpson (Frances Gibson, Sydney, 16 September 2016).
625 Jim Simpson, 'Intellectual Disability:

Intellectual Disability Rights Service' (1986) 11 (5) Legal Service Bulletin 237, 238.

626 Interview with Jim Simpson (Frances Gibson, Sydney, 16 September 2016).

627 For a shocking look at attitudes to sterilisation of people with an ID see Edgar A Doll, 'Community Control of the Feeble-Minded'(1930) 149(3) The Annals of the American Academy of Political and Social Science 167.

628 Regina Graycar, Mary Gaudron and Jenny Morgan, The Hidden Gender of Law (Federation Press, 2nd ed, 2002) 13.

629 Re A Teenager [1988] FamCA 17 (15 November 1988). See Jim Simpson, 'Judges at Odds' (1989) 14 Legal Service Bulletin 102.

630 The application was originally made to the Supreme Court of New South Wales and a person who was the secretary of a disabled persons' society was appointed the next friend of the child. That Court declined jurisdiction based on the situation, amongst other matters, that the child was the child of a marriage and therefore the Family Court of Australia was the Court, if any court had jurisdiction, to deal with the matter. Re A Teenager [1988] FamCA 17 (15 November 1988).

631 Re A Teenager [1988] Fam CA 17 (15 November 1988) 100.

632 For a shocking look at attitudes to sterilisation of people with an ID see Edgar A Doll, 'Community Control of the Feeble-Minded'(1930) 149(3) The Annals of the American Academy of Political and Social Science 167.

633 Regina Graycar, Mary Gaudron and Jenny Morgan, The Hidden Gender of Law (Federation Press, 2nd ed, 2002) 13.

634 Interview with Jim Simpson (Frances Gibson, Sydney, 16 September 2016). See Jim Simpson, 'Sterilisation and the Family Court' (1991) 5 Australian Journal of Family Law 1; Linda Steele, 'Making Sense of The Family Court's Decisions on the Non-Therapeutic Sterilisation of Girls with Intellectual Disability' (2008) 22 Australian Journal of Family Law 1.

635 Wendy Waller, 'Community Management: Has it Gone or Just Evolved? A Discussion on Where Community Management has Come From and Where it is Today' (2002) 4 Developing Practice: The Child, Youth and Family Work Journal 26. See also Susan Kenny, 'Contestations of Community Development in Australia' (1996) 31(2) Community Development Journal 104, 106.

636 Interview with Jim Simpson (Frances Gibson, Sydney, 16 September 2016)

637 Interview with Jim Simpson (Frances Gibson, Sydney, 16 September 2016). See also Five Years of Rights: 1986–1991: Further Up The Hill (Redfern Legal Centre, 1991).

638 Secretary, Department of Health and Community Services v JWB (Marion's Case) (1992) 175 CLR 218. Marion's Case provides that parental consent only suffices as authority when a procedure is performed for 'therapeutic' reasons. Conversely, any proposed non-therapeutic procedure requires approval from the Family Court and will be determined on the basis of an individual's best interests. See also Jeanne Snelling, 'Re-Visiting Re X: Hysterectomy, Removal of Reproductive Capacity and the Severely Intellectually Disabled Child in New Zealand' 22 Journal of Law and Medicine 679, 685.

639 Sally Robinson, Stand Up and Speak! Sit Up and Listen! (IDRS, 1997).

640 Janene Cootes, Roger West and Jim Simpson and Redfern Legal Centre, Intellectual Disability Rights Service. Rights in residence: a guide to the law and rights in group homes, hostels, institutions and other supported accommodation *Redfern Legal Cen-*

*tre Publishing,*1988

641  Mark Ierace and Redfern Legal Centre. Intellectual Disability Rights Service, Intellectual Disability: a Manual for Criminal Lawyers (Redfern Legal Centre1989).

642  Redfern Legal Centre. Intellectual Disability Rights Service and Julia Hall, Legal Rights & Intellectual Disability [microform]: A Short Guide (ERIC Clearinghouse [Washington, D.C.] 1986); Anne Rauch, and Redfern Legal Centre. Intellectual Disability Rights Service, Your rights at work (Redfern Legal Centre Publishing, 1987); Jenny Klause, and Anne Rauch, Legal rights: a course for people with a learning difficulty or an intellectual disability: a kit for trainers ( Redfern Legal Centre Publishing,1990); Redfern Legal Centre. Intellectual Disability Rights Service, Questions of rights: a guide to the law and rights of people with intellectual disability (Redfern Legal Centre Publishing,1992);Stephen Booth and Intellectual Disability Rights Service, When I'm gone: an introduction to wills and estate planning for parents of people with intellectual disability (Redfern Legal Centre Publishing,1999); Linda Steele, Intellectual Disability Rights Service and Coalition on Intellectual Disability and Criminal Justice and New South Wales Council for Intellectual Disability, Enabling justice: a report on the problems and solutions in relation to diversion of alleged offenders with intellectual disability from the New South Wales local courts system ( Intellectual Disability Rights Service Inc, 2008)

643  See Intellectual Disability Rights Service, Five Years of Rights: 1986–1991: Further up the Hill (Redfern Legal Centre, 1991).

644  ] 'About Us', Intellectual Disability Rights Service (Web Page, 2019) <http://www.idrs.org.au/s32/_about/aboutMain.php#.WZD4WncjGks>.

645  See for example in Tasmania: Chris Pippos, Burnie Advocate (Burnie, 17 May 2014) 4.

646  Michael L Shier and Femida Handy, 'Executive Leadership and Social Innovation in Direct-Service Nonprofits: Shaping the Organizational Culture to Create Social Change' (2016) 27(2) Journal of Progressive Human Services 111,114.

647  Morris L Cohen, 'The Legal Publishing Industry in the 20th Century and Beyond' (1992) 11 *Legal Reference Services* 9, 10.

648  Sol Encel, *Equality and Authority* (Cheshire, 1970) 123.

649  Email Ian Close to Frances Gibson (21 July 2021).RLCP was registered as a company limited by guarantee, (Redfern Legal Centre Publishing Ltd) on 17 July 1987. (ACN 003 333 597): 'Company Names Register', *Australian Securities and Investments Commission.*

650  The term 'poverty law' describes the broad areas of law and legal needs which arise by virtue of an individual's or a group's poverty: Ontario Ministry of the Attorney-General, 'Poverty Law', *Ontario Legal Aid Review* (Web Page) <https://www.attorneygeneral.jus.gov.on.ca/english/about/pubs/olar/ch11.php>. 'Poverty law' traditionally includes housing and consumer problems, social security and employment issues, and family matters.

651  Ros Macdonald, 'Plain English in the Law: A New Model for the 21st Century' 30 (2004) *Commonwealth Law Bulletin* 922, 923.

652  See Brian Keon-Cohen, 'Community Legal Education in Australia' (1978) 4(4) *Monash University Law Review* 292; Bryan Keon-Cohen 'Community Legal Education in Australia, Philosophies and Programmes for the Future' (Speech, Law for Non-Lawyers: The Newcastle

Conference, University of Newcastle, 22–24 August 1978).
653 Australian Law Reform Commission, *Plain English and the Law* (Report No 9, 1987) 15.
654 B Danet, 'Language in the Legal Process' (1980) 14(3) *Law and Society Review* 445, 452.
655 Carl Felsenfeld, 'The Plain English Movement: Panel Discussion 6' [1981–1982] *Canadian Business Law Journal* 408.
656 Tom McArthur, 'The Pedigree of Plain English' (1991) 7(3) *English Today* 13, 19. Moves towards Plain English legal writing in the USA precede this however, such as Citibank of New York's introduction of a Plain English consumer promissory note in 1975, and legislation from New York in 1977 which required that every contract of $50,000 or less 'primarily for personal, family or household purposes' be: '1. Written in a clear and coherent manner using words with common and every day meanings' and '2. Appropriately divided and captioned by its various sections.' See also Ros Macdonald, 'Plain English in the Law: A New Model for the 21st Century' (2004) 30 *Commonwealth Law Bulletin* 922, 923.
657 B Danet, 'Language in the Legal Process' (1980) 14(3) *Law and Society Review*, 445, 452.
658 Carl Felsenfeld, 'The Plain English Movement: Panel Discussion 6' [1981–1982] *Canadian Business Law Journa*l 408, 411.
659 Marie R Haug and Marvin B Sussman, 'Professional Autonomy and the Revolt of the Client' (1969) 17 *Social Problems* 153.
660 I Marie R Haug and Marvin B Sussman, 'Professional Autonomy and the Revolt of the Client' (1969) 17 *Social Problems* 153.156.
661 Nina Toren, 'Deprofessionalization and its Sources: A Preliminary Analysis' (1975) 2(4) *Sociology of Work and Occupations* 323, 332.
662 Ivan Illich, 'The Professions as a Form of Imperialism' (1973) 25 *New Society* 633.
663 Paul Fink and Stephen Weinstein, 'Whatever Happened to Psychiatry? The Deprofessionalization of Community Mental Health Centers' (1979) 136(4) *American Journal of Psychiatry* 406.
664 Harry Specht, 'The Deprofessionalization Of Social Work' (1972) 17 *Social Work* 3.
665 Francine Bernard and Pierre Hamel, 'Toward a Deprofessionalization of the Profession of Accountant? The Situation in Quebec' (1982) 24(2) *Sociologie du Travail*, 117.
666 Thomas McDaniel, 'The Deprofessionalization of Teachers' (1979) 43(2) *The Educational Forum* 229.
667 Marie R Haug, 'Deprofessionalization: An Alternate Hypothesis for the Future' (1972) 20 *The Sociological Review* 195, 197.
668 Marie R Haug and Marvin B Sussman, 'Professional Autonomy and the Revolt of the Client' (1969) 17 *Social Problems* 153.204.
669 See Eliot Friedson, *Professional Dominance: The Social Structure of Medical Care* (Atherton Press, 1970); Terence James Johnson, *Professions and Power* (Macmillan 1972); Ivan Ilich, *Disabling Professions* (Marion Boyers, 1977).
670 Mary Anne Noone and Stephen Tomsen, *Lawyers in Conflict* (Federation Press, 2006) 15.
671 John Basten, 'Conference on Legal Services' (1975) 9 *Legal Service Bulletin* 246.
672 Sidney M Bliss, 'Preventive Law' (1940) 16(2) *The Journal of Business Education* 23.
673 Louis M Brown is often acknowledged as the father of preventive law. See Avrom Sherr, 'Professor Louis Brown: The Father of Preventive Law' (1996) 3 *International Journal of the Legal Profession* 253. Brown was the author of the 1950 textbook *Preventive Law* (Prentice-Hall, *1950*)

and *Lawyering Through Life: The Origin of Preventive Law* (Fred B Rothman & Co, 1986).
674 Louis M Brown, 'From Preventive Law to Mock Law Office Competition' (1972) 51 *Oregon Law Review* 343.
675 John Chesterman, *Law and the New Left: A History of The Fitzroy Legal Service 1972–1994*, (PhD Thesis, University of Melbourne, 1995) 67.
676 Jenny Hocking, *Lionel Murphy: A Political Biography* (Cambridge University Press, 2000) 175.
677 BA Keon-Cohen, 'Community Legal Education in Australia' (1978) 4 *Monash University Law Review* 292, 297.
678 I BA Keon-Cohen, 'Community Legal Education in Australia' (1978) 4 *Monash University Law Review* 292.
679 BA Keon-Cohen, 'Community Legal Education in Australia' (1978) 4 *Monash University Law Review* 292, 311.
680 John Chesterman, *Law and the New Left: A History of The Fitzroy Legal Service 1972–1994*, (PhD Thesis, University of Melbourne, 1995) 180.
681 Kathy Laster and Ryan Kornhauser, 'The Rise of DIY Law: Implications for Legal Aid', Asher Flynn and Jacqueline Hodgson (eds) *Access to Justice and Legal Aid*, (Bloomsbury Publishing PLC, 2017) 126.
682 Anne Riches and Garth Symonds, 'Redfern Legal Centre and Community Legal Education' in Ben Boer (ed) '*Community Legal Education Preventive Legal Aid, Proceedings of the Commonwealth Legal Aid Proceedings* (Commonwealth Legal Aid Commission, 1980) 60.
683 'Redfern Legal Centre: 15 Years On', *Sydney Morning Herald* (Sydney, 12 March 1992) 97.
684 Redfern Legal Centre, *Tenth Year Report 1977–1987* (Redfern Legal Centre, December 1987) 19.
685 *Legal Practitioners (Amendment) Bill 1967* (NSW).
686 See New South Wales, *Parliamentary Debates,* Legislative Assembly 23 March 1977, 5569 (Mr FJ Walker).
687 Email Terry Purcell to Frances Gibson (16 September 2019).
688 Attorney, activist and politician Ralph Nader is an auto-safety reformer and consumer advocate. He has run for president of the USA several times, as a candidate for the Green Party. 'Ralph Nader', *Biography.com* (Web Page) <https://www.biography.com/people/ralph-nader-9419799>. For Michael Mobb's current activities see Janine Israel, 'Sustainability Expert Michael Mobbs: I'm Leaving the City to Prep for the Apocalypse' *Guardian* (online, 19 September 2019) <https://www.theguardian.com/environment/2019/sep/29/sustainability-expert-michael-mobbs-im-leaving-the-city-to-prep-for-the-apocalypse?fbclid=IwAR1F5CHJsuKh1BESHErQZiV9_M1WQX_MnZsU7VWsK-6FySRjTQ4_OXvGYcjk>.
689 For a brief history of the Ranger Uranium Mine see Keri Phillips, 'The Long and Controversial History of Uranium Mining in Australia' *ABC Radio National* (Web Page, 14 July 2015) <http://www.abc.net.au/radionational/programs/rearvision/history-of-uranium-mining-in-australia/6607212>.
690 Interview with Michael Mobbs (Frances Gibson, Sydney, 29 April 2016).
691 William H Simon, 'Babbitt v Brandeis: The Decline of the Professional Ideal' (1985) 37 *Stanford Law Review* 565, 574.
692 Michael Mobbs (ed), *Legal Resources Book* (Redfern Legal Centre, 1978).
693 Interview with Virginia Bell (Frances Gibson, Sydney, 1 December 2016).
694 Email Sean Kidney to Frances Gibson (7 November 2018).
695 Interview with Anne Healey (Frances Gibson, Sydney, 24 July 2016).
696 Anne Riches and Garth Symonds,

'Redfern Legal Centre and Community Legal Education' in Ben Boer (ed) '*Community Legal Education Preventive Legal Aid, Proceedings of the Commonwealth Legal Aid Proceedings of the* (Commonwealth Legal Aid Commission, 1980) 60.
697 See John Terry, 'What's in a Name' (1983) 8 *Legal Service Bulletin* 181,182.
698 Interview with Anne Healey (Frances Gibson, Sydney, 24 July 2016).
699 Interview with Chris Ronalds (Frances Gibson, Bawley Point, 24 January 2017).
700 Interview with Chris Ronalds (Frances Gibson, Bawley Point, 24 January 2017).
701 See for instance Legal Australia, *Thomson Reuters* 'Lawyers Practice Manual' (Web Search Results) <https://legal.thomsonreuters.com.au/Search?keyword=Lawyers%20Practice%20manual>.
702 Interview with Chris Ronalds (Bawley Point, 24 January 2016).
703 http://legal.thomsonreuters.com.au/lawyers-practice-manual-nsw-online/productdetail/89430
704 Anne Riches and Garth Symonds, 'Redfern Legal Centre and Community Legal Education' in Ben Boer (ed) '*Community Legal Education Preventive Legal Aid, Proceedings of the Commonwealth Legal Aid Proceedings of the* (Commonwealth Legal Aid Commission, 1980) 60.
705 Interview with Sean Kidney (Frances Gibson, Boston, 17 September 2016).
706 Bill Wheeler, Review of The Law Handbook (1986) 11(5) *Legal Service Bulletin* 229.
707 Interview with Sean Kidney (Frances Gibson, Boston, 17 September 2016).
708 The Federal Attorney–General's Department considered a plan to establish courses for high school students and adult education groups on the law and its administration in 1975. 'It would emphasise the problems of disadvantaged groups in the community, and could be adapted for high school use, continuing education courses, and audio-visual public education campaigns.' It seems nothing came of this proposal. 'Community Legal Education' (1974–1976) *Legal Service Bulletin*. Note there had been a project aimed at young people in schools in 1978 in the form of a newspaper Legal Eagle and then the Eaglebook series. Legal Eagle was developed and trialled in the first year and the first Eaglebook appeared in 1978 At its peak, class sets of Legal Eagle went into a third of the high schools in Australia, and the Eaglebooks achieved a similar distribution in many States. Susan Churchman, 'Community Legal Education: The Last Ten Years, Socrates Revisited' (1987) 12 *Legal Service Bulletin* 198, 201.
709 Susan Churchman, 'Community Legal Education: The Last Ten Years, Socrates Revisited' (1987) 12 *Legal Service Bulletin* 198, 201.
710 See 'Streetwize Comics', *Museum of Applied Arts and Sciences* (Web Page, 9 August 2007) < https://collection.maas.museum/object/8499> which states: 'Streetwize began in 1984 as an initiative of Redfern Legal Centre, Redfern Legal Centre Publishing, NSW Legal Aid and the Youth Advocacy Service of Marrickville Legal Centre.' While the comics were initially conceived as a way of informing young people about their legal rights and responsibilities, it was soon realised that young people's problems are multifaceted and interconnected. The issues covered in the comics broadened out to include health, drugs, welfare, sexuality, employment and personal rights. Because streetwise comics are based on the philosophy that effective communication must be built around the perceptions and needs of the audience, in-depth research and consultation with target audiences informs the development of each comic, drafts are tested in workshops, and the final results are subject to evaluation. The comics were

initially distributed in youth refuges and institutions in NSW, but Streetwize Communications went on to produce specially adapted editions for other states. Funding comes from federal and state government departments, non-government and community organisations.'
711 Kurt Iveson, 'The Real-Life Adventures of Streetwize Comics' (1998) 151 *Overland* 59.
712 Kurt Iveson, 'The Real-Life Adventures of Streetwize Comics' (1998) 151 *Overland* 60.
713 Herbert Gintis, 'Alienation and Power' (1972) 4(5) *Review of Radical Political Economics* 1.
714 Kurt Iveson, 'The Real-Life Adventures of Streetwize Comics' (1998) 151 *Overland* 59, 60.
715 Interview with Sean Kidney (Frances Gibson, Boston 17 September 2016).
716 *RLC News* (Redfern Legal Centre, August/Sept 1986) 1.
717 Email Ian Close to Frances Gibson (27 July 2021).
718 Interview with Andrew Haesler (Frances Gibson, Sydney, 7 July 2015). See also Kidney on the split and aftermath: 'Initially funds from the publishing went back to RLC. When it separated, we had an agreement for royalties to go to RLC even after we split off.' Interview with Sean Kidney, (Frances Gibson, Boston 17 September 2016).
719 University of New South Wales Press Ltd, *UNSW Press a History: 1962–2012* (UNSW Press, 2012) 20.
720 Australian Securities and Investment Commission Records as at 3 July 2017 for Redfern Legal Centre Publishing ACN 003 333 597.
721 Interview with Sean Kidney (Frances Gibson, Boston 17 September 2016).
722 Interview with Chris Ronalds (Frances Gibson, Bawley Point, 24 January 2017).
723 Interview with Sean Kidney (Frances Gibson, Boston 17 September 2016).
724 Email Sean Kidney to Frances Gibson (7 November 2018).
725 M Herron and Christine Slattery, *Community Legal Education in Victoria 1980–1985: A Background Study* (Victoria Law Foundation, 1986); Ania Wilczynski, Maria Karras and Suzie Forell, 'The Outcomes of Community Legal Education: A Systematic Review' (2014) 18 *Justice Issues* 1, 4; Monica Ferrari and Angela Costi, 'Learnings from Community Legal Education' (2012) 37(1) *Alternative Law Journal* 52.
726 Neil Rees, 'How Should Law Schools Serve Their Communities?' (2001) 5(1) *University of Western Sydney Law Review* 111.
727 *North Coast Community Housing v Field* (Tenancy) [2010] NSWCTTT 446 (22 September 2010), *Australian Competition & Consumer Commission v Murray* [2002] FCA 1252 (11 October 2002).
728 See for instance *R v Fisher* [2011] ACTSC 56 (1 April 2011).
729 Legal Information Access Centre, 'Do You Need a Lawyer', *Hot Topic* (Web Page) <http://www.austlii.edu.au/cgi-bin/sinodisp/au/other/liac/hot_topic/hottopic/1999/5/2.html?stem=0&synonyms=0&query=%22Redfern%20Legal%20Centre%20Publishing%22>.
730 Stian Nygaard and Angeloantonio Russo, 'Trust, Coordination and Knowledge Flows in R&D Projects: The Case of Fuel Cell Technologies' (2008) 17(1) *Business Ethics* 23.
731 Giovany Cajaiba-Santana 'Social Innovation: Moving the Field Forward. A Conceptual Framework' (2014) 82 *Technological Forecasting & Social Change* 42, 47.
732 Fisk, Catherine L and Robert Gordon, [519] (2010) 1(3) UC Irvine Law Review 519 at 533.
733 See Kathleen J Tierney, 'The Battered Women Movement and The Creation of The Wife Beating Problem' (1981) 29 *Social Problems* 207.

734 Jalna Hanmer and Mary Maynard, *Women, Violence and Social Control* (Macmillan Press, 1987) 23.
735 Regina Graycar, Mary Gaudron and Jenny Morgan, *The Hidden Gender of Law* (Federation Press, 2nd ed., 2002) 12.
736 The Law Reform Commission (ACT) Report No 30 (Australian Government Publishing Service, 1986) 2.
737 Australian Law Reform Commission, *Inquiry into Domestic Violence No 30* (1986).
738 Australian Law Reform Commission, *Inquiry into Domestic Violence No 30* (1986) 34.
739 Department of the Prime Minister and Cabinet Office of the Status of Women, *The Effectiveness of Protection Orders in Australian Jurisdictions* (1993 Australian Government Publishing Service) 15.
740 *The Crimes Domestic Violence Amendment Act 1982* No. 166.
741 Department of the Prime Minister and Cabinet Office, 'Status of Women the Effectiveness of Protection Orders in Australian Jurisdictions' (Australian Government Publishing Service, 1993) 19.
742 See Australian Law Reform Commission, *Family Violence: A National Legal Response* (2010) 114, 155.
743 See Anna Matczak, Eleni Hatzidimitriadou, and Jo Lindsay, *Review of Domestic Violence Policies in England and Wales* (2011, University of London); Catherine Jacquet, 'Domestic Violence In The 1970s' *National Library of Medicine, National Institute of Health* (Web Page,2015) <https://circulatingnow.nlm.nih.gov/2015/10/15/domestic-violence-in-the-1970s/>; Michael P Johnson and Kathleen J Ferraro, 'Research on Domestic Violence in the 1990s: Making Distinctions' (2000) 6(4) *Journal of Marriage and the Family* 948–963.
744 See Anna Matczak, Eleni Hatzidimitriadou and Jo Lindsay, *Review of Domestic Violence Policies in England and Wales* (2011, University of London) 3.
745 Later to be The Hon Justice Virginia Bell AC, Justice of the High Court of Australia
746 Interview with Virginia Bell (Frances Gibson, Sydney, 1 December 2016).
747 I Interview with Virginia Bell (Frances Gibson, Sydney, 1 December 2016).
748 'Tenth Year Report 1977–1987', *Redfern Legal Centre* (Web Document, 1987) 25 <https://rlc.org.au/sites/default/files/attachments/1977-1987 RLC 10th year report.pdf>. As did CLCS in other states and the specialist Women's Legal Services.
749 Interview Jane Goddard (Frances Gibson, Sydney, 23 January 2016).
750 Interview Jane Goddard (Frances Gibson, Sydney, 23 January 2016).
751 The Chamber Magistrate provides information about legal options and court proceedings in New South Wales but cannot represent people appearing before the Court.
752 Interview Jane Goddard (Frances Gibson, Sydney, 23 January 2016).
753 Interview with Ben Slade (Frances Gibson, Sydney, 8 December 2015).
754 Interview Jane Goddard (Frances Gibson, Sydney, 23 January 2016).
755 Interview Jane Goddard (Frances Gibson, Sydney, 23 January 2016).
756 Interview with Mary Perkins (Frances Gibson, Sydney, 22 July 2016).
757 Marlene Krasovitsky and Denise Lynch, *Women's Domestic Violence Court Assistance Scheme: Evaluation* (Redfern Legal Centre Publishing, 1991).
758 Interview with Louise Blazejowska (Frances Gibson, Sydney, 11 February 2017).
759 Marlene Krasovitsky and Denise Lynch, *Women's Domestic Violence Court Assistance Scheme: Evaluation* (Redfern Legal Centre Publishing, 1991) 1.
760 Interview with Louise Blazejowska (Frances Gibson, Sydney, 11 February 2017); Janette Prichard and Sue Malcolm, 'Integrated Intervention: The Women's

Domestic Violence Court Assistance Program' (WDVCAP)' (Paper presented at the Second Australasian Women and Policing Conference, Brisbane, July 1999). See also J Bradfield and J Nyland, *Evaluation of the NSW Women's Domestic Violence Court Assistance Programme: A Report to the NSW Legal Aid Commission* (Bradfield Nyland Group, 1998).

761 Interview with Louise Blazejowska (Frances Gibson, Sydney, 11 February 2017).

762 Redfern Legal Centre, *Annual Report, 1995–1996* 17. See Jane Mulroney, *Women's Domestic Violence Court Assistance Program: Support Workers' Kit* (Harris Park, N.S.W, Domestic Violence Advocacy Service, 1999).

763 Interview with Louise Blazejowska (Frances Gibson, Sydney, 11 February 2017).

764 Australian Law Reform Commission, *Equality before the Law: Women's Equality Report No 69* (1994).

765 Ibid 668. The Report noted 'The model has been used and adapted in other areas to suit community needs … The Redfern Scheme is built upon an interactive, co-operative relationship between solicitor and support worker. Solicitors may be employed by a community legal Centre or be private practitioners or court appointed duty solicitors. The solicitor provides professional advice and follow up advice if necessary. The support persons are social welfare professionals usually from local community services. The support workers explain the court process, layout and personnel, take initial instructions and, since women seeking court intervention are often in crisis, investigate the non-legal aspects of the client's situation including housing, financial and counselling needs. Their role is integral to the legal process. Underpinning the Scheme is the belief that solicitors working hand in hand with trained support workers will provide a more effective service than either solicitors or support workers independently. The participants in the scheme acknowledge that the service should be run by women for women. In some circumstances, however, women solicitors may not be available and it may be necessary to have male solicitors appearing.'

766 'NSW Health Domestic Violence Discussion Paper' (NSW Health 1999).

767 Jane Mulroney, *Women's Domestic Violence Court Assistance Program Support Workers Kit*, WDVCAP Training and Resource Unit, (Domestic Violence Advocacy Service and Redfern Legal Centre Publishing, 1999) 35–54. See also *Domestic Violence: Impact of Legal Reform in NSW* 5 (NSW Bureau of Crime Statistics and Research Legislative Evaluation Series, 1989).

768 Interview with Louise Blazejowska (Frances Gibson, Sydney, 11 February 2017).

769 Interview with Helen Campbell (Frances Gibson, Sydney, 23 November 2016).

770 South Sydney Herald, 'Human Rights Award for Redfern Legal Centre', *Redwatch* (online, 2007) <http://www.redwatch.org.au/media/080205sshh/>.

771 Interview with Hilary Chesworth (Frances Gibson, Sydney, 9 July 2016).

772 Interview with Natalie Egan (Frances Gibson, Bendigo, 22 October 2016).

773 See Finance and Public Administration References Committee, Senate, *Inquiry into Family Violence in Australia* (2015); Victorian Royal Commission into Family Violence (2016); Mary Anne Noone, 'Challenges Facing the Legal Aid System in Australia' in Asher Flynn and Jacqueline Hodgson (eds) *Access to Justice and Legal Aid* (Bloomsbury Publishing PLC, 2017) 23, 32.

774 See Talina Drabsch, Domestic Violence in NSW (2007) NSW Parliament Briefing Paper no 7/07, 28.

775 Facebook, *Womens Domestic Violence Court Advocacy Service NSW Inc* (Web Page) <https://www.facebook.com/wdvcasnsw/>.

776 See 'Walgett To Receive Women's Domestic Violence Court Advocacy Service', *The Nationals for Regionals NSW* (Web Page, 12 April 2017) <https://web.archive.org/web/20180330154312/http://www.nswnationals.org.au/walgett_to_receive_women_s_domestic_violence_court_advocacy_service >.

777 NSW Ombudsman, *Domestic Violence: Improving Police Practice* (2006) Report to Parliament, iv.

778 Australian Law Reform Commission, *Family Violence Improving Legal Frameworks*, ALRC Consultation Paper Summary 1, 226.

779 See for instance Jane Wangman, 'Gender and Intimate Partner Violence: A Case Study from NSW' (2010) 33(3) *UNSW Law Journal* 945; Robyn Edwards, 'Staying Home Leaving Violence: Listening to Women's Experiences' (2011) *Social Policy Research Centre Report* 4, 11.

780 Lisa Valentin, 'Concern for Clients as Domestic Violence Court Services put Out for Tender', *Sydney Morning Herald* (online, 10 September 2018) <https://www.smh.com.au/politics/nsw/concern-for-clients-as-domestic-violence-court-services-put-out-for-tender-20180904-p501mq.html>.

781 This concept of a multi-disciplinary approach to matters dealt with in courts was replicated in later developments such as the drug courts in NSW, Queensland and Victoria. See Rob Hull, 'Victoria's New Drug Court' [2002] (120) *Victorian Bar News* 10.

782 Ronald S Burt, *Structural Holes* (Harvard University Press, 1992).

783 Meric S Gertler, David A Wolfe and David Garkut, 'No Place Like Home? The Embeddedness of Innovation in a Regional Economy' (2000) 7(4) *Review of International Political Economy* 688.

784 Commonwealth, *Commission of Inquiry into Poverty, Law and Poverty in Australia: Second Main Report* (Australian Government Publishing Service, 1975) 164.

785 'Commonwealth Role: Social Security and Benefits System', *Parliament of Australia* <https://www.aph.gov.au/Parliamentary_Business/Committees/Senate/Community_Affairs/Completed_inquiries/2010-13/commcontribformerforcedadoption/report/c05>.

786 Commonwealth, *Commission of Inquiry into Poverty, Law and Poverty in Australia: Second Main Report*, (Australian Government Publishing Service, 1975) 166.

787 Commonwealth, *Commission of Inquiry into Poverty, Law and Poverty in Australia: Second Main Report*, (Australian Government Publishing Service, 1975) 165.

788 Commonwealth, *Commission of Inquiry into Poverty, Law and Poverty in Australia: Second Main Report*, (Australian Government Publishing Service, 1975) 167.

789 I Commonwealth, *Commission of Inquiry into Poverty, Law and Poverty in Australia: Second Main Report*, (Australian Government Publishing Service, 1975) 170.

790 Interview with Anne Healey (Frances Gibson, Sydney, 24 July 2016).

791 'The Great Social Security Conspiracy Case', *Australian Institute of Criminology* (Web Page, 1989) <https://aic.gov.au/publications/lcj/wayward/chapter-6-great-social-security-conspiracy-case>.

792 John Basten, 'Neighbourhood Legal Centres in Australia: A legacy of the Vietnam war?, (Papers delivered at Annual Meeting of Law and Society association and ISA Research Committee on Sociology of Law (Wisconsin June 5-8 1980) 17.

793 'The Greek Conspiracy', *PIAC* (Web Page, 22 February 2013) <https://piac.asn.au/2013/02/22/the-greek-conspiracy/>.

794 Stephen Tomsen, 'Professionalism and State Engagement: Lawyers and Legal Aid Policy in Australia in the 1970s and 1980s' (1992) 28(3) *Australian and New*

*Zealand Journal of Sociology* 316.
795 Interview with Philippa Smith (Frances Gibson, Melbourne, 6 September 2018).
796 Interview with Julian Disney (Frances Gibson, Sydney, 25 July 2016).
797 Interview with Philippa Smith (Frances Gibson, Melbourne, 6 September 2018).
798 Email Roger West to Frances Gibson (29 August 2017).
799 Graham Williams, '14 Refuges for Runaways', *Sydney Morning Herald* (Sydney, 2 October 1982) 2. See also New South Wales, *Parliamentary Debates*, Legislative Assembly, 27 September 1982, 1269 (Mr. Booth, Treasurer).
800 Mark Coultan, 'City Backs Welfare Centre', *Sydney Morning Herald* (Sydney, 2 February 1983) 14.
801 'Diary', *Sydney Morning Herald* (Sydney, 5 May 1983) 16 and see Michael Raper (ed), *Welfare Rights in Black and White* (Welfare Rights Centre Sydney, 2003) vi.
802 Interview with Philippa Smith (Frances Gibson, Melbourne, 6 September 2018).
803 Philippa Smith, 'New Centre Fills Gap in Welfare Rights Aid', *Sydney Morning Herald* (Sydney, 5 June 1983) 103.
804 Legal Service Bulletin, 'Briefs, Welfare Rights Centre' (1983) 8 *Legal Service Bulletin* 130, 142.
805 Interview with Philippa Smith (Frances Gibson, Melbourne, 6 September 2018).
806 Lina Sonne, *Innovation in Finance to Finance Innovation: Supporting Pro-Poor Entrepreneur-Based Innovation* (PhD thesis, University of Maastricht, 2007) 57.
807 Note that in 1979, the Brotherhood of St Laurence operated a specialist service to help people to deal with social security matters and established the Unemployment Rights Service assisted by students from the then Phillip Institute of Technology (now RMIT Bundoora). Funding for the service was discontinued in 1984. Centres operated on differing models see the Victorian Welfare Rights Centre which was established on different model based of no casework but being a service to other workers. See 'Social Security Rights Victoria' *History* (Web Page) <http://www.ssrv.org.au/about/history/>. See also Charles Livingstone, 'Welfare Rights: A Proposed Model for Their Better Protection' (1986) 11(1) *Legal Service Bulletin* 24.
808 John Barber and Helen Kiel, 'Redfern Legal Centre and Australian Consumers' in Association & Combined Pensioners' Association of N.S.W et al. *Prisoners of neglect: A Report on the Phone-in Survey on Abuse of the Elderly 6th–7th March 1982* (Social Welfare Action Group, 1982).
809 Dorothy Cora, *Noreen Hewitt: Portrait of a Grassroots Activist* (Older Womens Network NSW, 2010).
810 Michael Fine, 'TARS: Its Beginnings' *TARS Annual Report 2010–2011*.
811 Interview with Dominic Gibson (Frances Gibson, Sydney, 4 July 2015).
812 Kathryn Freytag, *If Only I'd Known: A Study of The Experiences of Elderly Residents in Boarding Homes, Hostels and Self-Care Units* (Aged Care Coalition NSW, 1986).
813 Peter Grimshaw, "Horror' Conditions in Boarding Houses' *Daily Telegraph*, (Sydney 6 March 1986).
814 Linda Adamson and John Barber, *Beyond Benevolence* (Australian Pensioners Federation, 1989) 5.
815 Interview with Ben Slade (Frances Gibson, (Sydney, 8 December 2015).
816 Interview with Ben Slade (Frances Gibson, (Sydney, 8 December 2015).
817 Interview with Gerard Craddock (Frances Gibson, 1 May 2013).
818 Interview with Robyn Lansdowne (Melbourne, 6 July 2016).
819 Interview with Terry Buddin (Frances Gibson, Sydney, 26 July 2016).
820 Regular Records was an Australian record label based in Sydney that operated from 1978 until the mid-1990s.
821 Interview with Terry Buddin (Frances Gibson, Sydney, 26 July 2016).

822 Interview with Andrew Haesler (Frances Gibson, Sydney, 26 July 2016).Sydney, 7 July 2015).
823 Interview with Dominic Gibson Frances Gibson, Sydney, 4 July 2015).
824 Interview with Shivaun Inglis (Frances Gibson, Sydney, 26 July 2016).Bendigo, 2 September 2016). Inglis also recalls the Olympic fervour of some workers. 'I also remember I was going overseas on Friday 23 September 1993 and this was the night of the announcement as to who was going to get the 2000 Olympics. We had a party at Redfern Street and went into town. Everyone was kissing and hugging. Jane kissed a policemen then stood on a hill and shouted at the jubilant masses 'What about the tenants.' There were thousands of people walking through the streets. Then I remember coming back at the early hours of the morning. Jane and Ben and Frances came out to the airport and made me phone the Centre and say Ben, Jane and Fran were not coming to work. They insisted we made separate calls. Ben was lying on the floor of the airport with eyeliner on. Mary Perkins answered all the calls. She did not seem particularly pleased.'
825 Interview with Katherine Biber (Frances Gibson, Sydney, (7 September 2016).
826 Interview with Andy Nehl (Frances Gibson, Sydney, 26 July 2016). Sydney, 9 February 2017).
827 Interview with Bill Dickens (Frances Gibson, Sydney, 26 July 2016). Dubbo, 8 February 2017).
828 Interview with Andy Nehl (Frances Gibson, Sydney, 26 July 2016).Sydney, 9 February 2017).
829 Rice, Simon, 'Simon Rice on Police Verbals by Mutant Death' (2009) 34(1) *Alternative Law Journal* 68
830 The Cannanes, History Part 4 <https://www.cannanes.com/history_part4.html>.
831 The pub was established by Australian cricketer, John Louis Kettle in 1867. Kettle advertised his new pub in the Bell's Life in Sydney and Sporting Chronicle on Saturday December 21 1867: Cricketer's Rest Pitt Street, Redfern Opposite Albert Cricket Ground. J. L. Kettle, proprietor of the above Hotel, having just purchased a large parcel of the finest wines, Spirits, and Beers for cash is determined at this festive season to supply the inhabitants of Redfern and visitors to the Albert Cricket Ground during the holidays at prices not to be competed with. The Hotel being in such close proximity to the Albert Cricket Ground, affords J. K. every possible advantage of supplying Cricket Clubs and gentlemen players with Luncheons, Dinners, and every accommodation on the most reasonable terms, and being himself, perhaps, one of the oldest cricketers in the colony, he ventures to hope for a liberal share of support. N.B. Private Entrances and Waiting Parlours for passengers by the Omnibuses, which leave the Hotel every ten minutes.
832 Interview with Gerard Craddock (Frances Gibson, 1 May 2013).

www.ingramcontent.com/pod-product-compliance
Lightning Source LLC
Chambersburg PA
CBHW051534010526
44107CB00064B/2729